Revolutionary After Effects 5.5
Enhancing Digital Video

George J. Kingsnorth
Christian Darkin
Peter Reynolds
Ned Soltz
Darren Smith
Mark Welland
Paul Logan

Cover photograph of Acme Dunn printer appears by kind permission
of Mr. Kiel, President of Photo-Sonics Inc. http://www.photosonics.com
Thanks also to Buckey Grimm http://members.tripod.com/~cinefan/home.html

friendsof

DESIGNER TO DESIGNER™

Revolutionary After Effects 5.5
Enhancing Digital Video

First published March 2002

Trademark Acknowledgments

friends of ED has endeavored to provide trademark information about all the companies and products mentioned in this book by the appropriate use of capitals. However, friends of ED cannot guarantee the accuracy of this information.

Published by friends of ED
30-32 Lincoln Road, Olton, Birmingham. B27 6PA. UK.

Printed in USA

ISBN: 1-903450-78-0

Revolutionary After Effects 5.5
Enhancing Digital Video

Credits

Authors
George J. Kingsnorth
Christian Darkin
Peter Reynolds
Ned Soltz
Darren Smith
Mark Welland
Paul Logan

Commissioning Editor
Alan McCann

Lead Editor
Jake Manning

Editor
Adam Dutton

Additional Material
Tom Muller

Author Agent
Chris Matterface

Technical Reviewers
Vibha Roy
George J. Kingsnorth
Tom Muller
Peter Reynolds
Christian Darkin

Project Manager
Jenni Harvey

Graphic Editors
Chantal Hepworth
Katy Freer

Proof Reader
Keith Small

Cover Design
Deb Murray

Index
Simon Collins

Special Thanks
Mel Jehs

CD Design
Corné van Dooren

Managing Editor
Dave Galloway

Christian Darkin

Christian Darkin is a writer, animator, and filmmaker. He has written on video editing for dozens of magazines including Computer Arts, Camcorder User, and Digit, as well as The Times, The Guardian, and the FT. He's written, directed, and edited several short films and written two plays for the Edinburgh Festival, and comedy sketches for TV and BBC radio. He's also the author of the Darwin plug-in for 3D Studio Max, and a desktop version of Prime Minister Tony Blair.

George J. Kingsnorth   www.bluesphere.co.uk

George J. Kingsnorth gained an HND in Film and Television at Bournemouth & Poole College of Art & Design in 1983. He moved to Belfast in 1984 to join the BBC as an assistant film editor and later moved to Anglia Television in 1988 to become a film editor. Returning to Belfast in 1989 he has continued to work as a freelancer in television and corporate production and pos-tproduction, working on over 200 projects. In 1994 he gained a Post-graduate Diploma in Media Studies and later finished an Open University degree in 1997, the same year hes set up Blue Sphere Productions Ltd as a film and video development company. In the last three years he has produced nine short video dramas and directed three of them. Currently he is developing a number of feature films.

Peter Reynolds   www.alkamy.com

Peter started his career in fine arts, but the lure of animation and motion graphics proved to be irresistible (or too much fun!). He is the founder of alkamy studio (www.alkamy.com) which at times feels more like a playground than a work place, allowing the fusion of traditional art techniques with the latest in digital thingamajigs. Alkamy was recently nominated as a finalist in the Australian Effects and Animation Festival for a title credit sequence Peter designed and animated in After Effects.

Peter leads a very animated life with his wife and studio partner Marie, Kimi the Director of Entertainment and resident Samoyed, and his imaginary friend, HAL. Everything is running smoothly. And you?

Ned Soltz

Ned Soltz has been involved with computer-based NLE (Non-Linear Editing) since the days of Premiere 1.0 and CoSA After Effects. He is an educator, writer, consultant and resource to creative people. He only wishes that he were more creative himself. In recent years, Ned was one of the organizers of the Los Angeles Final Cut Pro Users Group, and he is a "guide" on the 2-pop.com web site, helping people with After Effects, Final Cut Pro and general computer hardware issues.

Mark Welland   www.newmediaworks.co.uk

Before the days of the digital revolution Mark Welland was using an array of media to complete design and illustration projects, particularly influenced by the likes of artist Russell Mills. When Photoshop arrived it was great to put into practice those skills, without getting his hands dirty. Mark set up THE NEW MEDIA WORKS in 1993 away from print and corporate identity to concentrate purely on creative digital media solutions.

Darren Smith   www.newmediaworks.co.uk

Coming from a background in photo-media, Darren has been designing at The New Media Works for 19 months, working on projects offering design solutions for various clients, ranging from Photoshop visuals/3D to After Effects projects.

He sees the beauty of using a time-based application is that core skills such as timing are transferable, whether you are working in Flash, QuickTime, Director, or in this case After Effects.

Paul Logan   www.newmediaworks.co.uk

Paul completed his degree in Design & Art Direction at Manchester Metropolitan University in 1999 and went on to work with an amazing organisation called IDEA where multi-media training and workshops propelled him into this industry. He has been working at The New Media Works for over two years doing everything from interactive design to video animation. Paul hopes to develop his skills further in After Effects and other time-based media to push exciting creative ideology in innovative directions.

Revolutionary After Effects 5.5

Revolutionary After Effects 5.5

Table of Contents

Revolutionary After Effects 5.5

Table of Contents

Table of Contents

Welcome

"When Indy descends into the Well of Souls, he's confronted by a big bad cobra. But you can actually see the plexiglass used to protect Harrison Ford and Karen Allen from the snake!"

All it takes is one reminiscent viewing of a classic like *Raiders of the Lost Ark* to realize that we've been spoiled by digital effects. There was a time when *Terminator 2*'s liquid metal antagonist was a silvery glint in James Cameron's eye, a time when the *Star Wars* movies had to make do with midgets in teddy bear costumes because digitally animated characters were an impossibility, and a time when some stories like Tolkien's *Lord of the Rings* were too fantastical for the screen to live up to.

Movies now made from such books, written not far from where this one was put together, continue to break barriers in visual effects every day, barriers that previously held even the deep pockets of Hollywood in check.

But we don't all have those resources, and so we can't ever hope to achieve such spectacle in our DV productions. Or can we? Enter After Effects 5.5...

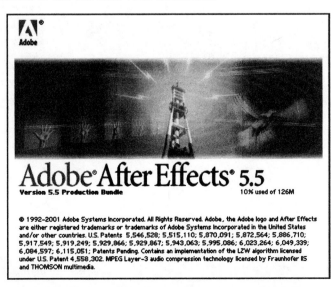

Revolutionary After Effects 5.5

Nowadays film students and aspiring filmmakers the world over can, without any capital at all, bring monsters to life in their desktop videos. With After Effects, it's quite possible to turn a family video of two young boys fighting with plastic swords in the back yard into an epic laser sword battle in a barren desert. The possibilities are now only limited by your own imagination, but how do you actually make it happen?

That's where this book comes in. After Effects is a huge and powerful tool, and just getting started can be daunting and hard work. Even once you understand how After Effects works, there's still a long way to go before you learn how to apply effects subtly and realistically. A long way that is, say, till about Chapter 9...

We hope to cut away one of the two remaining barriers to making stunning effects at home, by teaching you how to use this amazing technology. Then it really *is* all down to your imagination.

The Revolutionary Approach to After Effects

This book will bring you a mastery of After Effects whatever your background and level of DV expertise. You'll quickly see how to set up your hardware and configure the package for your system, moving on to discover the range of files you can import and composite in After Effects, before embarking on some of the more advanced features, such as layering and animation.

Throughout, as with all friends of ED books, the emphasis is on the professional and the practical, and there won't be very many pages of theory. We believe the best way to get you on the road to stunning motion graphics for DV is to let *you* get your feet wet with cutting edge tutorial projects and exciting practical examples.

Take a sneak peek at the kinds of projects you'll be building, rendering and learning from. Recreate an alien invasion, remove an actor from a shot in spectacular fashion, or turn a juggling boy into a silhouetted enigma!

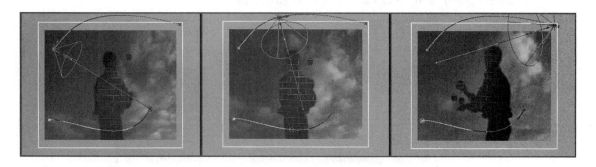

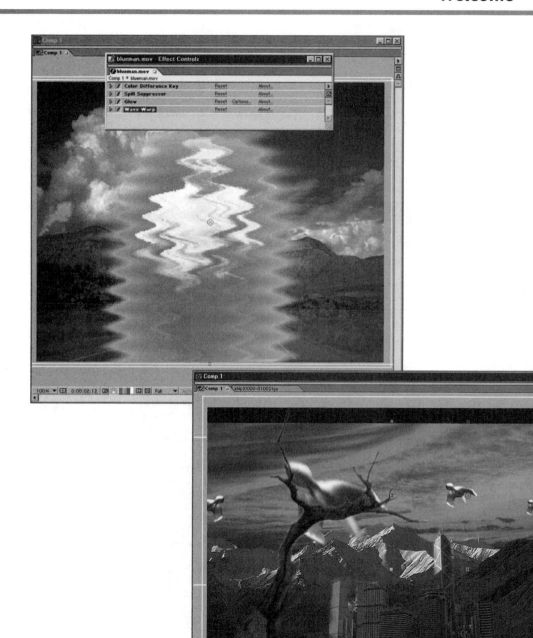

You'll see how to manipulate lighting and shadows to achieve the shot you need, and also how to use After Effects layers and visual guides to animate your virtual camera to perfection.

But *Revolutionary After Effects* isn't exclusively for high-end digital video productions. What if you're streaming your digital videos from your web site and want a banner to advertise your productions? Well, one of our case studies will cover just that – injecting some electricity into your web pages with After Effects-powered banners.

And if all you want to do is create the Terminator 2-style villains we mentioned earlier, well, we've even got some of that. Learn how to composite a CGI android into your live-action shots in another of our case studies.

The CD-ROM

The book comes with a CD-ROM which contains all the source files you'll use in the tutorials throughout the book. Alongside After Effects 5.5 project files and source footage, you'll also find Photoshop files and images which have been used or imported to create the final effects, so everything you need is there!

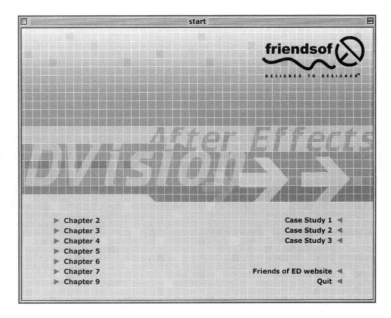

The Standard Version and the Production Bundle

We'll be showing you the best of After Effects 5.5 in both the Standard edition and the Production Bundle. In the occasional exercise where the Production Bundle's extra features are used, we'll offer alternative steps to achieving similar effects wherever possible.

How the Book Looks

We use a few layout conventions to make things clearer throughout the book.

- If we introduce a new **important term** or reference another **Chapter Number** then these will be in **bold**.

- We'll use different styles to emphasize things that appear on the screen, KEYSTROKES or SHORTCUTS and also hyperlinks.

> *If there's something you shouldn't miss, it will be highlighted like this!*
> *When you see the bubble, pay attention!*

■ When we want you to click on a menu, and then through subsequent sub-menus we will indicate to like so: File > Import > File... This would translate to:

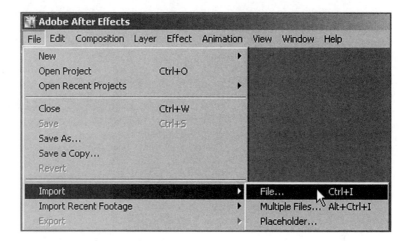

Build this Movie now

1. Finally, as the book is tutorial driven, much of the practical content will be built into examples and exercises which you should follow through:

2. If you see the exercise numbers, switch on your computer, launch After Effects and get ready.

3. Follow the steps through and check the screenshots and diagrams for more hints.

4. When you get to the end, give yourself a pat on the back.

Support – Just In Case

DVision books from friends of ED aim to be easy to follow and error-free. However, if you do run into problems, don't hesitate to get in touch – our crack team of reader support professionals will have you sorted in no time at all!

You can reach us at support@friendsofed.com, and we'd love to hear from you, even if it's just to request future books, ask about DVision, or tell us how much you loved *Revolutionary After Effects*!

> *To tell us a bit about yourself and make comments about the book,*
> *why not fill out the little reply card at the back and pop it in the post!*

You can also check out our web site for news, more books, downloads and, of course, our packed message boards! Point your browser at www.friendsofed.com/DVision.

Time to Set Off

Well, there's nothing more you need to know about the book before getting underway. You'll soon see that whatever the complexities of the package, whatever the limitations on your budget ... you have After Effects, you have this book, and that's all you'll need to add a stunning sheen to your digital video projects.

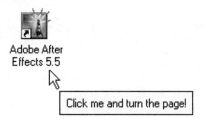

Adobe After
Effects 5.5

Click me and turn the page!

In 500 pages time, you really will see that the final cut is only the beginning...

1 Getting Started

Who is After Effects for? Well, if you want to produce special effects for video and film, or create title sequences, graphical stings, and logos, if you're an animator, a 3D designer, a Flash designer, or a web-page designer, After Effects is for you!

The package has found a place in some of the most important and impressive Hollywood films such as *Blood - The Last Vampire*, *The Iron Giant* (animatics), and *The Talented Mr Ripley* (titles), but has also been used in cartoons, animations, and some of the most impressive sites on the Internet.

So what is it that makes After Effects so essential to anyone working with moving images? Well, to say it's a special effects package would be to only understand part of the program's work. To say it's an animation package neglects a huge area of the programs capabilities as well. You could, however, say that After Effects is a compositor. Its job is to take all kinds of media – still images, animations, video clips, and even Flash movies, and compose them into a single video, adding effects, and altering the nature of the images (and sounds) in loads of different ways. If you enjoyed collage in your early art class days, you're going to love After Effects – it's a digital collage powerhouse!

With it, you can create strange alien landscapes, transport people and objects from one environment to another, combine CG (Computer Graphics) and real life footage, and animate it all together. You can fly video clips around the screen, add and animate text, overlay one image onto another, and even create cartoons.

You can work in 2D or 3D, or combine the two, and you can output your finished work as anything from an animated GIF for the Internet, right up to a cinema quality effect for the big screen.

In this book, we'll take you from the basics of the package right through to advanced animation techniques.

Web designers have had their eye on After Effects and the range of tools available within it for a long time. It was only with the release of version 5 that After Effects has become a real Internet tool. With version 5.5 came the ability to load in Flash movies, and it became possible to use the package to author and edit web content. Amongst other things, this book will provide an easy way in to understanding how to use After Effects to create and manipulate Internet videos and

Flash animations. We'll use tutorials and examples (all of which you'll find on the enclosed CD) to explore every aspect of this powerful and complex tool. More specifically, we'll look at:

- How to prepare elements for use in After Effects

- The process of constructing compositions

- How to import and combine various types of footage

- How to add effects to layers

- The 3D possibilities of After Effects

- Using keyframing to create animations

- Creating advanced animation with parenting and expressions

- How to use text, and graphical objects in our work, as well as particle systems, motion tracking, and chromakey

- Finally, we'll learn to output our finished work for all kinds of audiences and media.

Before we begin, however, it's worth taking a look at the three main ways in which After Effects is used within a production:

- For compositing

- For effects

- For post-production

Compositing

By taking two or more scene elements (which could be video clips, still images, animations, or Flash movies to name but a few), and combining them into a single scene, we create an entirely new animation. This is a composite.

Sometimes, compositing is very obvious. A picture-in-picture display, for example, or a string of text superimposed over a video clip.

Sometimes, the idea is to make your composite blend realistically into the background. For example, you might want to combine a 3D animated creature with a filmed background. To "sell" the effect (convince the audience), the join between the real and CG elements would have to be as subtle as possible, and various techniques, including color matching, keying, and the addition of grain would have to be used to get the best possible result.

Then again, sometimes, a composite is designed to be completely undetectable. For example, a boom mic might need to be removed from a shot. In this case, all the After Effects operator's efforts would go into trying to ensure that the audience didn't even know a special effect had been necessary!

There are several techniques with which a composite can be created. Here are a few of the most important ones:

Transformation – A shot is moved out of the way, rotated, or scaled to show another scene underneath it. This is often used to create picture-in-picture and transition effects.

Alpha channels – Part of an image is made transparent before it's imported into After Effects. It's then saved with an alpha channel – an additional layer to the red, green and blue colors that create the spectrum of 24-bit color. In the alpha channel, black is used as a mask, and white is used as a transparent color to allow the image containing the alpha channel to be seen. When it's placed into a composition, anything underneath the image will be seen through the transparent parts.

Overlay modes – An image is placed on top of another using a special mode, which makes parts of the top image semi-transparent. These modes are available in a number of packages, Photoshop being one of the more familiar. Often, using modes like add, luminance or soft light produce ghostly effects where images appear half-faded over each other.

Masking – A shape is literally drawn onto the image, using the pen tool, and acts like a cut-out, making anything outside the shape transparent. Masks can be animated over time so that, for example, if you draw a mask around a person in one shot, and animate it to follow their movements, then you can simply place another shot underneath it, and that person will appear in the new scene.

Keying – A particular color, or selection of colors in an image is made transparent. Typically, a person or object is filmed against a blue (or green, or yellow) backdrop. Keying is then used to make the screen transparent, and another scene can be simply dropped in behind them.

Matting – A matte is a grayscale image used to define the areas you want to become transparent in another image. For example, if you've got a title written in black on a white background, you can use it as a matte so that the white areas are replaced by one image, and the black areas by another. Mattes can be animated, and shades of gray can create half-fades and semi-transparent areas.

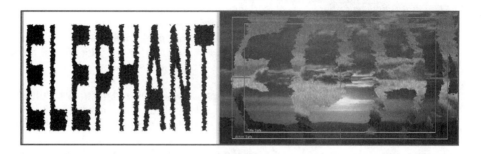

Effects

Effects are where After Effects is used to process an image, or create one entirely from scratch. On-screen text is an effect, and so is changing the brightness of a video clip. More exotic effects include warping and distorting the image, creating lens flares, glows, and smoke effects, and shattering the image into a thousand shards of glass.

In addition, there are some very sophisticated particle effects (for creating and animating dozens of objects at once). There are animation effects for tracking the motion of objects, or creating random movement, and there are audio effects for creating and manipulating sound in various weird and wonderful ways.

Effects cover a massive range of tools, all of which can be animated over time, and layered one on top of another to produce an enormous range of possibilities. In addition, they can be added to with various plug-in modules, which can be brought from third-party companies, and are occasionally given away for free download on the Net. As well as that, most Photoshop compatible plug-ins can be used with After Effects.

You're probably now either dribbling at the thought of all the amazing effects you're going to produce, or trembling at the thought of the thousands of controls to be learnt. If you're trembling, don't worry! After Effects really simplifies the effects process by making all but a couple of the effects into filters. Filters cover a vast range of tools, but they're carefully filed away, and designed to all be self contained and quick to apply. You can just click on the image you want to apply them to, and select the filter on the Effects menu. There's so much in common between the controls of one filter, and the next that you'll very quickly pick up how to use them all once you've mastered the basics.

Post Production

After Effects is rarely the only package used in a production. Often, material is created in a 3D animator, a stills package, or a video editor, and then transferred to After Effects for compositing or effects work, before being brought back into a video editor and cut into a longer scene or sequence.

Sometimes, however, there's another stage after the final cut is produced. Scenes often need to be processed to create a uniform look, or a series of scrolling subtitles, or an effect that spans the length of the production may need to be added. A shot might need to be given a colored tint, or be given a grain so that it looks as though it was shot on film, or the color or brightness levels may need to be altered to make a sequence look as though it was shot at night.

It's worth recognizing this kind of work as a separate task in After Effects, as it's often done at the final 'polishing' stage in a production, and is usually applied to an entire scene, or even the whole program, rather than a sequence of just a few seconds as most effects tend to be.

Differences between the Standard version and the Production Bundle

After Effects comes in two flavors: The Standard version and the Production Bundle. The difference between them is that the Production Bundle comes with everything found in the Standard version plus a range of features, tools, and extra Effects Filters designed for the more demanding user.

Predictably, this makes it about half as expensive again as the Standard version. Whether that extra money is justified depends almost entirely on what you intend to use the product for. Here's a quick rundown of what you get for your extra money:

Motion tracking

The Production Bundle's motion tracking tools allow you to pick a point on an image, and automatically trace its movement throughout the length of the clip. You can then use this motion path to apply to another image. Practical uses for this include superimposing a new object into a scene where the camera is moving, attaching an object or effect to a moving object (such as blurring out the face of a passer-by in a shot), or removing movement from a shaky camera shot.

Extra filters

Several additional Effects Filters are included in the Production Bundle. In **Chapter 7**, you will get a more thorough explanation of these effects, but here's a brief list of them for now:

- 3D channel filters – several filters to make use of 3D information stored in some image files. Useful for producing 3D fog, distance blur, or other effects on 3D animations.

- Alpha levels – changes the transparency level on images with transparent areas.

- Bezier warp – lets you bend and distort your image as though it was on a rubber sheet.

- Bulge – bulges or pinches an image at a specific point.

- Corner pin – keeps your image as a four sided polygon, but lets you place each corner anywhere you like. Good for perspective effects.

- Displacement map – moves pixels around in your image based on the brightness of the equivalent pixel in another image. This allows you to create masks which will distort the shot in very controllable ways. Good for etched glass effects.

- Mesh warp – your image is covered with a grid, and you can move the corners of the grid to re-shape your image. Good for warping and morphing effects.

- Optics compensation – tries to correct the fish-eye, or other optical effects, created by extremely wide, or extreme zoom lenses. Can also be used to fake those effects.

- Reshape – distorts your image based on shapes you draw on the screen. Useful for morphing effects.

- Ripple – creates ripples as though a pebble has been thrown into a pond.

- Twirl – spins your image around a given point, as though it's being sucked into a vortex.

- Wave warp – good for creating waves and ripples of all kinds.

- Vector Paint – lets you do simple painting jobs using a variety of brush sizes on an image. It also lets you animate your brush strokes so you can have strokes painted onto the screen over time.

- Lightning – creates lightning effects.

- Fractal noise – creates basic smoke, explosive, or liquid effects.

- Particle playground – lets you produce particle effects where multiple objects are animated without the need to create keyframes for each one. You can create effects like rain, meteor storms, or a herd of cattle, and control the motion in various ways.

- Glow – makes objects glow, either depending on their brightness, or on their shape

- Scatter – dissolves your object into pixels.

Audio effects

Additional audio effects are included too:

- Flange and chorus – powerful effects creation tool for a variety of sounds.

- High, low pass – removes very high, or very low frequency sounds from your audio.

- Modulator – for creating warbling, vibrato, and DALEK-type effects.

- Parametric equalizer – a more sophisticated version of the graphic equalizer.

- Reverb – powerful echo effects to make your audio sound as though it was recorded in a concert hall.

- Tone – synthesizes a sound. Combine this with effects filters to make more complex noises.

Better keying

The keying tools in the Production Bundle are significantly better than in the Standard version. They allow you to create better bluescreen and other keying effects:

- Color difference key, color range key, and linear color key – three color keyers designed to offer more sophisticated control over which colors are made transparent, and which are left opaque.

- Difference matte – takes two images and makes only those pixels which are the same in both transparent. If you've got a person in a street, and a shot of the street empty, you can use the two images to separate the background and the actor, then place them into another shot.

- Extract – a more sophisticated version of the luma key (used for making areas transparent based on their brightness).

- Inner outer – masking tool for getting good cut-outs where objects have complex, or feathery shapes.

- Spill suppresser – used to remove the halo of color often left around a subject after they've been filmed against a blue screen, which has then been keyed out.

- Simple choker and matte choker – two filters used in conjunction with a keying filter to improve the edges of keyed objects.

16 bit per channel color

Film uses a much wider range of colors than video. Much closer, in fact, to the range of colors the human eye can distinguish. If you're working with film, and your finished production will end up on cinema screens, you'll probably want to preserve as much of your original vibrancy as you can – 16 bit per channel color mode lets you do this.

Network rendering

With network rendering, you can use multiple computers on a network to render a project. If you've got a group of computers all linked together, you can use the power of all of them to render much faster. You can also leave some to render while you get on with your next project on another system.

Version 5 vs 5.5

At the end of 2001, Adobe released After Effects 5.5. Although not a complete rewrite of the package, it did alter a few of the finer points, and it did add some brilliant new functions. In this book, we do cover the new possibilities offered by 5.5, but always make it clear in the text when we're talking specifically about AE 5.5. **Whichever version you're using, you'll find this book equally useful**.

If you're thinking of upgrading from 5 to 5.5, here's a quick rundown of the new features you'll get:

New filters

Several new filters have been introduced with version 5.5. Some others have been downgraded from the Production Bundle to the Standard version:

Color stabilizer (Production Bundle only)

This goes through your video clip trying to compensate for changes in lighting or color temperature (like when the sun goes behind a cloud, or the camera moves from indoors to outdoors).

Levels (individual controls)

This gives you very tight control over the brightness and contrast of all parts of your image. You can control the levels of the red, blue, and green parts of your image separately.

4 color gradient

Use a blend of four colors to create a smooth shaded backdrop. You can animate the positions and colors of each of the four colors. That way you can produce softly shaded backdrops, and lighting effects.

Cell pattern

This creates animated cells, and crazy-paving effects. A range of different backdrops and textures can be set up with this filter.

Grid

With this, you can create grids of any size, shape and thickness. Useful for backdrops, sci-fi screens, matrix effects, and so on.

Roughen edges

This decays and roughens the edges of an object (especially effective when used on text).

Time difference

This is a color correction tool which changes colors based on the colors of an image at different points in time.

Advanced Lightning (Production Bundle only)

Very controllable lightning strikes on which you can animate literally dozens of parameters. Lightening can also be made to "stick" to the outline of a layer, making it easy to make it interact with objects in your scene.

Downgraded filters

Four filters have been 'downgraded' from the Production Bundle, so they're now available in the Standard Version of the package. These are Lightning, Ripple, Twirl, and Wave Warp.

3D layers

These can now cast colored shadows, and project images onto each other, creating effects like that of light through a stained glass window. You can also have several views of your production open at once, making it easier to work with 3D compositions, because you can see them from the camera's point of view, as well as being able to manipulate objects in other views.

Import compatibility

You can now import 3D camera motion from 3D Studio and Maya (Production Bundle only). You can also import far more 16 bit color image types, and Macromedia Flash and MPEG formats. Plus, you can export directly to Realmedia web video format.

Post-rendering

Post rendering actions now allow you to have finished renders automatically reloaded into your project. This is useful if you're producing a shot in which you need to create several slightly different versions of the same shot (as in a title sequence for a series). You can set AE up to render each version in turn, and then load it into a composition before rendering that.

Smart mask (Production Bundle only)

This helps with complex masking jobs by automatically adding points to smooth out a mask, which can then be animated more finely.

Expressions update

The expressions have been updated, giving you more options for automating your animations, and wiring the animation of several features together so they can be controlled easily with a single adjustment.

Setting up a post-production studio

After Effects isn't a post-production studio on its own. In order to create one, you'll need a lot of extra hardware and software to feed into it. Exactly what products you're going to include in your set-up will depend very much on your own needs and budget; and available hardware and software is changing all the time. Here's a breakdown of some of the current options you can consider when building your own set-up:

Hardware

Video camera

DV cameras give us a cost effective means of producing results good enough for Broadcast TV without having to deal with bulky and expensive SP Betacam Cameras. It's also digital, so you don't lose any quality when you copy your material from tape, to computer, and back to tape. However, that doesn't mean that all DV camcorders are the same, or that they all have good enough quality lenses and image reproduction hardware to satisfy clients. How to choose a camcorder is unfortunately beyond the scope of this book, but many professionals use the Canon XL1, the Canon XM1 (called the GL1 in the US) or the Sony VX series.

Capture card

Any old thing will do. You can get a DV capture card for about $40 if you shop around, and it will give you DV in and out. If you've got a Mac, the chances are there's already one built into your computer (check for a firewire port). The only reason to go for a more expensive card is that it might allow you to capture analogue as well as digital material, it might come bundled with useful editing software, or it might allow you use real-time effects and transitions within your editing package (this doesn't apply to After Effects).

Scanner

If you think you're going to end up using photos in your productions, and will need to scan them in, you can do it at much better quality and much more easily with a scanner than by trying to muck about pointing a camcorder at them. Virtually any scanner on the market today will be up to producing images well beyond TV (and even HDTV) quality.

Hard disk space

If there's one thing working with video does well, it's eat disk space! One second of DV material takes up 3.6 Mb. That's just over 4.5 minutes per Gb. Add to that the fact that for each minute of finished program, you'll probably have 5 minutes of raw footage, and things begin to mount up. Start using uncompressed image sequences and it gets worse: 1.2mb for every frame, which is 9Gb for 5 minutes! Just try to get as much hard drive space as you can afford. And bare in mind that 20Gb is the smallest hard drive you can now buy – that's approximately 80 minutes of DV video, so it's not all bad!

External TV monitor

If you're working for video, it makes sense to have a TV plugged into your system on which you can watch the finished movies. You can't see AE works-in-progress on a TV, but you can render in a format which will play back to a TV plugged into your capture card (or camcorder).

VCR

For recording your finished production onto. If your DV camcorder has a 'video in' function, you can use this to get a good quality master copy onto DV tape. It's not the best quality you can get (for that you'd need to store uncompressed footage), but if your original footage is on DV, you won't gain anything. If you can't write to your camera tapes, you'll need a high quality VCR.

Software

Non Linear Editor

Such as Adobe Premiere (which can export projects directly to After Effects), Final Cut Pro, Avid, and Media Studio. The editing package is the center point of any post production set-up, and you'll probably have experience with various editors before you even think about getting hold of After Effects. Choose one you're comfortable with, and make sure it can import and export files compatible with AE.

3D animation package

Such as 3DS Max, Strata 3D, Maya, Movie3D, Carrara, Poser and Lightwave. 3D animation is a tough business, and learning it should not to be undertaken by the faint-hearted. Having said that, once you master it, you can create almost anything, and when combined with AE, a whole realm of complex effects are possible.

Photo editing package

Such as Photoshop, Photoshop Elements, and Paint Shop Pro. A good still image processing package is absolutely essential to any video workshop. Use it to create fancy text, to build mattes and masks, for grayscale images and textures, to paint onto frames of video, and to create the elements for animation.

Vector graphics package

Such as Illustrator, Corel Draw, and Freehand. Vector graphics are good for creating images which can be scaled without losing quality. Use them for graphical 2D animations such as title sequences, and idents (graphical stings featuring logos, product names, or program titles).

Video painting package

Such as Aura, Ulead Video Paint, and Commotion. Video painting or rotoscoping packages treat video in the same way that Photoshop treats still images. You can paint onto individual frames of video, or onto a whole range of frames at once. Most packages offer a range of natural looking painting tools from watercolor brushes, through to lightening, plants, and text effects. A video painter is useful if you need very fine control over each frame of video, if you want to create freehand animations, or if you want to 'clone' parts of a shot into another shot, or another time (for example, to paint out an unwanted passer-by, or to clone in a character from another shot).

Video processing package

Such as Media Cleaner Pro. After Effects produces some good output formats, but if you want to compress your finished product for different media (like the Internet, CD ROM, or DV) then a processing package can automate the whole job.

Setting up a Web studio

After Effects can now be used as a web design package. However, it's not a replacement for any of the current tools on the market. It's something entirely new, and so opens up new possibilities for designers.

In a web design environment, After Effects becomes more of a graphical tool. You're more likely to use it more to produce interesting 2D animations, vector graphics, and text-based sequences, than the video intensive, complexly layered effects created for TV and film.

Generally, you'll need to add it to a fully functioning web design suite, which could consist of:

Still image package

Such as Photoshop, Photoshop Elements, and Paint Shop Pro. This is essential for creating and manipulating bitmap images for use in After Effects.

Vector image package

Such as Illustrator, and Corel Draw. In web design, the most important consideration is file size. Vector images tend to be smaller than bitmaps, and they can be scaled infinitely without becoming blocky. Use these in your AE projects, and the resulting Flash animations should be smaller.

Macromedia Flash

Although After Effects produces Flash movies, it can't create interactivity. If you want to do that (and lets face it, most of the time you do), then you'll need Flash. After Effects 5.5 can import Flash movies, so you can use Flash to create content for AE and vice-versa.

Web-page design package

Such as Dreamweaver. Of course, once you've created your content, whether it's Flash, QuickTime, or Realmedia, you'll still need to create a web site to place it onto.

Conclusion

Now that we've taken a look at what After Effects is used for, and seen where it fits into a design or post production suite, we can start to get down to the real business of learning how to use the package. In the next chapter, we'll find our way around the package, working out what the extensive (and sometimes intimidating) array of buttons and controls actually do. We'll see how easy it is to start creating projects, and really get our hands dirty with a selection of quick projects.

2 An Overview of After Effects

So now you know the difference between the Standard and Production versions of After Effects and hopefully have purchased the proper version to achieve the results you require. You have set up After Effects on your computer, but you still need an overview of how an actual project comes together.

Getting started in After Effects as a complete beginner can be a daunting task. There is a huge number of tools and buttons and windows and menus and terms like keying and alpha channels and argh!!! Furthermore all of these elements are interlaced in After Effects. For this reason we're going to throw you in at the deep end and take you quickly through a project in After Effects. This way you can start to get an overall idea of what After Effects is doing straight away and this will help when you're learning about its many facets in more depth.

You should definitely sit next to your computer and work step by step through this chapter. Don't worry if you don't understand everything right now, as we'll delve deeper into the various topics later on. For now I'll take you by the hand, and trust me, soon we'll be making a couple in Middle Eastern costume fly on their carpet around the Pyramids.

Opening a new project

On launching After Effects you are presented with a **Project Window**. I like to save that project immediately and give it a name, in this case I simply called my project RevolutionaryAEProject.aep. Make certain that the .aep extension is appended to your project if you will need to work cross-platform between Mac and Windows. In this case, I am working in Mac OS X (a new capability of AE 5.5). But, should I desire to open this project in a Microsoft Windows environment (and AE 5.5 now supports Windows XP), the file extension will allow Windows to recognize the file as an After Effects document.

This blank Project Window will be the repository of all media that you will be using in your project. This could be video, still images, audio, animations, or compositions. We'll deal with compositions next, but just for a moment familiarize yourself with all of the controls within this Project Window.

Help Bubbles: Whenever you wish to know the function of any of those icons you see in a particular window, just pass your cursor over it. A Help Bubble (or Tool Tip for Windows) will appear and tell you what it does.

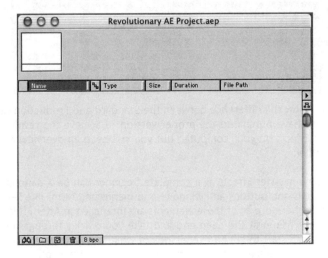

At the lower left corner of the Project Window are four little buttons, which are of the utmost importance. Moving from left to right:

- The binoculars icon enables a search for specific files.

- The folder icon creates a new folder.

- The middle icon might be the most important; it provides a simple way of creating a **composition**, the core of working in After Effects.

- The trash icon may not be as obvious as you think. Dragging media to the trash icon deletes it from the project, but not from your disk.

At this point it's important to remember that After Effects is non-destructive to your media unless you choose to edit the original media. That simply means that absolutely no changes are made to your original footage. After Effects creates a link to those original files, ultimately to create an entirely new file when you make your movie. Remember, then, not to delete original files while still working on your project!

Importing files

You can now bring media files into the Project Window. This is known as importing and can be done in one of two ways.

- You may locate your media files directly on your hard drive(s), select them and then drag the icons into the project window.

- Or import them directly using the File > Import > File... command, and locate the media by browsing through your files. Alternatively press COMMAND I (Mac) or CTRL I (PC)

Of course, I have prepared for my AE project by carefully organizing all of the files I may need into a folder which I can find easily, and all of the files have reference-able or descriptive names!

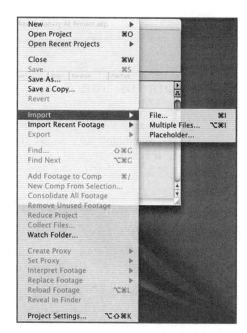

Starting the project

1. Open up After Effects, choose File > Save and save the new project as `Revolutionary AE Project`. Make certain that the file extension `.aep` remains appended to the file name.

2. Choose File> Import > File…, and browse to the **Chapter 2** folder on the CD. Open this and import the Pyramid5 QuickTime movie.

3. Repeat step 2 but this time, import the Sheik_Good QuickTime movie.

    Your project folder should now look like this:

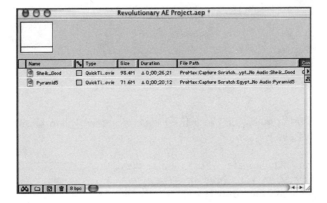

A new composition

You may create your composition either by selecting a file or files from the Project Window and dragging them on top of the composition icon, or by selecting Composition > New Composition.

Creating a new composition from the composition menu will bring up a dialog box called the **Composition Settings** window. The new composition window allows adjustment of key parameters for the project:

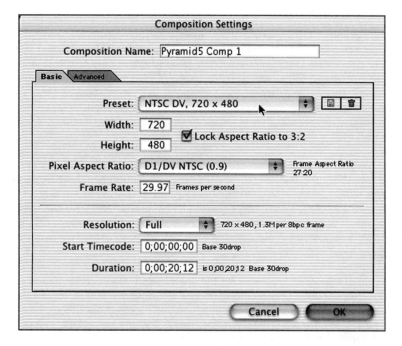

At the very top you can enter a name for your composition. Below this are settings for the size of your screen and how many frames per second the movie will show, these can be either be preset or you can make your own custom settings. Then at the bottom there are three fields which deal with resolution, at what time the composition starts, and its duration. **Chapter 3** discusses this window in more detail.

Clicking OK you find some new windows have opened. Of immediate importance are the Composition window, and the Timeline.

Timeline window

The Timeline window contains a number of important controls.

Let's just look briefly at some of these controls. They will be explained in greater detail in **Chapter 5**.

In the upper left corner, you will note the **timecode** in blue. That indicates the current position of the **playhead**, which is the blue triangle and red line to the right of the window with all the numbers. You can click on the timecode and enter a specific timecode where you wish the playhead to jump.

Now, let's use the help bubbles/tool tips again. Pass your cursor over each of the options to learn what they do. Other than the timecode position, one of the most useful features initially is the **visibility** switch (the eye). There are often times where you wish to hide a layer so that you can work unobstructed on another layer. Turning this switch on or off accomplishes that. The only other switch that is significant at this early point in your mastery of After Effects is the **quality** switch, indicated by the broken diagonal line. In this position, your preview will be of lower resolution, thereby speeding up previews. If you need to view the preview in full resolution, then toggle high quality by clicking in the box.

As you run your cursor over the icons and let the bubbles/tips tell their story, stop for a moment on the "M" above the layer check box. This enables motion blur for that particular layer. Motion blur adds realism to layers in motion. Should you wish to use motion blur, I recommend that you enable it only when you are in later stages of your project and wish to preview the effect of the motion blur. It slows previews considerably. At first while making your rough cut, you are generally looking for position and other significant factors. At later stages, you will wish to fine tune and perhaps preview in greater similarity to final output.

Here's something just to tuck away for the moment but which I consider to be the coolest feature of AE 5.5. You will use it later on in this book and throughout your After Effects life. Note that little cube just to the left of the Parent heading (don't worry about Parents for now). Checking that box enables the layer to act as a 3D layer. That means that the entire layer can be moved in 3D space along all three axes, that it can cast or receive shadows to or from another layer, and in general can be manipulated in 3D space. This does not mean that the layer itself is three dimensional; it remains a two dimensional object while having three dimensional properties. As I said, don't concern yourself with this for now, it's something to look forward to later.

Composition window

The Composition window is the space where you will preview your video as well as being one of the vehicles for adding media to your timeline. This is done by dragging media into the window from the Project Window. When you place your playhead in the timeline at a specific point, that moment in time will appear in your Composition window. Likewise, when you play the timeline or preview your project with one of the preview tools available to you, you will see your playback in the Composition window. Controls at the bottom of the window allow you to change

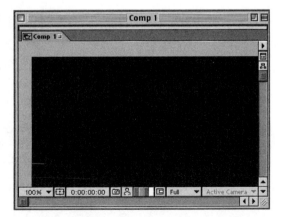

the display ratio of the image, to show title safe/action safe areas, and to change the resolution of the preview. **Chapter 3** deals with this in more detail.

Creating your new composition

1. Create a new composition. Under the basic tab choose the following settings:

    - **Preset** to NTSC DV, 720x480. This sets width, height, aspect ratio and frame rate.

    - **Resolution** to full.

    - **Duration** to 0;00;20;12.

    Now click OK.

    > *NTSC represents the video standard for North America and Japan. PAL is the standard for most of the rest of the world with the exception of certain countries on the SECAM standard. The sample files for this chapter are in NTSC format.*

2. Select the Sheik_Good file from the Project window and drag it onto the Timeline.

    Now the Composition window should look more like this screenshot:

    OK. Don't laugh too hard, this is my wife and I in Bedouin costume (fortunately you can't see the bottle of Kosher wine she is serving me) using our foyer as a set.

3. Looking at the Composition window, set the display to 50% size in order to save screen real estate and for faster previewing.

4. For now set the preview resolution to full. You might wish to lower that resolution for faster previewing once you begin the composite operation.

5. Pull the playhead (also known as the "Timeline Marker" and "Current Frame Marker") to the beginning of the clip (all zeroes on my timecode).

6. Click and hold on the Pyramid5 file in the Project window, then drag it into the Composition window.

    You will now see the pyramids in the Project window. Obviously we want our characters to be in front of the Pyramid so...

7. Click and hold on the Sheik_Good layer in the timeline, and then drag it so that a dark line appears above the Pyramid5 layer. Now let the mouse button go.

    Your Timeline window should now look like this:

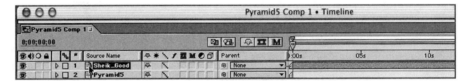

Contextual menus

A good way to save time in After Effects is to use contextual menus. Just CONTROL and click (Mac) or right click (PC) within any window, and a series of menus will appear related to the context of that window. Open up the contextual menu in the composition window and have a look.

Your menu may look slightly different depending upon whether you have purchased the Standard or Production Bundle. The After Effects Production Bundle includes the Keyframe Assistant as well as the Motion Tracker/Stabilizer. These features will be discussed later.

In this case, all of the options available to a specific **layer** become available without pulling down any menus from the top menu bar. The concept of layers here is crucial. What you are doing in After Effects is compositing one layer of media upon another and through the interaction of these layers, (their motion and effects) you create your video magic. Remember that layers are visible from the top down. You can look in your timeline to determine the order of the layers and even alter them by dragging the layer up or down in the timeline. You probably don't know what most of those options do right now. Don't worry though, you will soon enough.

More on the timeline

You'll also wish to zoom in and out of your timeline alternating between a view which compresses the entire composition into the Timeline window or which zooms into the single frame level. Control the level of zoom with the triangles at the bottom of the timeline. The best way to see what I mean is to play with the arrow you can see in the screenshot. Just slide it back and forth.

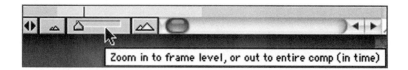

Generally you may not want to utilize the entire duration of footage you have imported into your project. If you double-click the media file, you will bring up a window which plays the media.

On the extreme upper right corner of the timeline, you'll see an arrow. Pull it down to expose the Panels menu and open that menu to show **In** and **Out**. Select both In and Out and two new columns will appear.

You will note that for each clip, the in point is 0, meaning that the clip begins at timecode 0 of the composition's timeline and its outpoint corresponds to the length of the media.

The first way of setting in/out points is using these timecode boxes. Click on an in or an out point and you will then be presented a dialog box. Type the desired timecode into the box. That's a little difficult unless you know the exact spot you wish to hit.

Here's a shortcut. Position your playhead on the desired in or out point. Here's where zooming to frame level might help. Then ALT-CLICK (Windows) or OPTION-CLICK (Mac) on the in/out box. After Effects will then set that position as your in/out point.

Alternatively, simply grab one of the ends of the clip and drag right or left to change in or out points.

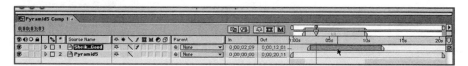

Once you have set your in/out points, you may drag the highlighted clip duration indicator left or right in your timeline to determine its position in time within your composition.

Clipping the movie

As you play the Sheik_Good clip, you will see a little flash at the beginning. That's where the DP (director of photography) in this case our teenage daughter, switched on the lighting. This will affect what we need to do later, and it's best to get rid of this bit.

1. Select the `Sheik_Good` layer in the timeline.

2. Drag the playhead along so that you can see the lights turn on, and leave it positioned just after this point. This should be just after one second.

3. Click on the gray shape at the beginning of the clip and drag it up to where the playhead is.

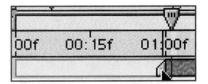

4. Now click on the main mass of the layer and drag it back so that it starts at zero on the timeline.

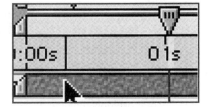

Cutting out the living room

1. Select the **rectangular mask** tool from the tool box window and draw a rectangle around the blue screen and oriental rug (our flying carpet).

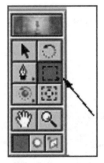

2.   This has now eliminated all of the extraneous background. At this point, should you wish to reposition the masked layer, you may move it with the Arrow tool. For that matter, you could resize the image by grabbing a corner handle and dragging (click then hold SHIFT and drag to maintain proportion).

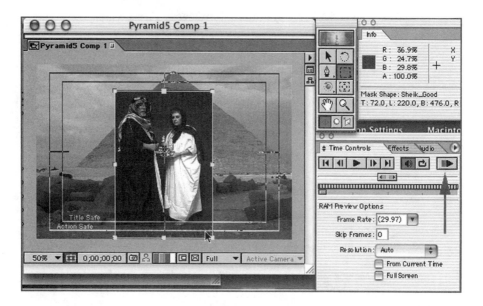

3.   Enable the Title Safe/Action Safe indicators by clicking on the icon in the Composition window between the composition display size, and the current time indicator. The icon has been selected and appears darkened and depressed. This function will be fully explained in the next chapter.

Have a quick look at the window that says Time Control on it. That arrow on the right is the important one! Click it and AE will create a RAM preview of the entire timeline or the workspace which you have set, caching into RAM as many frames as possible depending upon the amount of RAM which you have in your computer and is available to After Effects. Remember that After Effects is very memory intensive and this applies to whatever environment in which you operate: Windows, MacOS9

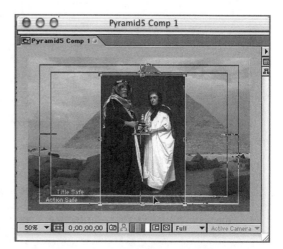

or MacOSX. Regardless of your environment, load up your computer with as much RAM as possible.

We want to move the image slightly, to within the Action Safe guideline.

4. Select the Sheik layer in the Timeline.

There is now a box (called a bounding box) around the masked layer.

5. Use the Selection tool to move the layer into place. I chose to move the image a little higher. But you're the editor... move it where you wish or just leave it where it is.

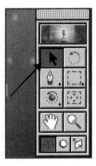

6. Click on the triangle to the left of the layer name to reveal the drop down list. Now click on the arrow next to where it says Transforms to reveal its properties.

7. Making sure the playhead is at 0, now click on the stop watch to the left of the Position property.

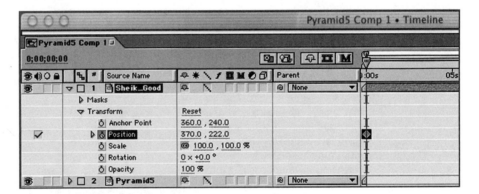

A diamond has now appeared on the timeline, known as a **keyframe**. A keyframe represents a point in the timeline where a specific parameter has been specified – size, rotation, opacity, anything which can be manipulated in After Effects. By default, After Effects will interpolate the parameters which you have set in each respective keyframe. For example, if your first keyframe is set for 50% scale of your image and the second keyframe, let's say 5 seconds later, is set for 100%, then within that duration of time the image will grow from 50% to 100%. You will learn later in the book about the various options available for each keyframe. But for now, know that the concept of keyframing is the very basis of the art of motion graphics in After Effects.

My intent is to leave the clip in the same place and create the illusion of motion by the moving video underneath. It's a really rather lousy home-movie style of panning the camera so your audience gets sea-sick, but it is effective for this scene.

The Effects window

Now it's time to apply an effect to get rid of the blue screen and really place us in the Giza Plateau. Once you select an effect to apply to a layer, another window will appear on your screen – the Effect Control window. It is in this window that all of the adjustments and settings specific to the effect you have selected may be controlled. You can also access all of the effects parameters by clicking down the arrow beside your layer name in the timeline.

Keying out the bluescreen

1. Making sure the Sheik is still selected, choose Effect > Keying > Color Key and a new window should open called the Effect Controls window.

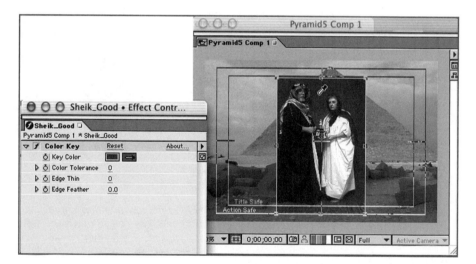

2. Click on the little eye dropper in the effect window and then click on the blue screen to select its color. Be sure to click either in the position where I have clicked or anywhere else the blue is darkest. That's because... well, I have to confess... this is not the best-shot blue screen in the history of the big screen. There are a few lighting variations which make it difficult to pull a clean key.

3. Now hold the cursor over the blue 0 next to where it says Color Tolerance, just under the eye dropper. This will make a little hand appear.

4. Now click and drag to the right until the number reaches 56. This is known as the rub text approach. There are other ways to change values such as these, which you will learn in **Chapter 5**.

> *These effects values can also be accessed from the timeline by clicking the little arrow next to the layer name, and then clicking the arrow next to where it says* Effects, *and then the arrow next to the effect name.*

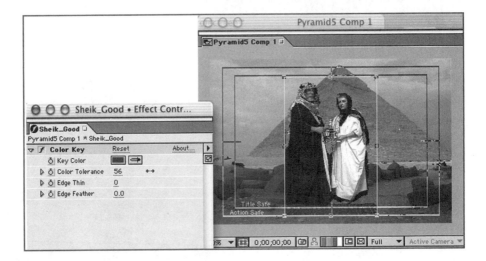

It should now look like we're really there as After Effects provides immediate visual feedback in the Composition window. It may not be perfect, but hey you've only been using After Effects for about two minutes. In **Chapters 4** and **6** there are similar examples providing clever ways to clean up the edges.

Rendering

Now everything has been set, tweaked, arranged, and composited, I'm satisfied that this will be cinema's greatest flying carpet scene in the history of filmmaking. So, it's time to make the movie.

Make your movie

1. From the Composition menu, choose Make Movie.

2. In the following window change the file name to `Pyramid5 Comp 1.mov`. Make certain that the final output will be directed to a drive which has adequate space for the resulting After Effects render, and press Save.

Immediately the Render Queue window will appear.

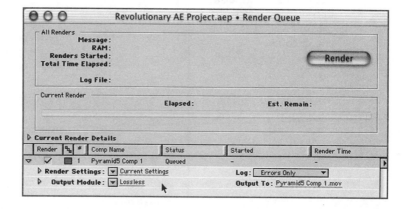

3. Click the blue text next to Render Settings, and the following window will appear:

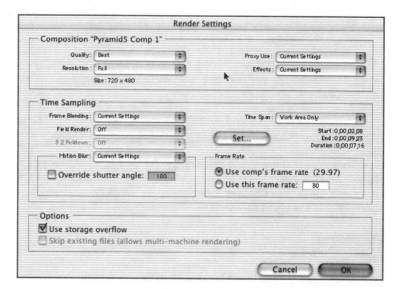

4. Alter your Render Settings window so that it matches the previous screenshot and click OK.

5. Back in the Render Queue window click on Lossless.

6. Alter the Output Module Settings window to match mine and click OK

7. The Render Queue window will now be the front most window. Click Render, watch the progress bar, or go get a cup of coffee.

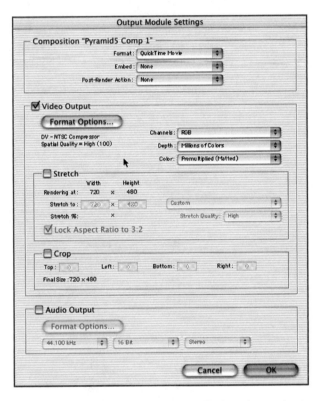

You should now find Pyramid5 Comp 1.mov in the folder which you specified, and can play it using QuickTime. If you haven't got QuickTime, download it from the Apple web site: www.apple.com.

After Effects is a powerful and subtle tool, and to really master it takes a lot of time and effort. However, if you don't want to put in any of that just now, try out some of these exercises.

Save your project and create a new one by clicking File > New Project. Now, just right click on the Project window, select File > Import > Multiple Files… and locate and import everything from the quickies folder in the **Chapter 2** section of the CD. A finished version of each of these effects is also available to look at on the CD.

Ghost

1. Drop the file ghost.mov onto the new composition icon in the Project window.

2. Select the image `background for ghost.bmp` and drag it into the timeline below the ghost movie layer.

3. On the timeline, click Switches/modes – the button at the bottom of the timeline about one third of the way along. The mode button for each layer now appears, labeled Normal right now. Click the mode button (where it says Normal) for the top layer (`ghost.mov`), and select lighten.

4. If you move the playhead to a point at which the actor is in shot, you'll see he has now become a ghost.

Alien eyes

1. Drag the file `hunter.mov` to the new composition icon, in the Project window.

2. With `hunter.mov` selected on the timeline, pick Effect > Channel > Invert, and the image is turned into a negative.

3. Select Effect > Blur & Sharpen > Radial blur, and another effect appears in the Effect Controls window. This time we pick Type and change it from spin to zoom to create a tunnel vision type effect. Our point of view shot is beginning to look very much like that of a sci-fi robot.

4. We finish up with a final effect filter. Choose Effect > Render > Audio Waveform. This creates an oscilloscope type effect, which will modulate with the sound of the clip. On the Composition window, we can drag its start and end points so it covers the entire screen from left to right, and in the Effect Controls window at the bottom, we click the composite on original box.

Star text

1. Create a new composition via the menus Composition > New Composition. Make it 720x540 in size, and about 20 seconds in duration.

2. Click inside the Composition window, hold down CTRL and click. Then choose New > Solid. Make it the same size as the composition and click OK.

3. Immediately select Effect > Text > Basic Text, and type in several lines of text to the window that appears. Hit return between each line of text. When you're finished, click OK.

4. Depending on the size of your text, you may need to use the Size control in the Effect Controls window which appears to reduce it until it fits within the solid you created.

5. Click the stopwatch icon next to the Position label in the Effect Controls window. Now click on the crosshairs in the center and drag it to the bottom of the composition window, such that you can no longer see the text.

6. Click the last frame button on the Time Controls window, and then use the crosshairs again – this time to choose a point just off the top of the composition window. Playing through the composition you can see the text now scrolls up the screen.

7. Now move to the timeline, and click the fifth box in the switches/modes section of the timeline, just under the 3D box icon.

8. Choose the Rotation tool from the toolbox window. Now click and hold on the small square in the Composition window, which is central at the top of the solid.

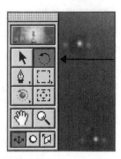

9. Now push forward, to angle the text layer so the text is scrolling away into the distance.

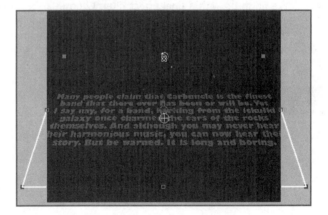

10.   Playing through this, you'll see the words heading off into the distance in true *Star Wars* fashion.

Summary

So, there is a basic overview of the features of After Effects. You should now have at least a feel for After Effects and how it works. Right now you will probably have a thousand questions, but you are able to use After Effects right the way through a small project. In the remainder of this volume, you will have the chance to explore these features in greater detail as you learn to apply the power of this revolutionary application to realize your creative dreams.

3 Starting Up a New Project in After Effects

In this chapter we will be looking at the various settings and options we need to consider for files and footage that we bring into After Effects. It is important to specify how After Effects will treat these inputs as it will influence the way in which elements are combined. This in turn will influence the quality of our final rendered output so it is essential to take the time to set things up correctly. There's no denying this part of the process is not as much fun as applying animation and effects, but if we want our work to look its best, taking the time to set things up correctly is critical.

A project is a single file that stores references to all the footage that is used in that particular video project. It's like a folder that contains all of the research and chapters of our manuscript. It also holds our compositions and contains the information about the arrangement of footage within those **compositions**. A project will often contain several compositions.

Composition settings

Compositions are one of the key components of any After Effects project. It is within a composition that you will organize footage, images, audio, and effects and bring them all together for final rendering and output. Let's take a closer look at what makes up a composition.

Composing your settings

1. Open a new project.

2. Create a new composition.

This brings up a Composition Settings dialog box with a number of options for us to consider.

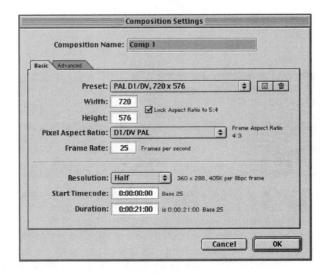

By default these options will be set to the same settings as any previous composition we have created.

3. Beginning at the top of the dialog box, we can name our compositions whatever we like (although for complex projects it is good to get into the habit of using a simple and ordered naming system to save yourself time, and to avoid confusion as the project gets larger and larger). For this exercise name the new composition Symphony Number 5.

   Moving down the Composition Settings dialog box you will notice two tabs titled **basic** and **advanced** settings. Starting with the basic tab, the first option we have is Preset options. After Effects comes with a number of preset options. These options determine the size of the composition frame, the pixel aspect ratio and the frame rate. Different media formats use different resolutions, frame rates and aspect ratios. For example, film speed is 24 frames per second, PAL video uses 25 frames per second, and NTSC video uses 29.97 frames per second. For the most commonly used formats we can use the preset options that come with After Effects. And we can also create our own presets, for output formats which are not covered.

4.   Click on the current preset and you can scroll through a number of other presets including PAL, NTSC, High Definition Television, and even Film.

Custom
Small, 160 x 120
Medium, 320 x 240
NTSC, 640 x 480
NTSC, 648 x 486
NTSC DV, 720 x 480
NTSC DV Widescreen, 720 x 480
NTSC D1, 720 x 486
NTSC D1 Square Pix, 720 x 540
✓ **PAL D1/DV, 720 x 576**
PAL D1/DV Square Pix, 768 x 576
PAL D1/DV Widescreen, 720 x 576
HDTV, 1280 x 720
D4, 1440 x 1024
Cineon Half, 1828 x 1332
HDTV, 1920 x 1080
Film (2K), 2048 x 1536
D16, 2880 x 2048
Cineon Full, 3656 x 2664

*For most projects in print, multimedia, web, film, and TV, it's a good idea to "begin with the end in mind" and it's no different with After Effects. By doing this, we will ensure our After Effects project will look good on what ever platform it is delivered on. If we were working on a project like a movie teaser/trailer to be used for the promotion of an up coming film, and the teaser/trailer was to be released and seen simultaneously at cinemas, TV and the web, we would most likely set up our project for film output, which is a much higher resolution than for TV or the web. We could then adapt this project for TV and the web and maintain a high quality output. However, if we set up our project for a web movie output with a resolution of 160 x 120 pixels, this file would look terrible blown up to TV resolution and even worse on film. So always use the **highest** resolution **needed** for your project's output. I stress **needed,** because we don't want to use the highest resolution possible all the time. The higher the resolution; the longer our render times are. Working to tight deadlines (an unfortunately common occurrence!) means we need to be able to work fast and render fast, whilst maintaining quality.*

5.   For the moment, select PAL D1/DV, 720 x 576 or NTSC D1, 720 x 486, depending upon which region you are in (re-cap **Chapter 2** for more clarification about this).

You will notice the details below: Width, Height, Pixel Aspect Ratio, and Frame Rate have automatically been set. You may have also noticed that to the side of the Preset option there is a grayed out save icon and a trash icon. If you are using specific settings for a project, particularly ones you want to apply to different compositions and projects, you can change all the details for Width, Height, and so on and then save your new settings as a preset to apply to other compositions. You can also delete presets you no longer require by selecting them and hitting the trash icon. Don't worry if you delete any of the standard presets accidentally, you can reset all of the factory presets by holding OPTION (Mac) or ALT (Windows) and clicking the trash icon.

Leaving the Composition Settings window open, let's look at each of the basic settings in more detail, before going on to look at the advanced settings.

Basic composition settings

Frame size

The frame size determines the viewable area of a composition. Only items inside the frame are visible, and it is only these items that are previewed and rendered by After Effects. You are able to set the Width and Height parameters separately, although this time, they have been set for us because we selected one of the preset options. The frame is surrounded by a work area, which allows you to position items outside of the frame and bring them into the frame as required.

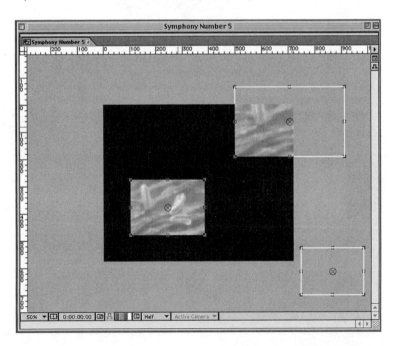

After Effects also allows you to place compositions within other compositions, called "nested compositions" (this is covered in detail in **Chapter 8**).

The Lock Aspect Ratio check box allows you to change the width or the height of a composition while maintaining the aspect ratio. When this box is checked, if you change the width, After Effects will change the height automatically and vice versa. Say we wanted a composition that had a film aspect ratio but we actually wanted the composition frame smaller than a normal film frame (lower resolution). We select the film preset, check the Lock Aspect Ratio box and then change the width or height to the new dimension we require. After Effects will automatically update the other dimension to give us a smaller composition with the same proportions as film. This also allows you to place smaller compositions within the main compositions that are proportional to the main composition.

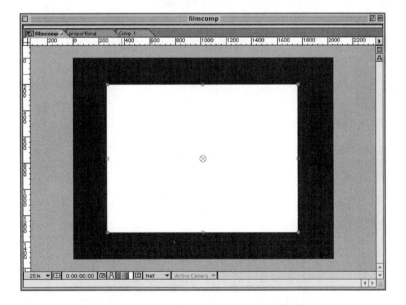

Pixel aspect ratio

Different devices use different size and shape pixels. Computer monitors often use square pixels, whereas D1 format and DV video use rectangular pixels. The pixel aspect ratio compensates for the difference between your system and the final output format. Choose a pixel aspect ratio that corresponds to your final output format. In our case, we selected the Preset for PAL D1 DV, or NTSC D1 DV, so the correct pixel aspect ratio has already been set for us.

In most instances, we would be using one of the present options, which means After Effects will select the corresponding pixel aspect ratio automatically. However, should you encounter situations in which the presets do not cover your required output format, determine the correct pixel aspect ratio for that format. Pixel aspect ratios are covered later on in this chapter (see Pixel Aspect Ratio information under the Interpret Footage window section).

Frame Rate

The frame rate is the number of frames per second (fps) that are displayed to the viewer. **Persistence of vision** is a term often used to describe the process by which a series of still images can be presented to a viewer, and each image is retained on the back of the retina long enough to create the illusion that the viewer is watching something in motion. For persistence of vision to work we need a projection speed of 10 fps or more.

The frame rate we set in our After Effects project, like so many other considerations, usually depends upon the final output we wish to produce.
Generally:

- we can go as low as **12 fps** for the **web**,

- **CD presentations** often fall somewhere **between 12 and 24 fps**,

- **film** for motion pictures/cinema is **24 fps**,

- **PAL** video is **25 fps**

- and **NTSC** video is **29.97 fps**.

We should also consider the frame rate of any footage we have imported for use. For example, if we imported a web animation as footage that was 12 fps, and our composition needs to be 24 fps for cinema release, then as we move along the timeline to see our animation footage advance 1 frame, we will need to move the composition timeline 2 frames. So each frame repeats itself once. Repeating each frame once is something animators sometimes do intentionally, and is referred to as **"animating on two's"**.

But often we don't want frames to repeat themselves, so we can either make sure the composition frame rate matches the footage frame rate, or we can use **frame blending,** which is covered further in **Chapter 9**.

Resolution

Resolution settings can be your best friend, particularly if you're a bit short on memory or processing power. Resolution determines the dimensions of the image in pixels, which affects the image quality of the rendered composition that you view. When it comes time to do your final render, or to check the detail of individual frames, full resolution will give you the image quality you need for TV, Film etc. In the meantime, you can use half, third, quarter, or custom resolution, which allows you to reduce the number of pixels rendered while you are working. This decreases render times dramatically, giving you faster previews and allowing you to get instant feedback on your composition.

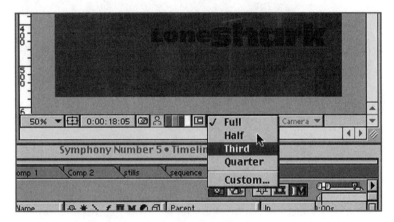

As you decrease the resolution of your composition, images will become pixelated, and have lots of jagged edges, but in the main composition window, you can change the resolution and the viewing size at any time, to check how it will ultimately look. The viewing size is indicated in the bottom left hand corner of the composition window and defaults to 100%. Say you're working at half resolution, you can eliminate the pixelation by setting your viewing window to 50%.

For example, if we start out with PAL footage in a composition that is set to 720 x 576 pixels, our footage will occupy 720 pixels across the screen and 576 pixels down.

If we reduce the resolution in the Composition window to quarter resolution, this reduces the composition to 180 x 144 pixels. The image becomes pixelated because although there is only information for 180 pixels across and 144 pixels down the screen, the image is still occupying a space of 720 x 576 pixels. This is because our viewing window is still set to 100% which is the full image size, and 720 x 576 pixels.

If we reduce the viewing window to match our resolution (i.e. a quarter of 100% = 25%) we end up with a smaller image on screen without the highly pixelated effect.

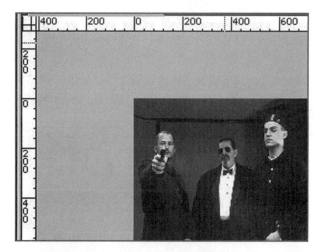

The size of the viewing window can be set to automatically adjust to changes in resolution using the After Effects display preferences, which we will look at later in this chapter.

Start timecode or start frame

Towards the bottom of the set of basic tab options, we come across either Start Timecode or Start Frame. Here we can specify when the composition starts, either at what time, on which frame, or at how many feet and frames, depending on what Display Style we have selected in the Project Settings

Time Options

After Effects has a number of ways to display time, which can be selected from among the Display Style options found in File > Project Settings...

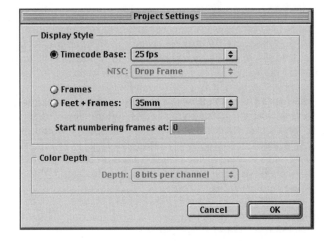

You can display time in terms of **Timecode**, **Frames**, or **Feet + Frames**. Using Timecode is excellent for synchronizing sound and music. However, you may find that sometimes, you want to switch between options. For example, if you come from a traditional animation background, you may intuitively think in terms of frames, (how many frames you would use for a particular walk cycle or wing flap...). You might also find yourself working on a film project, where the edit decision list has been mapped out in Feet + Frames. So it is not unusual to switch between time displays for different tasks.

Timecode Base

By default, time is displayed in hours, minutes, and seconds using the SMPTE timecode. SMPTE timecode is a standard set by the Society of Motion Picture and Television Engineers, and is used widely throughout the film and TV industry. To specify the Timecode Base, ensure the Timecode Base button is selected, and click on the pop-up list to choose from a variety of speeds ranging from 24 fps to 100 fps.

Setting the time display

Return to your project, and for now, lets stick with the Timecode Base.

1.   Select the Timecode Base button

2.   Choose 25 fps for PAL or 30 fps for NTSC.

NTSC drop frame options

If you select 30 fps, the option below for NTSC becomes available and you can choose between Drop Frame or Non-Drop Frame. Video for NTSC television actually plays at 29.97 frames per second, and these options are numbering systems used to adjust for the 29.97 fps running speed of NTSC video. Despite what the terms indicate, no frames are actually lost or skipped, instead frames are merely numbered differently. After Effects defaults to using the SMPTE Drop Frame method of renumbering the first two frame numbers of every minute, except every 10th minute. At a rate of 29.97 fps, After Effects would have to give 0.97 of frame to us every second, which could become very frustrating. The renumbering system allows us to work on whole frames and still output at the correct frames per second. At 30 fps we would get 18,000 frames every ten minutes. With the SMPTE renumbering method we get 17,982 frames every ten minutes. Ten minutes = 600 seconds, so if we divide 17,982 frames by 600 we get 29.97, which is 29.97 fps which is the broadcast speed we need for NTSC. You can also select the Non-Drop Frame timecode, which assumes the rate of 30 fps.

Now lets get back to the Composition Settings dialogue box. Below the Start Timecode, or Start Frame box we come to Duration.

Duration

Duration is the total length of the composition, which we can specify in terms of time, frames, or feet and frames. Once again, this depends on what Display Style we have selected in the Project Settings.

That's it for the basic settings! Click on the Advance tab and we'll continue with the advanced settings.

Advanced composition settings

```
╔══════════════ Composition Settings ══════════════╗
║                                                    ║
║   Composition Name: [ Symphony Number 5 ]          ║
║                                                    ║
║  ┌ Basic ┌ Advanced ┐──────────────────────────┐  ║
║  │                                              │  ║
║  │        Anchor:   [  grid  ]                  │  ║
║  │                                              │  ║
║  │  Shutter Angle:  [ 180 ]                     │  ║
║  │  Shutter Phase:  [ 0 ]                       │  ║
║  │ Nesting Options: ☐ Preserve Frame Rate       │  ║
║  │                  ☐ Preserve Resolution       │  ║
║  │ Rendering Plug-in: [ Standard 3D      ▼ ]    │  ║
║  │                  [ About... ]                │  ║
║  │                                              │  ║
║  └──────────────────────────────────────────────┘  ║
║                                                    ║
║                          [ Cancel ]  [[  OK  ]]    ║
╚════════════════════════════════════════════════════╝
```

Anchor

The first thing we come across is the Anchor setting. The anchor setting determines how the layers in your project are positioned. The default setting for the anchor is the center, which works well most of the time. If you need to change the frame size of a composition, the Anchor setting will determine how the different layers of that composition will be placed within the new frame size. Usually the layers are centered, however you can anchor the layers to the edges or corners of the frame before it is resized.

Shutter Angle

The settings for the shutter angle only come into play if you are using motion blur. The Motion Blur we are referring to is not a filter from the effects menu, although those filters are certainly available. In this case After Effects applies a blur to a layer in movement. The faster the layer is moved, the more blur will be applied. The shutter angle also influences the amount of blur. The shutter angle is measured in degrees, from 1 degree, giving us very little motion blur, to 720 degrees, which gives us intense motion blur. By default, the shutter angle is set to 180 degrees.

Below, motion blur has been enabled for an image which we are moving off the stage over a period of 1 second. The shutter angle is set to 1 degree.

Using the same image and motion, the shutter angle is set to 180 degrees.

Using the same image and motion, the shutter angle is set to 720 degrees.

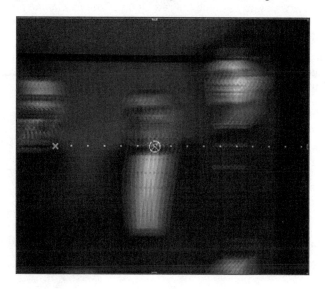

Shutter Phase

You can specify a number up to 360, which determines when the shutter will open relative to the frame start. This will give a smearing or streaking effect on moving layers. It works best on bright items with a dark background. If the background is bright the smears will be difficult to see, and probably not noticeable.

The best way to get a feel for the shutter angle, and shutter phase settings, is to experiment with footage when you require motion blur. Often you may find the default settings are close to what you require, with only minor or no adjustments needed.

Nesting Options

As mentioned earlier, you can place one composition inside another. This is then termed a *nested* composition.

The nesting options present us with two check boxes:

- Preserve Frame Rate

- Preserve Resolution

If Preserve Frame Rate is checked, then the nested composition will maintain its original frame rate, otherwise it will assume the frame rate of the parent composition, in which it is nested.

Similarly, if Preserve Resolution is checked, the nested composition will maintain its original resolution, otherwise it will assume the resolution of the parent composition.

Rendering Plug-in

The default 3D renderer is **Standard**, which allows you to animate layers in 3 dimensions, including shadows and lighting. Clicking the About… button will give you a bit more information about the plug-in.

That just about covers all the options you can play with when creating a new composition. Ordinarily, you'd have planned your project out, and already know which settings you want to use. However, this is probably not the case at this stage. Don't worry if you later want to change some of the composition settings, because the great thing is you can change them at anytime. All you need to do is to simply select Composition > Composition Settings…, or press CTRL + K (Windows) or COMMAND + K (Mac), and the Composition Settings dialogue box will await your command!

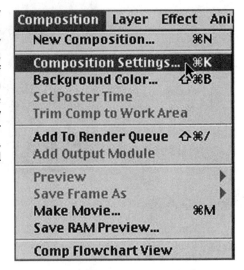

Setting preferences

After Effects is already set up with default preferences, which we will now begin to customize. Don't worry about setting the wrong preferences, as default preferences can be restored at any time by deleting the After Effects **Prefs** file, while After Effects is shut down. Upon starting After Effects, a new default preferences file will be created.

To begin setting preferences, choose Edit > Preferences and then make a selection from the numerous sub-menus.

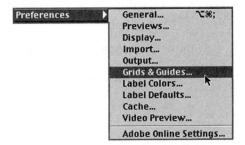

Before we go any further, let's run through the options we have here and look at what each one does. Let's start with the **General** options.

Edit > Preferences > General options

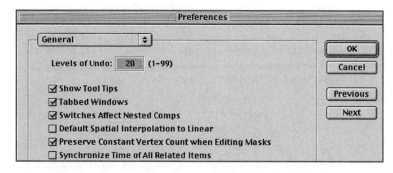

From this dialogue box, you can move to other preference sub-menus by selecting from the pop-up list at the top, which is currently set to General. *You can also use the* Previous *or* Next *buttons to the side.*

The first option we can set is the levels of undo. For mistakes, accidents and experiments that yield less than satisfactory results, you can rely on the undo command (Edit > Undo or CTRL + Z for Windows, and COMMAND + Z for Mac) to sequentially undo up to 99 of the most recent changes to your work. The default undo level is 20 which I find is more than adequate, I can often get away with 10 or less. The thing to keep in mind when setting the level of undo is the higher you set it, the more memory it requires, and that's memory you may need to be working on other areas of your project.

We can also turn a number of check box options on and off. These options include:

Tabbed windows

This places a newly opened composition in the comp and timeline windows, each composition separated by their own tab. If this option is turned off, each composition you open will be placed in a separate new window.

Switches Affect Nested Comps

On the main timeline, there are a number of switches. The switches allow you to turn various levels of functionality on and off for each layer, which is useful in allowing you to work faster. By having this option turned on, any switches we turn on or off for a composition will affect any other compositions that are nested within it.

Default spatial interpolation to linear

Interpolation is the way in which After Effects defines changes between keyframes in an animation. Spatial interpolation is the interpolation between motion path keyframes through space. After Effects uses Auto Bezier curves to define changes/motion between keyframes as a default. The default interpolation can be changed to linear if this check box is selected.

Preserve constant vertex count when editing masks

This option, when checked, will have After Effects add or delete control points to a mask's entire duration, when you add or delete control points. Note that the mask is only reshaped at the time the control point was added or deleted.

Synchronize time of all related items

When checked, this option will update the current time markers of all windows of nested compositions, when you move the current time marker in any of them.

Edit > Preferences > Previews

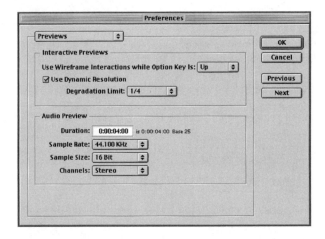

From here, we can specify settings for Interactive Previews and Audio Preview.

The Interactive Previews section allows us to select how wireframe interactions are used. Wireframe interactions, replaces the images/footage of a layer with a wireframe rectangle when a layer is being moved. The layer is updated in the Composition window after you have finished moving it.

Another useful option is the Dynamic Resolution, which allows After Effects to substitute a lower resolution for a layer while the layer is being manipulated. This can improve the ease and speed of working.

In the Previews dialog box, we are also able to specify the quality at which our audio will play for previews, without affecting the audio quality when we render the project. CD audio quality is 16 bit, 44kHz sample rate, DV audio quality is 16 bit, 48 kHz. So if we are going to use sound from our DV recording, it is a good idea to match the sample rate.

Changing the sample rate

Open a sample project to try changing the sample rate.

1.   Select Edit > Preferences > Previews…

2.   In the Audio Preview section, change the Sample Rate to 48.000kHz.

Edit > Preferences > Display

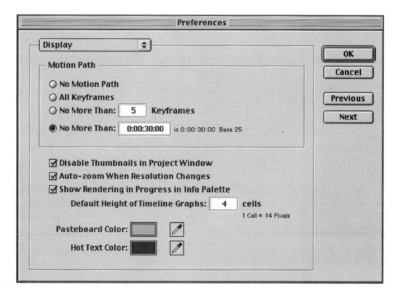

The window presents us with a number of display options as follows:

Motion Path

When you are animating the movement of an object or layer, (in other words, changing its movement/position over time), After Effects can display paths that describe that movement. These paths are displayed as a series of little dots, like a trail of bread crumbs.

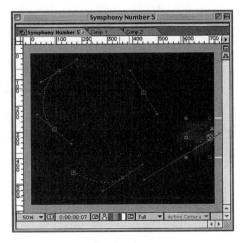

We will deal with the animation of movement and other attributes further throughout the rest of the book. For now we will look at the options we have available for how After Effects displays motion paths. From the Motion *Path* box you can select one of the following buttons:

- No Motion Path – which will hide motion paths and their key frames

- All Keyframes – which will show all keyframes in the composition frame

- No More Than: __ Keyframes – which will limit the number of keyframes displayed around the current time marker

- No More Than: 0:00:15:00 – which sets the time range within which keyframes are displayed, 15 seconds would show us keyframes within 7.5 seconds either side of the current-time marker.

Why do we need all these options? For a complex animation, with a lot of movement going on, it can become confusing when we are animating or refining animation if there are motion paths from different objects/layers intersecting and overlapping all over the screen. This is when the motion path display options come in very handy.

Disable Thumbnails in Project Window

This option is a memory saver. Thumbnails are nice to have, so that you can readily see footage and images in the project window, but if you're short on memory, you don't really need thumbnails, particularly if you've named all the files you import sensibly.

Auto Zoom When Resolution Changes

As we discussed earlier, when you reduce a composition's resolution, the image becomes pixilated, which is quite ok, particularly if you need to work rough and fast. If you still want a clear image once you have reduced the resolution, you need to reduce the display size of the composition accordingly. If you have the Auto Zoom When Resolution Changes option selected, After Effects will do this for you automatically.

Show rendering in progress in info palette

This will display the progress of your rendering in the Info palette, which is useful when you have a lot of renders to get through.

You can also set the default height of timeline graphs. The timeline graphs will be covered in more detail in **Chapter 5** as they are often used to fine tune the animation of layer properties. This option allows you.to specify how high these graphs will appear in the Timeline window.

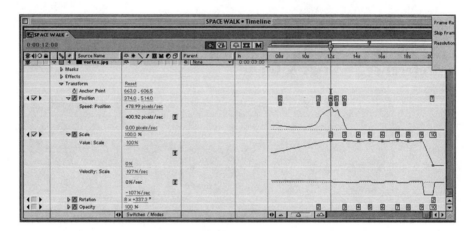

Pasteboard Color

The color around the project's frame can be set by clicking on the color swatch, or using the eyedropper. The default grey is often a good color as it allows you to concentrate on what is taking place within the composition, without adversely attracting attention to itself or drastically interfering with color perception. The main considerations when setting the Pasteboard color is it should be easy to work with, and should contrast enough with the layers within the composition. If you had a lot of snow footage, it's probably not a good idea to set the Pasteboard to white.

Hot Text Color

Hot text is the colored text and numbers that can be clicked on for further options, or edited to change variables when animating. For example, in a composition timeline window, the current time indicator that sits to the top left in the format 0:00:00:00, is hot text and should be a blue color by default. This option allows you to change the color of the text. Hot text makes setting and changing variables such as an objects position, rotation, or alpha setting, very convenient.

Edit > Preferences > Grids & Guides

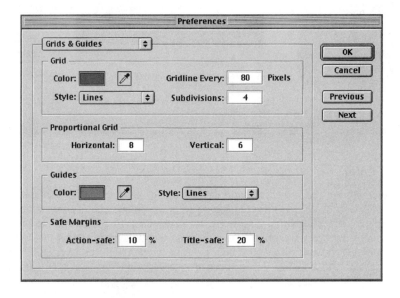

When it comes to a composition's layout, we can find a number of useful options in the Grids and Guides preferences window. Grids and guides are very handy for organizing, positioning and aligning the various layers within a composition. From here, we can set the options for standard grids, proportional grids, guides, and safe margins.

Grid

Standard grids will remain the same size that we set them, no matter how we change the composition size. We set the distance between grid lines in pixels. For standard grid lines, we can also specify subdivisions, which are thinner lines between main grid lines.

To reveal the standard grid select View > Show Grid. Now that the grid is visible, if you go back to the View menu, you'll see that the option has changed to Hide Grid.

Proportional Grid

Proportional grids increase or decrease to correspond with any change in the composition size, and we can specify how many horizontal or vertical columns the grid is divided into.

To reveal the proportional grid, hold down ALT (Windows) or OPTION (Mac) and click the safe areas icon on the composition window.

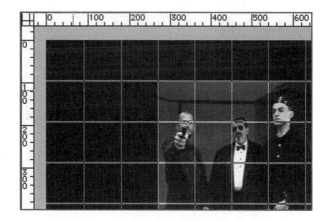

When choosing the color for grids or guides, consider the footage or images you will be working with. Say you were working with footage of a lush green hillside, green grids or guides are probably not your best option!

When you are positioning layers within a composition, you can also have them snap to the grid lines (select View > Snap to Grid).

Guides

Guides are a very flexible tool to use when laying out your composition because you can quickly position them to where ever you want.

The left hand side and the top of the Composition window have rulers. If you cannot see rulers in your Composition window choose View > Show Rulers. If you move the mouse over these rulers you will notice it changes from a normal pointer to "double arrows". When this happens, click and drag back into the Composition window and a vertical or horizontal line will move with your mouse. Release the mouse to drop it in position. If you are not happy with the position you can move the mouse over the guide and the "double arrows" will appear again, indicating you can move it by pressing and dragging again.

The Info window gives you feed back on where the Guide Position is within the composition. If your Info window is not open choose Window > Info.

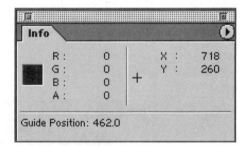

Safe Margins

Towards the bottom of the Grids and Guides options panel, you will find another important composition/layout tool, the Safe Margins settings. When dealing with video images for television, we need to consider overscan, which is what happens when television monitors enlarge an image, and often cause the edges of it to be cut off. Different television monitors handle images differently, and there is a wide variety of televisions in use, so to counter this problem we use action-safe and title safe areas.

Safe-action is the area in which it is safe to display any important action, elements, scenery, and so on, we wish to be seen, which is very handy when animating objects around the screen.

Safe-title is the area in which we can safely display any titles/text we wish to be readable, essential for title credit sequences and the like. The safe-title area is typically smaller than the safe-action area.

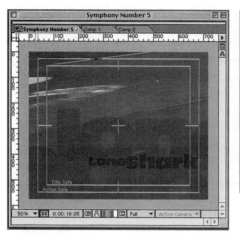 

In After Effects, we can set the size of safe-titles and safe-action as a percentage of the composition that falls outside of the safe area. This gives us an "unsafe" area, that runs inside the edge of the compositions frame.

It is sometimes a good idea to run off some test plates or test footage to work out your safe titles and safe action areas, as this may change depending upon your final output.

Edit > Preferences > Import...

After Effects is able to import a wide variety of different file types, including image files, still image sequences, movie files, audio, Photoshop files, Illustrator files, and Adobe Premiere projects. When After Effects imports files, it does not copy the whole file, which is why After Effects files remain relatively small. Instead, After Effects makes a link to the original file. So it is important to organize your files, to maintain your links. Although broken links are easily fixed, you don't want it to happen to a whole project if you can avoid it.

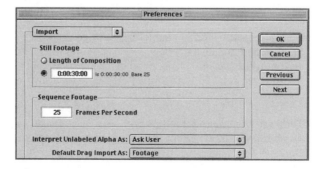

There are a few options we can set in the Import preferences window for importing images and footage files. In this window, we can set options for

- still footage

- sequence footage

- unlabeled alpha channel interpretation

- drag import default settings

Still footage

If you import a still image to use with a composition, and then drag that image into the composition, the default image's time on screen will be the entire time of the composition. To change the default screen time of imported images, make sure the Import Preferences windows is open. You will notice that in the Still Footage box, Length of Composition is selected. Let's play with this feature in our own project.

Importing into the project

1. If it is not still open, open up the project you've been playing with, in the Import preferences window, select the time option, and set it to 30 seconds, so that it reads 0:00:30:00 (SPMTE timecode format is hours:minutes:seconds:frames). Click OK.

2. Now import the still image `thirty_sec.jpg` by selecting File > Import > File...

3. Next, revisit Edit > Preferences > Import... and change the Still Footage time option to 10 seconds (0:00:10:00).

4. Import another still image, `ten_sec.jpg`. You should now be able to see `thirty_sec.jpg` and `ten_sec.jpg` in the project window.

5. Now create a new composition (Composition > New Composition...) with either the PAL or NTSC preset, and with a Duration of at least 1 minute (0:01:00:00). Call it `stills`.

6. In the project window, double click the composition `stills`, and the composition window and timeline will open. Now click and hold while you drag `thirty_sec.jpg` to the right hand side of the timeline, and you will notice that a time indicator follows your movements, and that the current time indicator to the left updates itself as you move back and forth along the time line.

7. Let's say we wanted the `thirty_sec.jpg` image to begin 15 seconds into our composition. Drag it along the timeline to around the 15 second mark and let go. Because we originally set the still import options to 30 seconds, the `thirty_sec.jpg`

image should sit on the timeline from around the 15 second mark to around the 45 second mark.

8. Now drag the `ten_sec.jpg` image onto the timeline, and you will notice as you drag it above or below the existing layer, that a dark line appears on, above, or below the existing layer.

9. Place the `ten_sec.jpg` above the `thirty_sec.jpg`, drag the `ten_sec.jpg` so the dark line is above the existing layer and the current time indicator is around the 15 seconds mark, then let go. The `ten_sec.jpg` layer should now sit above the `thirty_sec.jpg` layer, and should have a third of the duration of the `thirty_sec.jpg` layer.

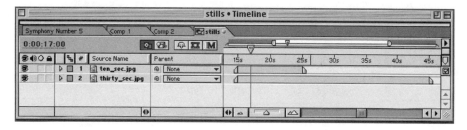

As you now scroll along the timeline, you should see 15 seconds worth of blank, followed by 10 seconds of the `ten_sec.jpg` image, and then the layer underneath should be exposed to reveal the remaining 20 seconds of the `thirty_sec.jpg` image.

In the Import preferences window, below the Still Footage box, we come to the Sequence Footage box.

Sequence Footage

After Effects is able to import a series, or sequence, of still images and will treat it as one file, as if it were a footage file. Each image is treated as if it were a frame of footage and will be imported in numeric, or alphabetic order. I recommend numbering the files in the order you wish them to appear to avoid confusion. The files must also have the same file name pattern and be of the same file type.

For example, the sequence below will import correctly:

- image001.jpg
- image002.jpg
- image003.jpg
- image004.jpg
- image005.jpg

But, the following sequences will not import correctly due to the various inconsistencies highlighted:

- image01.jpg
- image02.jpg
- image03.tif – **different file type**
- image04.jpg
- image05.jpg

- image001.jpg
- image002.jpg
- image3.jpg – **different numbering system**
- image004.jpg
- image005.jpg

- image1.jpg
- image2.jpg
- imack3.jpg – **different file name**
- image4.jpg
- image5.jpg

When dealing with a sequence of images, we can set what its frame rate will be when imported in the Import Preferences window. Setting the frame rate will determine how fast or slow the sequence footage plays. Say we had a sequence of rendered images from a 3D animation which we had animated at 24 fps for a film project. We would usually set the Sequence Footage to match the 24 fps so that the speed and timing of our animation is accurate. If at the last minute, the project changed from film to PAL video, we might decide that the small increase in speed to 25 fps was acceptable. In this case, in the first second of the sequence file the first 24 frames of the animation would play, plus the first frame of the next second of the animation. The sequence would play slightly faster than the original animation.

> *This is separate from setting the frame rate of imported footage. Imported footage should always be set to the original frame rate of the footage. (File > Interpret Footage > Main...)*

Importing images

1. Select Edit > Preferences > Import... If you are using PAL, set the Sequence Footage box to 25 Frames Per Second. If you are using NTSC, set the Sequence Footage box to 30 Frames Per Second. Click OK.

   Now lets import some images as a sequence.

2. Select File > Import > File...

3. Select any one of the following sequence files:

   - surprise001.jpg
   - surprise002.jpg
   - surprise003.jpg
   - surprise004.jpg
   - surprise005.jpg
   - surprise006.jpg
   - surprise007.jpg
   - surprise008.jpg
   - surprise009.jpg
   - surprise010.jpg

4. Check the JPEG Sequence box and click Import.

5. Create a new composition called `sequence` and use a PAL DV or NTSC DV preset. Open the sequence composition, and drag the `surprise` sequence onto the timeline.

Because we set the import preference frame rate to 25 or 30 fps to match our PAL or NTSC settings, when you scroll through the timeline, you'll notice that our sequence file displays 1 separate image on each frame of the timeline.

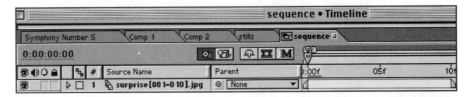

But what if we wanted each image to hold for say... 2 frames ("animating on twos", as we saw earlier)? In that case, we could have set our Sequence Footage Frames per second to half the speed of our composition in the import preferences before we imported the images. But the other thing we can do is actually change the frame rate of our imported files. Let's do this now.

6. Select the `surprise` sequence in the project window, and then select File > Interpret Footage > Main.... (We'll be looking at this window in more detail at the end of the chapter.)

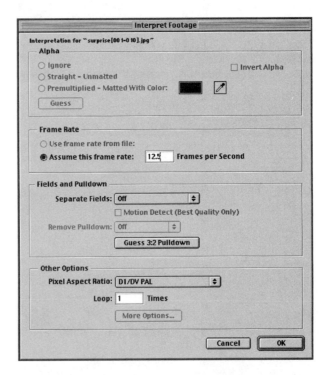

7. In the Frame Rate box, change the Assume this frame rate value to 12.5 fps for PAL, or 15 fps for NTSC. Click OK.

Now, returning to our sequence composition, you will notice the surprise[001-010].jpg sequence layer now has twice the duration as it had before but the Out point has remained in the same position.

Drag the Out point to the right, so the entire sequence layer is visible. Now as you scroll through the timeline, each image of the surprise sequence layer should remain on screen for 2 frames.

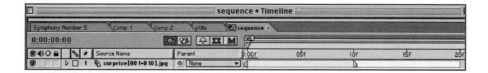

Interpret unlabeled alpha

Another option we can specify in the import preferences is how After Effects interprets unlabeled alpha channels.

The alpha channel handles image transparency information. When After Effects imports a file with an alpha channel, it will check to see if the alpha channel should be handled as straight alpha, or premultiplied. If, however, the alpha channel is unlabeled (not specified), After Effects can handle the situation in a variety of ways, which can be preset, or set at the time of import.

In the Edit > Preferences > Import... window you can determine how After Effects deals with unlabeled alpha channels for imported files. The Interpret Unlabeled Alpha category has a pop-up list with a variety of options.

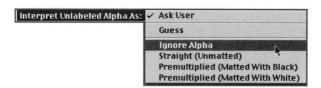

By default, After Effects is set to Ask User, which lets you decide the best interpretation method every time you import images with an alpha channel. This option is often the most useful if you are importing a variety of images that handle alpha information in different ways.

Another option is also to have After Effects guess the best interpretation method. You can also choose to ignore alpha channels.

However, if you are importing a large number of a particular type of image that all handle unlabeled alpha information in the same way, you can also select from three interpretation methods:

- Straight

- Premultiplied (Matted with Black)

- Premultiplied (Matted with White)

Check with the application you used to create the image to determine how it handles the alpha channel.

When an image has a straight alpha channel, the transparency information is stored in a separate channel from the color channels, and is termed unmatted alpha. If Straight is selected as the unlabeled alpha import option, the alpha channel is interpreted as straight alpha.

An image with a premultiplied alpha channel stores the transparency information in the alpha channel, but it also stores the same data in the RGB channels, which are multiplied with a background color. This is termed matted alpha. The colors are shifted toward the background color in proportion to their level of transparency. Often, the background color is black or white.

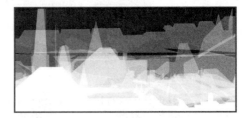

If Premultiplied (Matted with Black) is selected, After Effects interprets the alpha channel as premultiplied with a black background. If Premultiplied(Matted with White) is selected, After Effects interprets the alpha channel as premultiplied with a white background.

If your project required highest quality imaging, say for film quality, straight alpha channels produce the best results. However, premultiplied alpha channels still produce satisfactory results for many applications. Problems that may arise from alpha channel misinterpretation include halos around objects, or incorrect colors at the edges of image transparencies. Should you encounter this, try a different alpha interpretation option.

Default Drag Import As

Another way to import items is to drag them into the project window. If you drag a folder into the project window, its contents will be imported as a sequence by default. However, if you wish the contents to be imported as individual footage files, hold down Alt (Windows) or Option (Mac) as you drag. The other option you have available is to have dragged items imported as compositions.

You can specify this in the import preferences by changing the Default Drag Import As, from Footage to Comp. This last option is useful if you are using Photoshop files that have a lot of layers. If you drag the photoshop.psd file into the project window, it will create a new composition with each Photoshop layer converted into an After Effects layer. The new composition will have the same dimensions as the original Photoshop file.

Linked to our import preferences are the options housed in the Interpret Footage window that we looked at in the last exercise. So before we go on to look at the rest of the options available from the Edit > Preferences menu, we're just going to take a bit of time to look more closely at what we can do with the Interpret Footage window.

Exploring the Interpret Footage window

To modify how After Effects interprets imported footage files choose File > Interpret Footage > Main... Here, you can change the way After Effects handles and interprets footage regarding

- alpha channels

- frame rates

- fields and pulldown

- pixel aspect ratio

- looping

Let's take a look at what each of these does.

Alpha Channel

The first box we come to is Alpha, in which we can specify how the alpha channel (if any) of a footage file is interpreted by After Effects, in the same way we dealt with *unlabeled alpha* in the import options dialog box, choosing between Ignore, Straight, and Premultiplied.

Frame Rate

The Frame Rate of any footage item defaults to the Use Frame Rate from File option. Usually we want footage to assume its original frame rate as the relationship between the footage frame rate and the composition frame rate determines how smoothly the layer plays. If our footage is 24 fps and our composition is 24 fps, then for every frame we progress in the composition timeline, the footage also progresses one frame. If our footage is 18 fps and our composition is 24 fps, then for every frame we progress in the composition timeline, the footage will progress 0.75 of a frame, which means our playback won't be as smooth.

You can also change the frame rate at which footage plays within After Effects by selecting Conform to frame rate, and then typing in the desired frame rate as we explored previously with the surprise[001-010].jpg image sequence. Just keep in mind that if your footage contains audio you wish to use, the synchronization will be out for the new frame rate.

Fields and Pulldown

After Effects also allows us to specify how it interprets Fields and Pulldown.

Most broadcast video is known as interlaced footage because it does not display an entire frame of footage in one instance. Instead, the frame is divided into two fields of alternating horizontal lines (called the upper field and the lower field), as if you put the frame through a paper shredder and separated it into a collection of odd strips and a collection of even strips. The two fields are then flashed in quick succession on the screen to give the impression of a single image. We won't be covering fields in any more depth until **Chapter 9**, but feel free to take a look if you want to know more about this now.

The important part of it for us is to know whether our footage is interlaced, and if it is, which of the two fields flash on the screen first. Fortunately, controlling this in the Interpret Footage window is a lot less complicated than explaining it!

In the Separate Fields pop-up list, select Upper Field First for Avid video. Select Lower Field First for DV footage, or footage captured from an IEEE 1394 FireWire / iLink.

We can leave Separate Fields off if we have footage which uses progressive scan, as this is non-interlaced. Progressive Scan is where each frame is displayed in its entirety from top to bottom. Much like a film projector displays each frame of film, one after the other. A computer monitor uses progressive scan, as do some of the more expensive DV cameras.

If you are unsure of which field is flashed first, just select Upper Field First, and then open the footage from the project window by holding down ALT (Windows) or OPTION (Mac) and double-clicking the footage. This will open the footage in the Footage window. Make sure the time controls are visible (Window > Show Time Controls) and then find a segment of the footage that contains some moving elements that should continue in a constant direction. Step forward through 6 or so frames and observe that the moving elements do in fact move consistently in the one direction. If they do, we made the right selection. If the moving areas move back every second frame, then open the Interpret Footage window again and select Lower Field First instead.

When to use 3:2 pulldown

Because film runs at 24 fps and NTSC runs at 29.97 fps, if we tried to transfer the film footage frame for frame, the video version would run at approximately 125% of the original movies speed. To avoid this problem, film is transferred to NTSC video by a process called 3:2 pulldown.

3:2 pulldown works by having the first frame of film transferred to fields 1 and 2 of the first video frame and also to field 1 of the second video frame. The second frame of film is then transferred to the field 2 of the second video frame and field 1 of the third video frame. This 3:2 distribution pattern is then repeated for the entire footage. Again, we'll talk about this a little more in **Chapter 9**.

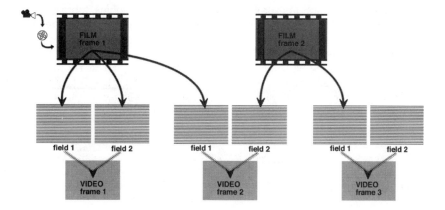

If this has been applied to the footage you are using, you will need to inform After Effects to ensure that any work you do in After Effects will synchronize properly with the film frame rate (After Effects will work with the footage as if it was still at 29.9fps unless you tell it you have applied a 3:2 pulldown to it).

To inform After Effects, we use the Interpret Footage dialog box, and after selecting the field separation method, we click the Guess 3:2 Pulldown button, and After Effects will determine the 3:2 pulldown phase order. We could specify the pulldown phase order ourselves if we know it by selecting from the Remove Pulldown pop-up list.

Why PAL does not use 3:2 Pulldown

PAL runs at 25 fps, which is a closer speed to film, and uses a different method to accommodate the difference. One method is to show 24 frames of the film and then repeat the 24th frame. This fits 24 + 1 film images into the 25 PAL video frames, however, this method is not often used as it results in a slight stutter every second because of the extra inserted image. A more common method is to transfer the images frame to frame, which means the film will now play on PAL video slightly faster (4% faster). This is less of a problem than the 24 + 1 stutter, and is not noticeable by the vast majority of viewers.

Other Options

In the Other Options section of the Interpret Footage window, we can specify the pixel aspect ratio, and also whether we wish footage to loop within a composition.

Pixel Aspect Ratio

Pixel Aspect Ratio, is the ratio of width to height of a pixel. The main thing to remember when setting the pixel aspect ratio for the interpret footage dialog box is that we match the ratio for the imported footage, not the ratio for final output. In the interpret footage dialog box, you can choose a setting from the pixel aspect ratio pop-up menu.

When all footage files are interpreted correctly, you can combine footage with different pixel aspect ratios within the same composition and render output that plays correctly.

The other thing to note is that if you import a computer image file, from say Photoshop or Illustrator, that has the same resolution (frame dimensions) as D1 or DV, then After Effects may set the wrong pixel aspect ratio because it mistakes the file for D1 or DV format footage, in which case you will need to change it back to square pixels so the image will not be distorted.

The following table can be used as a guide:

SETTING	PIXEL ASPECT RATIO	FRAME SIZE	FRAME ASPECT RATIO
Square Pixels	1.0	640 x 480, or 648 x 486	
D1/DV NTSC	0.9	720 x 480, or 720 x 486	4:3
D1/DV NTSC widescreen	1.2	720 x 480, or 720 x 486	16:9
D1/DV PAL	1.0666	720 x 576	4:3
D1/DV PAL widescreen	1.422	720 x 576	16:9
Anamorphic 2:1	2.0		*use for footage shot with anamorphic film lens
D4/D16 Standard	0.948	1440 x 1024, or 2880 x 2048	4:3
D4/D16 Anamorphic	1.896	1440 x 1024, or 2880 x 2048	8:3

Loop

Say we had some insect wings that needed animating, or a character's walk cycle, or some rain effects. Rather than animate every single wing flap, or each step, or each drop of rain, we can have the footage loop within a composition, for however long we need by specifying the number of loops in the Interpret Footage window.

That about covers it for the Interpret Footage window. Now we'll return to our Edit > Preferences options, and the Output window.

Edit > Preferences > Output...

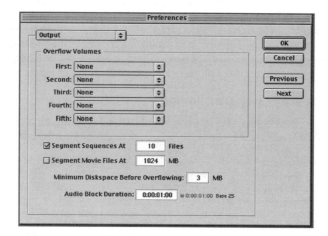

The After Effects output options window allows you to set up a project's render characteristics to take into account limited hard disk space, the need to divide a render into segments, and to specify the Audio Block Duration (see below).

Specifying output options is critical, particularly for rendering large projects and ensuring you don't completely clog up your hard drives. When rendering even modest projects, at PAL or NTSC resolution, the file size of each frame can quickly add up from frames, to seconds, to minutes, to gigabytes. This is the engine room that ensures we don't get a runaway train!

Overflow Volumes

In the Overflow Volumes box, you can specify up to 5 different hard drives / storage locations which a project can overflow to when free hard disk space runs low. Space constraints can be a real pain, so having one or more additional hard disks is a good idea, and you can now pick up decent size firewire hard disks for a reasonable price. After Effects will store the overflowed files in a folder on the root directory of the specified volume.

Segment Sequences

At times, you may need to render compositions as a sequence of single frames, perhaps to import into a film recorder, or to use a networked rendering process for large projects.

Looking again at the preferences Output window, you can see you are able to Segment Sequences, and specify the number of files it should segment at. If you wanted to separate the project into segments of 100 frames, you would select the Segment Sequences check box and specify 100 files. For every 100 frames, After Effects will create a separate folder to store the files.

Segment Movie files

Sometimes, you may also need to segment your composition into separate movie files. For example, you may have a movie that renders greater than 650MB, which means if you want to distribute it on CD without changing composition size, image quality or compression settings, you need to distribute it on more than one CD. To segment the movie, in the preferences Output window, you can tick the Segment Movie Files At checkbox and specify a segment size, say 600MB, leaving us 50 MB for menu information. This will place each 600MB chunk of video on separate CDs.

Minimum Disk space Before Overflowing

To help After Effects determine when it should start rendering on another drive, we can specify how much free space must be left untouched, at which point AfterEffects will begin rendering on the next drive. Let's try this with our own project.

Getting ready to render

1. Return to our `Project AEStudioEx.aep` file, open Edit > Preferences > Output... and set the Minimum Disk space Before Overflowing to 100MB.

    This gives the drive a comfort zone of 100MB which allows for other files, particularly system files, to be written to, without worrying about running out of disk space, but is still not a large chunk considering hard disks are typically now 10 gig or more!

    When it is time to render, there are a variety of ways to go about it. You can select the relevant composition in the project window and select Composition > Make Movie... From the dialog box, you can specify the hard drive, folder location, and movie name for your render. Alternatively, you can select File > Export..., and then choose from a variety of formats. You can also select Edit > Add To Render Queue, or Window > Render Queue, and then drag the composition from the project window to the Render Queue window. We'll look at rendering in much more detail in **Chapter 8**. A basic understanding of the process involved is all we need for now.

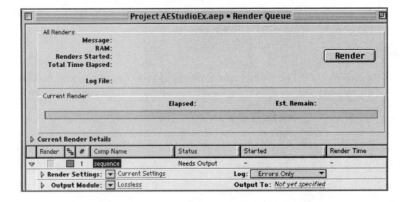

2. Open the Render Queue window, and drag the composition sequence from the project window to the Render Queue window.

In the Render Queue window, you will need to specify where you wish the render to be output to. You will notice that currently, the render item has Output To: listed as Not yet specified.

3. Click on Not yet specified, and then set the hard drive location you wish the composition to be rendered to.

Audio block duration

Audio Block Duration is where you can specify audio interleaving, which can be important for working with large movie files. Audio interleaving is used to protect an audio stream from data loss. This is achieved by breaking the audio data up and distributing it over a larger physical area of a disk, which is then re-assembled during playback. The result is that the distribution of errors becomes random, and an error occupies $1/75^{th}$ of a second, which makes it easy for the missing audio to be interpolated and played correctly.

This is often not an issue when using After Effects, but if you find you are having problems, consult with the documentation from you video card manufacturer.

Although you can create AVI files larger than 1 GB in After Effects, the AVI file may not open or play due to file format limitations in Video for Windows. However, some video cards permit playback of 1GB or bigger movies, if audio interleaving is set to 1 frame. To set audio interleaving to 1 frame set the Audio Block duration (0:00:00:01).

Edit > Preferences > Label Colors...

After Effects uses a label system to indicate what type of media a layer contains, assigning different colors to compositions, footage, stills, and so on. This kind of color-coding provides a very useful visual cue when working with complex projects or compositions, allowing you to sort through a vast amount of layers and a wide variety of footage and image formats.

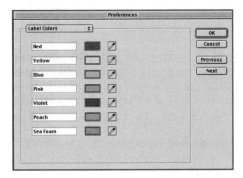
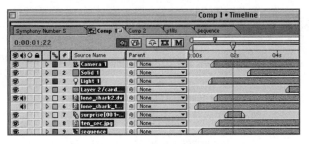

You can assign different colors to the label system by selecting Edit > Preferences > Label Colors... You can then rename colors, select the color swatch to bring up the color picker, or use the eyedropper tool.

Edit > Preferences > Label Defaults...

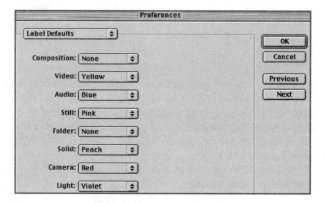

When you're happy with your color preferences, you can then assign the different colors to the different file / media types by selecting Edit > Preferences > Label Defaults... and then assigning different colors to different layer types.

While working in a composition, you can also assign labels to a layer by selecting the layer in the timeline, opening Edit > Label, and then assigning a color. You can also select a layer, and then select all layers of that type by choosing Edit > Label > Select Label Group. This is very handy for making changes to a number of layers of the same type at once.

Edit > Preferences > Cache...

Anyone working as an editor or compositor on a non linear system will tell you, with wide and anxious eyes, "get as much memory as you can afford!". Working with large image files and footage that naturally has many frames is often very memory and processor intensive.

After Effects speeds up the process of previewing and editing by storing image files and rendered compositions in memory (RAM). When you view a frame on the timeline, the rendered image is stored in memory. This means that when you view the image again, instead of recreating it, After Effects just calls up the one it generated earlier from its memory. You will notice that a green line will form at the top of the timeline for the frames you have viewed.

To set the image cache options (the cache is just a part of the memory that can temporarily store information), open Edit > Preferences > Cache...

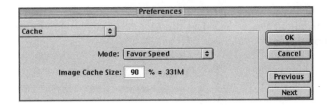

For the Mode setting, you can either select Favor Speed or Favor Memory. The Favor Speed option will make rendering and editing faster, as After Effects will only reorganize the cache as it runs out of memory. After Effects will continue to store more frames until in runs out of memory, when it will start discarding the earlier viewed frames in favor of the latest frames.

The Favor Memory option will reorganize the cache as you work, keeping it smaller, and making rendering more memory efficient. However, this will often slow After Effects down.

For either option, After Effects will automatically optimize the cache when you select a RAM preview, and when it is in between renders from the render queue.

Also in the cache preferences window, you can set the image cache size as a percentage of installed RAM, allocated to After Effects. A setting of over 90% is not recommended, unless you are using virtual memory, in which case a setting of over 200% is not recommended. However, Adobe does not recommend the use of virtual memory or applications such as RAM Doubler, because they significantly slow After Effects down. I'd have to agree. Avoid them if you can!

Edit > Preferences > Video Preview...

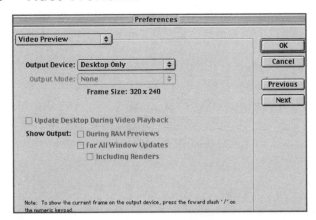

If you have an external video monitor with the relevant video card or fire wire device, you can use it to preview composition, footage or layer windows in After Effects. The Video Preview preferences window allows you to specify the device After Effects uses for output. Devices that are available for output will be listed in the Output Device menu. Output Mode settings will also depend upon the device you have selected.

The Update Desktop During Video Playback option will play previews on the external monitor and computer screen simultaneously.

You can also use the Video Preview preferences to specify the Show Output options. During RAM Previews will display RAM previews on the external monitor. For All Window Updates will update the video preview on the external monitor whenever there is a window update. Including Renders allows you to view each frame on the external monitor as it renders. Although render time is often 'time to find something else to do' time, even though you may feel like an anxious soon-to-be parent, impatiently waiting for the birth of your latest creation.

Summary

By now you should be familiar enough with composition settings, preference settings and project settings to allow you to set up a project that will produce the best results for your target output. We've covered a lot, so don't be concerned if you cannot remember it all. The more you use After Effects, the more familiar it will become. In the meantime, it's sufficient to have some idea of where to find things and from there you can cross each bridge as you come to it.

As I said at the beginning, setting up a project is not as much fun as getting your hands dirty with some animation or effects. To do that though we're going to need something to animate, so let's plough on into **Chapter 4** where well use some other tools to create something which we can actually import, and actually start to see what After Effects can do.

4 Importing and Compositing

After Effects is almost never used on its own. It's not easy to create an effect from scratch within the package. It is easy to use it to process images and clips produced in a range of other programs. It's also easy to implement some stunning effects, which are not available, or at least cannot be easily done, in any other program. Preparing the material you go on to use in After Effects is often the most significant part of an After Effects job, and it's essential you know how best to create and import files to get the best results.

This isn't always as simple as it sounds. There's a vast range of file types you can import into After Effects, and which of these you choose can often have an effect on the kind of results you can achieve, and the ease with which you can achieve them.

In this chapter, we'll take a look at some of the most common ways to create raw After Effects footage, and to composite it together into convincing clips. We'll use some practical examples to discover how still images, video clips, and animations combine to produce compelling work.

Get ready

The key to success, as with any process, is to think through your animation or effect in advance. What exactly do you need? Which elements of the shot need to be video clips, which can be constructed from stills, and which need to be graphical animations?

If you're creating a title, you'll need to decide whether it's best to generate it entirely within After Effects, or whether you need the beveling tools found in Photoshop. On the other hand, you might want the lighting on the text to change over time, in which case you might need to use a 3D package. If you're adding a building to a video shot of a landscape, you might well want to use a still shot for the building to make the compositing easier. On the other hand, if you're adding a tree blowing in the wind, it will need to move, so you'll probably need to bring it in as a video clip.

The question of exactly how much work to do before you take your elements into After Effects depends on your project specification

For example, say you've got a still shot of a landscape, which is going to form the backdrop of an effect. Before you can use it, it needs a little work:

- Its colors will need to be made much brighter.

- Its contrast will need to be increased.

- It will need to be blurred because it's to be placed in the distance.

- It will need to be shrunk to the resolution of the TV screen.

All of this could be done in a couple of minutes in Photoshop. In After Effects, it's likely to take a lot longer. Depending on your project, it's a good idea to work out how best to split the tasks between the programs you use.

The contrast and color saturation would probably be best done in Photoshop, because it's quick and easy. The blurring could also be done in Photoshop – but then what happens if you want to change the level of blur once you see all the elements of the shot together? You won't be able to, so perhaps this is actually best done in After Effects.

The re-sizing can be done in either package. If you're sure which portion of the scene you want to be displaying in the background of your shot, you might as well do it in Photoshop. However, if you want to change, distort, or even animate the backdrop to create a moving camera effect, keep it at full resolution, and re-size it in After Effects.

> *Another reason for doing things first in other applications is to increase your working speed, and decrease your render times. If you can get away with doing something first in Photoshop, then After Effects won't need to render it, so you decrease your render times. And when you're previewing something, After Effects doesn't need to render the effect for every frame in the composition window as you move around the timeline.*

These things may seem obvious, but we're only talking about a single background image here. You can imagine that with a complex project, more involved decisions have to be made about how to prepare your footage.

All in all, you just need to work out what you're likely to want to change about your video in After Effects. Anything you can lock down before you get there will reduce the complexity of your projects, and make rendering less of a pain. The idea is to produce the easiest possible footage to work with, but retain the flexibility to alter it in any way you like, and the only way to do that is to understand the shot you're trying to produce, and to know exactly what's required of each layer that will make it up.

The best way to achieve this is with good, strong planning, and the centerpiece of the kind of planning we need to do for After Effects is a storyboard that sketches out the way your effect will work.

All aboard the storyboard

Here we've got a complex sequence to put together. It's a title sequence for a television program, so naturally everyone involved in the production wants to put their ideas into it. With the wealth of ideas being thrown up, our job is more about trimming them down than anything else (if you want to see how the finished production went, take a look at the final tutorial in this chapter, where we put it all together).

Because this storyboard will later be used for real, the ideas and decisions detailed in it are somewhat predetermined. However, you can make the exercise more creative by using your own set of ideas as a starting point, and following the process laid out below. You don't have to produce a title sequence; you could make a short animation, or visual effect, for instance. Do try to keep it simple, though, as the focus of this exercise is the process, not the end product. If you decide to do this, have a quick brainstorm and get a collection of ideas together before you start the exercise.

1. First of all, we need to break down the production. What we've got right now is a list of ideas and we need to organize them in a way that will allow us to look at how we could combine them. We start by sketching out some of the ideas, and researching images we can use. Don't be too careful, or detailed. The idea at this stage is not to commit to an idea, but to throw out as many possibilities as we can.

2. Now we can start to concentrate and refine our ideas. We can junk those that won't work, and look at what remains to see how those ideas can be focused and combined. Our show is about elephants, so we'll need to have elephants in the title sequence!

However, rather than the textures and close-ups we've sketched out, we opt for a more mysterious look with just silhouetted shapes.

3. We decide the elephants will be in motion – walking slowly, but purposefully all in one direction throughout the sequence. We want the backdrop to be something strong, but the program is about the creatures being endangered, and the threats to their environment, so we want something that indicates this danger as well. Our initial idea is to use fire, but after a few sketches, we decide that this is too sensationalist. We want something gentler. We go for a time-lapsed sunset – it's quite dark, and red, and gives the impression of an ending, and it's stronger, subtler, and much more apt than the fire motif.

4. We now work on the titling – going through a number of typefaces, and eventually deciding on something big and bold. We decide to give this a scrolling motion in the opposite direction to the elephants roaming through the scene.

5. This is beginning to get quite complex, so to make sure everything will work, and to give ourselves a clearer idea of how we're going to achieve it, we now create a storyboard. A storyboard can be as simple or as complex as you like. Basically, it's a sequence of sketches. Here, we've done just three showing the progress of our shot. However, some sequences are a lot longer – a storyboard for a movie will contain thousands of images.

6. With the storyboard done, we can break down the elements of each shot more easily, and decide how we're going to produce each one.

   ■ We'll need a sunset, which we can either shoot ourselves, or take from a stock footage CD.

- We'll need some lettering, which should be easy to produce in Photoshop or After Effects.

- We'll need the elephants – they're the tricky part. Because we've produced our storyboard, we can see just what's needed from them. They'll have to be filmed, separately from their background somehow, duplicated, and superimposed into the shot. We either need to find exactly the right stock footage, then go through it frame by frame cutting out our elephant, or hire an elephant and a (very large) blue screen studio. Or, we need to find another solution. This is exactly the kind of problem that could halt your production halfway through if you haven't been through the design stage thoroughly enough.

7. Finally, we decide that since the elephants are only silhouettes, the best way around it is to produce them as animations. It's cheaper, quicker, more controllable, and we don't need a studio manager standing by with a shovel.

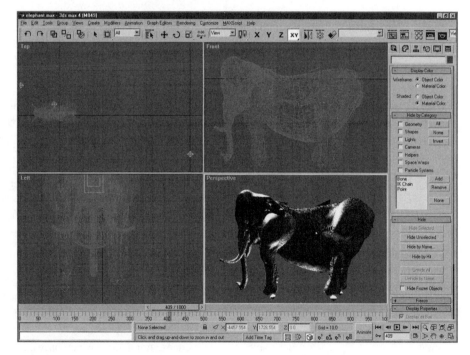

Job done! But before we take this project any further, we're going to look a bit more closely at what kind of files you can import into and use with After Effects.

Import formats

Throughout the first half of this chapter, we'll look at the various file-types you can import into After Effects, whether they will need to be compressed, and what extra information they can carry into After Effects for you. We'll then go through a set of examples detailing how to import and work with material from Photoshop, Premiere, 3D animation packages and Flash.

After Effects accepts a bewildering array of file-types reflecting the vast range of still and moving images you can combine within the package. For any job, there are a number of file types you can use, and it's often a difficult job choosing between them. Here's a list of some of the more common file-types you can use in After Effects, along with some information on how best to use them.

File type	Description	Best used for
AVI (Video for Windows)	Windows video format	CD and hard-disk based content only to be viewed on a PC
MOV (QuickTime)	Cross platform videos	DV, CD and Internet video for Mac and PC platforms. Quality and file size can be set at a wide range of levels.
RM (Realmedia)	Highly compressed video	Clips to be placed onto the Internet. Delivers acceptable quality even at the extremely low data rates used by most Internet connections
JPG, GIF	Compressed still image files. Compression can be varied	Images and sequences which need a small file size, but relatively good quality
Animated GIF	Animated image file	VERY small animations for the Internet using just a few frames.
Uncompressed images: TGA, TIFF, BMP	Still image sequences	Stills and short sequences with no sound. Clips which have to be preserved at the highest quality. In the case of TGA, images which have transparency that needs preserving.
SWF	Flash animation sequences	Animations which have been produced for the Web. Graphical animation sequences (especially good for those involving text). (Interactivity will not be preserved)

Compression

If you're importing straight video or animation, the best way to retain the quality of your original work is to import it as a series of sequentially uncompressed bitmaps.

You can use Targa files, BMP files, or any other uncompressed image type.

Any time you import a still image, you can check the Sequence button and the package will search the folder for any sequentially numbered series of images with that name. You can then treat that sequence within After Effects just as you would a video clip.

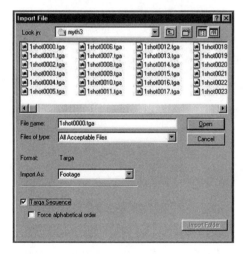

We've looked at After Effects import options in already in **Chapter 3**, but two things should be noted at this point:

■ After Effects doesn't know the frame rate of any still image sequence, so it specifies your project's frame rate by default. You can change this in the Interpret Footage > Main menu option.

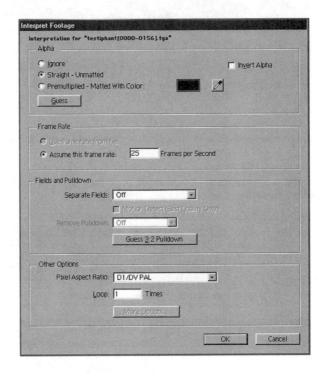

■ If your image sequence has a missing number, After Effects will assume it's got to the end of the sequence, and stop importing, so you'll just get part of your clip.

Working with uncompressed still image sequences means that nothing of the original quality of your images will be lost during the effects process. It also means that if your computer should crash during rendering, only the frame it's building at the time will be lost, previous frames have already been completed and saved so they won't be affected. You can also stop and start rendering at will without having to re-start from the beginning of a complex clip.

On the downside, you'll end up with a lot of files clogging up your hard drive, and they will be large and difficult to manage. For example, imagine you're creating a composite of a 1minute long 3D animated backdrop with an equivalent length of blue-screen video, and you're doing it at PAL resolution. At 25 frames per second, a minute of video is 1,500 frames. We have two sets of footage files, and we're producing 1 minute of completed video at the end, so say we have 4,500 files all in all. Each bitmap frame will be about 1.2mb in size, so our 1 minute of finished animation takes up 5.4Gb of disk space!

You won't want to be doing too much of that, unless you can afford a notably large hard drive.

You'll have to compromise a lot. A good compromise is often to work at DV quality. That's the highest quality your work will end up at most of the time, and DV compression comes in at 3.6 mb per second, so that's about 650mb for our example composite above. Plus you'll only be working with 3 files.

If your capture card imports video in a format After Effects can access – like QuickTime, or AVI format – then you don't even need to re-compress it, so you'll retain your original quality until you come to render the finished effect.

If your capture card produces its own file-type – which they often do – then you've got more of a problem. To get your video into After Effects you'll need to re-compress it. There are several software DV codecs that do this, and there's not a lot to choose between them. You'll probably find one or more on your system already. The problem is that each time you re-compress your picture you're degrading it slightly, and eventually the quality drop will become noticeable.

> *A Codec is a piece of software that compresses and decompresses images and audio. It stands for Coder/Decoder.*

For a normal project, you'll capture your footage, re-compress it to a software DV codec recognized by After Effects, render it out using the same codec (so you've recompressed it again) and then finally re-compress it back to the format your capture card prefers so you can record your finished project to DV.

In practice, the drop in quality when re-compressing from one DV format to another is very small, and you have to do a lot of re-compressing before it's noticeable. You'll probably get away with using this kind of technique, even a few times on the same clip, before you'll notice any difference.

Extra data

Some data formats, particularly still image ones, let you include extra information in your files. This can be terribly useful. The most common addition is the ability to include alpha channels (or transparency).

> *An alpha channel contains information about the extent to which the color of each pixel is to be blended with the background. If you have the image of a ball on a table, and you request the alpha channel blend the ball pixels completely with the background, the ball will disappear. If you request a blend of 50%, the ball will look transparent.*

If you create a TGA, TIFF image (as well as EPS, PDF and certain types of QuickTime files), then as well as recording the red blue and green components of each pixel, you can also store its transparency (the values of its alpha channel). This means that you can use all the finely tuned masking tools in Photoshop to create a very detailed mask, then drop the image straight into an After Effects composition, and its transparency will be retained. It also means you can render 3D animation sequences, and then replace their backgrounds in an instant.

Importing Photoshop files lets you go a stage further, and choose which layers of the image you want to bring in.

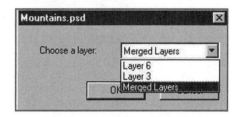

This is useful if you've got a complex set of layers you want to animate. For example, you can create a figure in Photoshop where each layer contains a single limb. Then you can then import each layer into After Effects, and easily animate the arms and legs.

RLA and Softimage PIC files created by 3D animation packages can also have additional properties. They can store alpha channels, but also offer z mattes, and several other types of data about objects in the 3D world, and the way their textures and materials are created. These are used to create effects which change according to their distance from the camera, and to allow you to adjust, in After Effects, some properties of a scene which might otherwise take days to re-render in 3D.

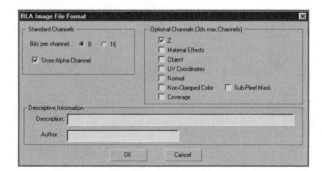

Premiere files offer yet another extra. You can directly import a Premiere project, and have it converted into an After Effects one (see the 'Working with Premiere' tutorial later). However, things get complex quickly if you try to import a very long or multi-tracked project. Also, bear in mind that Premiere can import some types of files that After Effects can't, so you might end up with gaps in your project.

You can now also import Flash files (see the 'Working with Flash' tutorial). However, in this instance, you lose information by importing into After Effects. Flash files lose all their interactivity, and any vector drawn objects become bitmaps, and are subject to becoming blocky if you move too close to them. In addition, there's no way to get at the animation within the Flash file, and change it. It's as though you've imported a straight video clip.

Now we've looked at some of the theory behind the different file types you can use in AE 5.5, we're going to get to the practical with a series of tutorials that demonstrate how to create and import a variety of file types, and then compose them within After Effects.

Working with Photoshop layers

Still images form a big part of the material used in After Effects. Not only are they commonly used for titles, captions and backdrops, they're also used in less obvious roles as black and white matte images, and even as elements of moving shots.

In this tutorial, we're going to use Photoshop to layer the elements of a landscape. The idea is to produce something which looks real, and which has both background and foreground elements, so that the animation we produce in After Effects can move through the picture. You can download the finished image from the CD, or you can build your own version of the scene as we go through the tutorial. Either way, be sure to read the tutorial through as it contains some really useful tips to help you with your own importing and compositing.

1. We start with a basic scene of a mountainous landscape:

The sky doesn't look very good at the moment, so we use the Magic Wand tool to replace it with a more dramatic one.

2. Next, we place a city into the shot using Photoshop's cloning tool. We use a soft-edged brush to paint the city directly from the other photograph into our picture. We paint it onto a new layer so we can easily go back if we create something that doesn't look right.

3.   If you're producing your own Photoshop composition, now would be a good time to adjust the brightness and color values of the city and its background so the colors blend correctly.

4.   Using the cloning brush created some soft edges, which we now clean up using the Eraser tool. We can be as careful about this as we like in Photoshop, spending time getting exactly the right composition for our shot.

5.   When this is done, we merge everything to a single layer.

6.   Next, we add a new layer. This will be the foreground – the portion of the shot which we want to place in front of any After Effects scenes. From yet another image, we cut out a dead tree. It's a complex shape, and takes quite a lot of work.

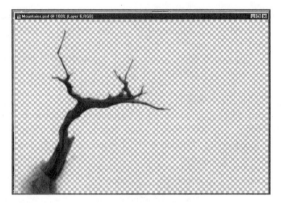

It's worth looking at your project at the planning stage, and taking this kind of work into account. The difference between matting a solid simple object like a rock or a building, and doing the same job with a complex shape like a tree is worth considering – and budgeting for!

7.   Now we place this tree into the layer by dragging it with the Move tool (at the top right of the Photoshop toolbar).

8. Finally, save the shot. We can save in any number of image formats which are loadable in After Effects, but if we use the standard Photoshop file format, then our layers can be preserved as they are, so we can have a lot more control over the image.

We're going to leave this example here for now, but we'll come back, pick it up, and take it into After Effects a little later on.

Each layer of our Photoshop file can be imported as an individual layer in our After Effects project. Then we can animate and apply effects to each of these layers individually. In our example, we could animate the foreground and background layers separately for a multi-planing effect, simulating the perspective change you experience in the real world so our shot doesn't feel so locked off

This kind of masking and color keying work is where Photoshop really comes into its own. The same kinds of tools are available in After Effects, but Photoshop allows you to work a lot more finely with them. It's so much easier to work in this detail with still images than with moving video shots, that it's well worth considering whether any of the elements of your scene can start out as still frames before you begin work on your effect.

The shot we've created here is clearly not the same shape as a TV screen (which is the format of our finished shot). We can distort, crop and even animate the position of our scene once we get it into After Effects, and it's often a good idea to produce elements at a resolution which is higher than your final output resolution, so that if you decide to, you can zoom into the image in After Effects without losing quality.

Working with Premiere

After Effects is usually used in conjunction with some kind of video editing package. Usually, a rough-cut of a production is produced, then small sections of it which need effects applied to them are exported so they can be manipulated in After Effects before being placed back onto the timeline to create the final edit. However, if you're using Adobe Premiere as your editor, the relationship between it and After Effects is somewhat deeper.

Here we have a short conversation between two 3D characters. We'll use Premiere to edit the production, then transfer the whole scene into After Effects where we can alter the backdrop for each. If you don't use Premiere, just read through the first part of the example, and pick up the practical when we import the finished PPJ file.

1. Load the video files from the CD into Premiere's project window. There's no audio to go with this project yet, but it would be a good idea to add some. Try recording a conversation from the television, and then load the audio files into Premiere's project window.

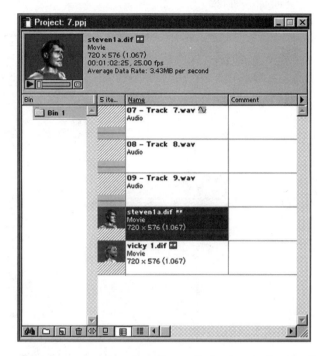

2. If you have recorded some audio, place the audio track onto the timeline so that we can start to cut the images to match it. Premiere's timeline is a little different from After Effects'. In fact, it's more interactive, and simpler to use.

3. Drop the first video shot into one of the empty video tracks, and drag to trim it to size. By dragging the middle of the clip, we can move it around the timeline. Dragging the playback head, or using the playback buttons as in After Effects, we can see the results of our work.

4. When you're happy, place the next shot. The major difference between Premiere's timeline, and that of After Effects is that here, you can place as many clips as you like on the same track. We build up our scene in this way, and then save the result as a Premiere PPJ file.

5. Loading up After Effects, go to the File menu and Import our scene as a piece of footage. The PPJ file is converted into an After Effects composition. If you just see a set of colored bars where the footage should be, go into the footage bin in the Project window, right click the footage files, and replace them with the MOV footage files from the CD.

Double click the PPJ file in the Project window, and we can examine the movie on the timeline. Each shot has been separated out as a track, and we can now go in and alter them in whatever way we like.

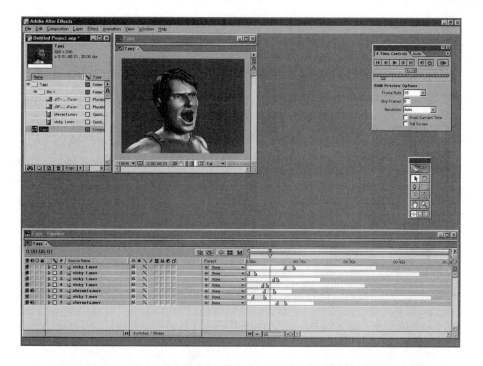

> It's useful to note here that After Effects can't handle Premiere's dissolves and wipes. However, it does replace them with solid layers, so you can see exactly where they would have appeared in the Premiere timeline. This provides a useful visual cue, so you can animate opacity or transform values to put your transitions back in.

6. Now load in the background image from the CD, which we'll use on our head shots. Place one instance of this onto the timeline below the first head shot. Shrink the length of the new background shot to match the length of the headshot it's covering. You can shrink the size of the clip by dragging the gray markers at each end of the footage bar in the timeline.

7. Now place another version of the background clip onto the timeline, and resize it to cover next headshot. Do this for each of the headshots.

8. We then select the Effects menu for each of our head clips, and select Keying > Color Key. Click on the Eyedropper tool, and with it, select the blue background color of each headshot. This allows us to make the blue background of the shot transparent, and lets the backdrop appear behind it. Play with the Color Key settings in the Effect Controls window to improve your effect.

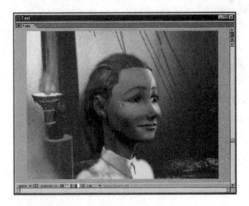

9.   Now you can see the background image, highlight each version of it on your timeline, and move the image to a different position for each character. This will make it look like they are in different parts of the room.

Don't worry, we'll be looking at color keying in more detail later on in the chapter, and throughout the book. This is really just a taster.

Working with 3D animations

One very common use of After Effects is to combine video footage with computer generated imagery, and the most convincing way to produce that imagery is often with a 3D modeling and animation package. Such packages tend to be expensive, and take a long time to learn. However, the results from them can be very rewarding.

Here, we're going to discover some of the common techniques and problems involved with this use of After Effects by attempting to build and fly a spaceship.

1. We're using 3DS Max. Starting with a basic box shape, use just the extrude and bevel tools on its individual faces to produce a basic spaceship shape. You can download my finished spaceship from the CD. It's nothing too impressive, but gives the idea of what we're looking for.

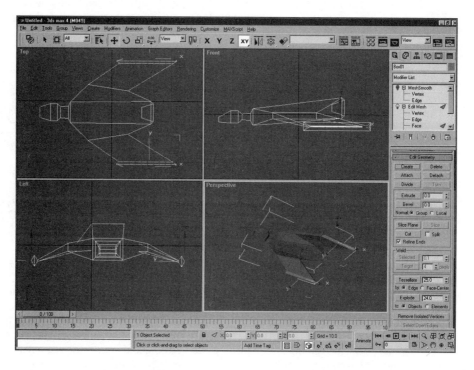

2. Add a mesh-smooth modifier to give the whole thing a sleeker, smoother look by rounding off all the hard edges. You can still drag control points around at various levels of detail until you get the shape you're looking for.

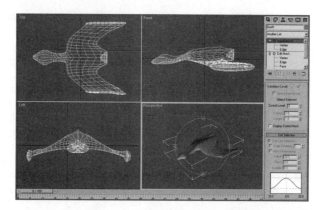

3.   To complete the model, add a material. Texturing is terribly important in 3D, and can make an otherwise unrealistic object look a lot more convincing. I went for a traditional look, metallic panels on a slightly shiny surface.

4.   The motion for the ship is easily created, with just two keyframes within Max, and we position the camera so the whole path is visible. Keeping the whole ship within the frame at all points in the animation gives us more choice about where we place it when we come to composite the shot in After Effects.

5.   Lighting is also important. In this shot, we want most of the light to come from above. To implement this, place a strong light high up in the shot so that it just catches the edges of the craft. We still want to illuminate the bottom of the craft, so place a softer light beneath it.

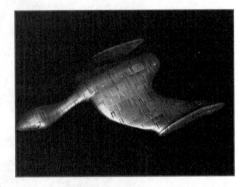

6.   Finally, add a motion blur and a flare from the engine, and render the shot.

7.   There's a big choice of output formats for a 3D animation file, but unfortunately, just exporting the 3D scene for direct use in After Effects isn't yet one of them. Instead, export the animation as a sequence of TGA files so that the background remains transparent, and we don't need to worry about keying all those soft edges caused by the motion blur. Next, load up After Effects, and import the sequence. Specify the alpha channel as straight.

> *Most image and video formats don't allow you to retain transparency, but TGA, RLA, PNG, and Photoshop files do, as do some QuickTime compression codecs.*

8.   You also need to import the file we're going to use as a backdrop. It's the cityscape we produced earlier on in the chapter! Because we saved this as a Photoshop file, we can import each layer separately. We import the file twice. Firstly, we bring in the background, then the tree layer, which will be our foreground.

9.   Assembling the shot is simplicity itself. First, create a new composition (Composition > New), drop the background onto the timeline, then the ship animation, then finally the foreground tree on top of that. The result appears instantly, and we can scrub through

it. The ship swoops in over the city, and zooms towards the camera, but always remains behind the tree.

10.   However, this is After Effects, so let's do a little more with our image. All the elements of the shot have been kept separate, so we can change anything we like. Try dropping in another copy of the ship animation between the background and foreground, and scale it down. You could also offset it in time compared to the first shot.

11. Now why not place another duplicate of the ship, but this time use the drag-handles to flip it over so it flies from right to left instead of left to right. You can also alter its speed with the time-stretch option on the Layer menu. Before long, we've got a whole fleet of ships flying over the city – all from just one short animation, and a couple of stills!

Working with Flash

Why use material created in Macromedia Flash as part of an After Effects production? Well, there are a couple of reasons.

- You can animate with it very easily, and very flexibly, and for many people used to producing web work, it's a very comfortable tool to use. Its ability to handle and animate text is probably better than that of After Effects, and it's also good for cartoon and graphical styles of animation.

- In addition, as the web and video grow closer together, the ability to make your work cross from one medium to another quickly and flawlessly becomes more important. A logo may have been developed for the web, and need to be transposed onto the screen, or vice-versa. If you can just drag and drop from one medium to the other, you can cut out hours, or even days or weeks of re-design work.

In this tutorial, a banner ad is being created which needs to appear on the web, but also has to be used in a slideshow displayed on a big screen at an exhibition we're attending.

1. In Flash, we need to assemble our banner. It's quite simple, and contains a bitmap image along with some text. We import the bitmap, create the text, and place the bitmap on the lower layer and the text on the upper layer, so that it lies on top of the image.

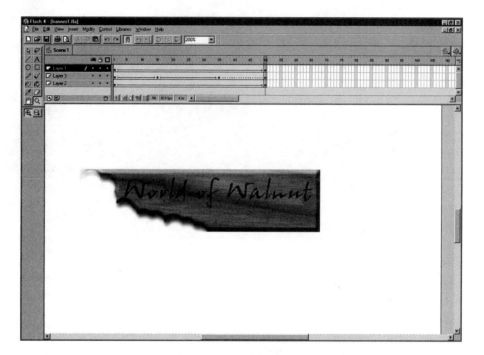

2. The animation side is quite simple as well. All we do is make the text and background fly in from different directions. We set up a couple of keyframes for the start and end position, rotation, and scale of each layer. Then we select Tween to create the in-between frames of the animation, and save the display as a SWF file. Take a look at the finished SWF file on the CD.

    Granted, it's not a particularly impressive animation, but it will give us an idea of what's possible. A little extra work might be needed on the Web version, but we're going to concentrate on the video side of the shot.

3. We now move to After Effects, where we import our SWF file. We also need to import a video backdrop for the shot. You could use the Pyramids movie from **Chapter 2**, or the cloudx2002.movie in the juggler folder of **Chapter 6** on the CD.

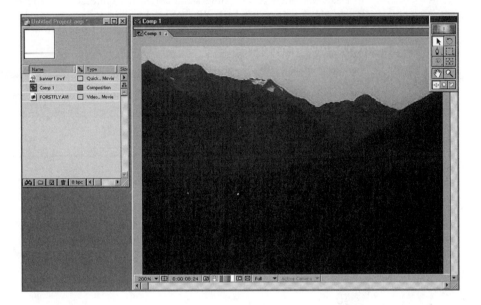

I used a relaxing countryside scene from the Premiere 5 source files.

4. Create a new composition, place the SWF file onto the timeline, and place the video beneath it. Add a luma key filter to the SWF file by selecting Effect > Keying > Luma key. This makes all the regions of a layer with a specified luminance or brightness transparent. Selecting it, we choose the Key Out Brighter option to make the white background vanish, so our project is superimposed onto the mountain shot. To specify the brightness, increase the Threshold value beneath the Key Type to about 130.

5. By increasing the feathering of the Luma key, we get a soft glow around the lettering which improves the look of the shot.

6. We can treat Flash files just like any other shot, adding whatever filters we like to them. Here, we've stuck in a Twirl filter, just for the fun of it.

7. We can now export the finished video as a QuickTime file. Of course, we could output it as a new SWF file, but with the video backdrop included, the file would be far too large to use as a web file. The problem with using After Effects to produce Flash output is that there's no way to judge the file size of your scene until it's been exported.

We've now looked at how to prepare and import material from particular programs to be modified in After Effects. Next, we're going to look at how to prepare material for particular kinds of After Effects modification.

Chromakey

One of the key skills in After Effects is that of keying: taking one image, and making a defined part of it transparent. This allows us to remove objects from one scene, and superimpose them into another.

Here, we're going to key using color. The idea is to create a shot in which a human hand is operating a computer generated console.

Our first job is to shoot the original footage. We're going to be using chromakey to remove the background from the hand, so we start by preparing a blue screen.

A good chromakey screen should be a flat, evenly lit backdrop in bright and pure green, blue, or yellow. The color you choose will depend on the make-up of the object you're putting in the foreground. For example, if you use a blue screen, and try to record a person wearing a blue shirt, their body will become transparent when you try to key.

But what if you don't have time to set up a good screen? If you can't prepare your footage cleanly enough does that mean the effect is impossible? Not with After Effects. The blue screen we're going to use in the following tutorial is, in fact, very poor. Often the conditions under which you're shooting will be less than perfect, and either there won't be time to set the blue screen up correctly, or the lighting won't be right, or there will be incorrect shadows.

Sometimes – as in this case – the shot was needed suddenly, and there was no chance of finding appropriate cloth or lights. The scene was shot with a table lamp, suspended over a blue drape.

This gives us some challenges and allows us to demonstrate some of the techniques After Effects offers for cleaning up a poor key.

A very handy exercise...

1. Once shot and captured, cut out the sequence of the shot, and import it into After Effects. You can find the finished sequence on the CD.

2. Then import the background (again, it's on the CD). This has been created using a 3D package, and animated so that the lights on the console flash.

3. Create a composition long enough to contain the entire shot (a duration of about 22 seconds should do it), and drop the backdrop onto it, with the blue screen video on top.

4. Right click (for PC, just click on a Mac) on the video clip, and select Effect > Keying > Color Key. This gives us a set of controls for our blue screen. The first is the key color. It's pretty obvious that this needs to be blue, so use the Eyedropper tool to select a representative pixel on the backdrop.

5. Using the next slider, we extend the tolerance, and watch as more and more of the backdrop vanishes. Ideally, this needs to be set so that the blue backdrop is removed, but the hand is retained. In this case, the key's not good enough for that, so we set it as high as we can before parts of the hand start disappearing.

6. Use the Edge Thin slider to remove the blue fringes around objects by slightly expanding the transparent areas. This is pretty good at knocking out small areas of the back-cloth like the horizontal lines on our fabric.

7. Now use the Feather slider to soften the blend between solid and transparent areas. This gives a more realistic composite, but the higher you set it, the less distinct your scene will be.

Our key is looking better, but it's a long way from being acceptable. You'll notice that much of the problem area is at the top of the screen, where the light on the backdrop isn't quite as bright. This is a job for a Garbage matte. A garbage matte is a rough mask used to exclude portions of the screen we don't want to have to mess about trying to key out.

8. To create your Garbage matte, select the Pen tool, and click around the hand (leaving it a little room to move).

This masks out the outside of the shot.

9.   We can then increase the feathering on the mask (by adjusting it on the mask section of the timeline), and most of our problems are removed.

So although the preparation of our footage in this case was not as good as it could have been, After Effects gives us options to deal with that.

Track Mattes

Another way to key out parts of your image is to use a Track Matte or Traveling Matte. A Track Matte is a black and white moving image, which acts as a transparency mask for other layers. With it, you can very accurately define an area of the screen which will become transparent, and you can have the shape of that area change or move on every frame.

Often, when creating a 3D animation, you'll render the output as a movie file, ready for After Effects. If you want your 3D object to be superimposed into another scene, then you'll also render another movie in which the object is completely white on a black background. This will produce a pixel-perfect replica of the shape of your object, which you can then use as your Track Matte. Often if you buy stock footage effects (like explosions), they'll be provided with a track-matte so you can place them easily into your scenes. This will all become clearer with a quick tutorial, so let's go.

Elephants

In the example below, we'll create a title sequence by using animated lettering in the foreground as a track matte to reveal a background image.

First, we need to create our initial footage. In this case, we're doing a title sequence for a documentary on elephants: we're realizing the storyboard we created in the first part of this chapter!

The footage I used consists of two backdrops of stock footage video (one of clouds, and the other of a sunset from the Premiere 5 stock footage), and a 3D rendered animation of an elephant walking (available for download on the CD). This has been rendered as a Targa series, and so has its transparency already embedded. We've done the elephant in 3D, because it turned out to be easier than hiring a real elephant and a blue-screen studio large enough to accommodate it.

Finally, there's our Traveling Matte:

It's not traveling very much yet, though: it's just a still image file. It was created in Photoshop by roughening the edges of a piece of text.

1. Open After Effects, and import the four files.

2. Drop the matte onto the timeline of a new composition, and expand it so it's a lot larger than the screen itself. To do this, select and drag out a corner node of the layer in the Composition window. Grab the layer in the Composition window and drag it across until you can see the first few letters of the title.

3. Go to the Timeline window, and expand the little triangle to the left of ELE MATTE.bmp. Expand the Transform section of the timeline, and turn on animation for the Position track by clicking the stopwatch. This will place a keyframe in the first frame of your composition.

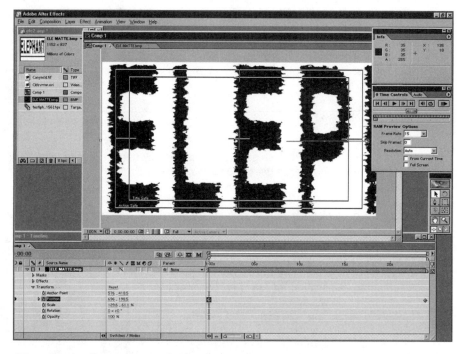

4. Move the timeline marker to the last frame of your movie, grab the matte layer in the Composition window, and drag it across to reveal the last letters of the title. This will place a keyframe at the end of the animation. Try playing the animation back now. You'll see that the text scrolls across the screen.

5. To make things a little more interesting, add a Bulge filter and animate that backwards across the screen. This creates a distortion in the lettering. Our matte is now quite a complex object. It's time to make it transparent.

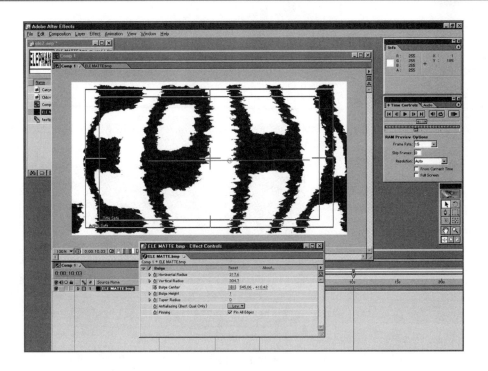

Drop some sunset background footage video onto the timeline under the text layer, and click the switches / modes button at the bottom of the timeline. This gives us our Track Matte options. On the video layer, click the right hand button in the trkmt column and select Luma Inverted Matte "Elematet.bmp".

6. Drop some clouds stock footage clip into a lower track. Cloudx2002 in the juggler folder of **Chapter 6** on the CD will do. The result is instant. The first clip replaces the letters, and the second replaces the backdrop.

7.   It's time to add the elephants. Drop in the elephant animation in front of all the others. Because it's been rendered as a Targa sequence, the background is already transparent.

8.   Just as in Photoshop, After Effects offers a number of ways to overlay objects. Our elephant looks OK, but for a more ephemeral effect, click the mode button next to the layer, and switch it to Soft Light.

9.   Then duplicate the layer until you have a whole herd of ghostly elephants walking across our lettering.

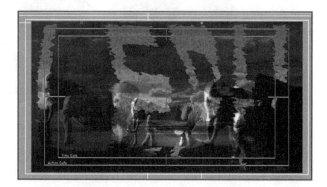

10.   Finally, create a new composition, and drag the old one into it. This puts everything on one layer and lets us use it like a pre-composed video clip. We can now add effects to the whole shot. We added a lens flare, a glow and some noise to soften the effect.

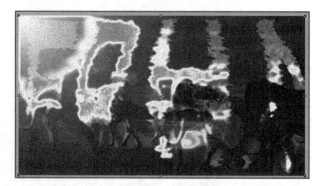

The result is a rather complex, but quite interesting composition, with enough going on to keep the viewer's interest.

If you created your own storyboard at the beginning of this chapter, now would be a good time to try to produce it. See how many of the techniques we discussed in this chapter you can incorporate into it.

Summary

So now we've looked at how other packages are used alongside After Effects. We've touched on creating the elements (and elephants) of our scenes in 2D and 3D animation packages, as well as looking at the importance of still images in our animations. We've found out how to import a range of different types of scene element, and the advantages and disadvantages of using certain types of material.

Armed with this information, you can now be more confident in your use of After Effects as a part of your post production studio. You can recognize it as not just an effects package, but as a compositor, bringing together very different types of material, and composing them seamlessly into a single frame.

In the next chapter, we'll look more closely at the After Effects environment and what we can do with the footage we bring into it.

5 Exploring the Timeline: Adding & Manipulating Grips

In this chapter, we're going to look at the various layer properties that can be changed over time, and how After Effects handles animation. After Effects is one of the best digital flip books money can buy!

The Timeline window is used to set up and manage the changes that will be applied to a composition and its layers over time. As such, it is the main window we rely on for animation. As we have already seen, when you add layers to a composition, the Timeline window displays them as layer blocks, allowing us to specify where a layer begins and ends on the timeline. Each layer contains properties, such as it's Position, Opacity, and Rotation. These properties can be set to a specific value, and also animated over time. Throughout this chapter, we'll be discovering how to access and use these properties to great effect.

We're going to develop an After Effects composition to demonstrate the practical side of what we learn in the chapter. So let's start by setting up our movie.

The first steps of SPACEWALK

To begin, let's import something we can play around with. We want to create a 30-second preview, or teaser for a movie.

1. First, select Edit > Preferences > Import... and in the Still Footage box, select the second button and specify 0:00:30:00. Click OK.

2. Copy the files for this chapter from the CD to your hard drive to increase work speed, and then import the vortex.jpg file.

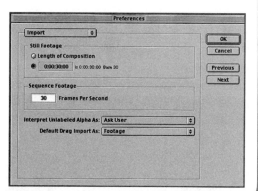

3. Create a new 35-second composition, and call it SPACEWALK. Use one of the presets for PAL DV, or NTSC (depending on where you live) so you can later export it to DV if you wish.

4. Drag vortex.jpg into the SPACEWALK timeline so it begins at the three-second point. The file has a duration of 30 seconds, and should therefore end at the 33-second mark of the timeline.

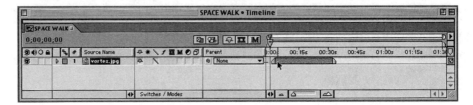

5. Our teaser cannot go over 30 seconds, so that's an extra three seconds we don't need. Grab the right-hand side of the layer on the timeline, and trim it back three seconds.

6. In the Composition window, notice that the size of vortex.jpg is quite large compared to the size of the frame. As we discussed in **Chapter 3**, starting off with the image being very large allows us to scale the image back up to its current size, without getting pixelation or resolution problems.

Now we've set ourselves up, it's time to learn a little more about layers and how they work in the Timeline window.

Expanding and collapsing layers

With some projects, you end up with so many layers in your timeline that you feel like you need an IMAX screen to work on it. Fortunately, After Effects has a number of intuitive functions and display methods that help us work with and sort through a large number of layers in a complex project. One of the most useful of these is the ability to expand and collapse layers.

Within each layer on the timeline are properties, which can be adjusted for the entire length of the footage or composition, or animated to change over time.

Looking at our vortex.jpg layer on the timeline, you'll notice that to the left of the source/layer name, there's a triangle that points to the right. Click on the triangle, and it will rotate to point downwards, revealing a category of layer properties: Transform. The category has another triangle pointing to the right.

> *You may see two other categories listed here:* Masks *and* Effects. *If you click on the triangle next to* Masks *or* Effects, *you will notice that apart from the triangle rotating, nothing much else happens. This is because we haven't added any masks or effects to the layer (we'll be adding masks and effects in* **Chapters 6** *and* **7***).*

Now click on the triangle to the left of Transform, and we are presented with five stopwatches, and five properties from Anchor Point to Opacity.

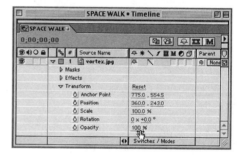

To the right of the Transform option, you can see the word Reset, and various numbers below it. This is all 'hot text', as discussed in **Chapter 3**. Move the mouse over the hot text for the Opacity property. Notice how the mouse cursor changes to a finger with double arrows pointing left and right. Click and hold down the mouse and drag the cursor to the left. The Opacity is reduced as you drag, all the way down to 0%, at which point, the vortex.jpg layer will have disappeared from view. You can also use the hot text to change the other layer properties' values.

If we were to change the values and leave the new values as they were, those values would remain that way for the entire composition, or at least for the duration of the layer on our timeline.

Drag the current time indicator to various positions along the timeline between 3 and 30 seconds. Notice that wherever you place the time indicator, it produces a series of "I" icons, that look like a profile view of iron girders stacked on top of each other, running vertically down beneath it.

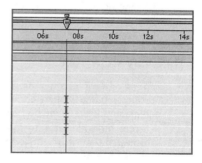

If we wanted to copy a property value to another layer, we can select the relevant "I" icon and choose Edit > Copy. Then expand the layer we wish to copy to, select the corresponding "I" icon, and choose Edit > Paste. This will copy the value of a property from one layer to another.

If we wanted to restore the original values for the various properties, we can click the Reset hot text. Click the Reset hot text for the vortex.jpg layer, and our vortex will reappear. As long as we have not set **keyframes**, the original layer property values will be restored.

If we want a layer's property values to change over time, rather than stay the same throughout the clip on the timeline, we need to set keyframes.

Keyframes

In After Effects, one of the main tools used to create and control animation, is the keyframe. The term 'keyframe' comes from traditional cel animation, the world of Mickey Mouse and Bugs Bunny. In the cel animation world, animators complete the drawings in which the most important part of the action occurs, these are the key drawings (or in After Effects terms, the keyframes). Then an assistant animator will complete all the drawings in between, which are termed in-betweens.

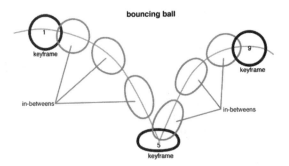

After Effects allows us to animate something frame by frame so that we can directly control every frame (all of the in-betweens). However, most of the time, it's worth taking advantage of After Effects interpolation, which will handle all the in-betweens for us. This leaves us free to concentrate on the keyframes.

In After Effects, when we set a keyframe, we are setting a value for a property of a layer at a specific point in time. To cause the property to change over time, we need to set at least two keyframes, a start value and finish value (although we can set as many keyframes in between as we like).

Time-vary stopwatch

As we saw when we were looking at the Transform properties of the vortex.jpg layer, each property has a stopwatch, or a 'time-vary stopwatch' icon. This is our starting point to begin animating. If we want the value of a property, say Opacity, to change over time, we move the current time indicator to the point at which we want the change to begin, and then click the stopwatch that sits to the left of Opacity. This sets a keyframe for Opacity, and a diamond appears on the timeline to indicate this. Opacity is automatically set to 100% for that point in time. If 100% is not what we want at this point, we can adjust the value of opacity with the hot text after we have set the keyframe. Alternatively, if we set the Opacity value to 50% before clicking the stopwatch, then an Opacity keyframe of 50% would have been set when we first clicked the stopwatch.

Using the stopwatch to set a keyframe

We want a two-second fade-in at the beginning of our movie.

1. Go back to our `vortex.jpg` layer, and set the current time marker to three seconds. Click on the stopwatch next to Opacity, and set this first keyframe to 0%.

2. Then move the current time marker to the five-second mark, and change the Opacity setting again, this time from 0% to 100%, and After Effects will automatically add a new keyframe at the new time position.

3. Now move the current time marker between the three-second mark and the five-second mark, and you should witness the `vortex.jpg` layer changing from invisible, through various levels of transparency, to completely visible.

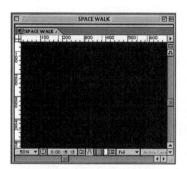 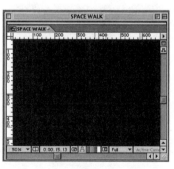 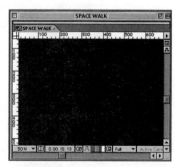

The other way we can add a keyframe is to select Animation > Add Opacity Keyframe. This menu option changes depending upon which property is selected, for example if we had Scale selected, to add a keyframe we can select Animation > Add Scale Keyframe. However, using the menu to add keyframes is not usually the quickest way to work.

Keyframe navigator

Now that we have added keyframes for the Opacity of our vortex.jpg layer, we can take a look at the **keyframe navigator**.

You may have noticed that when we added keyframes, to the left of the Opacity option, a check box appeared with a tick in it. This is the keyframe navigator. If you click on any of the other stopwatches that have not yet been selected, you'll notice that the keyframe navigator appears for each one you click. If you click on them again to turn them off, you will notice the keyframe navigator disappears. You can use the keyframe navigator to jump along the timeline from keyframe to keyframe, or to add or remove keyframes.

The tick indicates that a keyframe has been set at that point in time. If you move the current time indicator around, you will notice the ticks will appear and disappear, depending upon where keyframes have been set. You will also notice that back arrows will appear to the left, right or both sides of the check box. These arrows indicate there is a keyframe for that property to the left or right of the current time position. If you click on the arrow, the current time marker will be moved in the direction of the arrow, to the position of the next keyframe. Notice how a tick appears in the check box indicating a keyframe is set for that point in time.

Using the keyframe navigator to add keyframes is also easy. For our vortex.jpg layer, move the current time marker somewhere between the two Opacity keyframes, around four seconds on the timeline. The keyframe navigator should have an arrow on either side of an empty check box. To set a keyframe, just click the check box. To remove the keyframe, click the check box again. In this case, because we are setting a keyframe between two other keyframes, the Opacity value is set to an interpolated value based on the values of the two keyframes on either side.

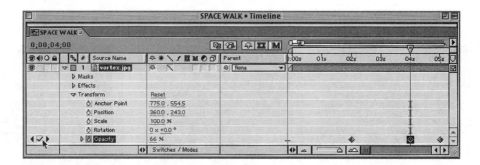

However, if we were to move the current time marker beyond the last keyframe for Opacity and then put a tick in the check box, we would get a new keyframe for Opacity with the same value as the keyframe before it. This is a way to set a keyframe without changing the property value.

Keyframe icons

Wherever you set a keyframe, you'll notice a diamond symbol on the timeline. These are the keyframe icons. When there is only one keyframe for a property, the keyframe diamond will be a dark gray color. Where there is more than one keyframe, the keyframes will appear to be half dark gray and half light gray if they are the first or last keyframes. Keyframes in between the start and end points will appear light gray.

The dark gray side indicates there is either no other keyframe (and so no interpolation) on that side of the keyframe and the light gray side indicates that interpolation is occurring on that side of the keyframe. A diamond symbol that is light gray on both sides indicates that interpolation is occurring on both sides of the keyframe.

Another way to modify a keyframe is to double-click the diamond keyframe icon to bring up a dialog box for that keyframe, irrespective of where the current time marker is.

You can also change keyframe icons from diamond symbols to numbers by selecting the Timeline window menu (the dark arrow to the right side of the Timeline window) and choosing Use Keyframe Indices.

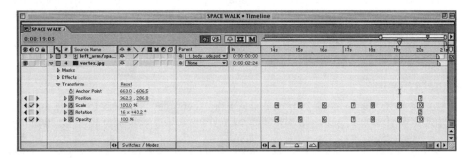

Copying and pasting keyframes

You can copy and paste keyframe values to different points in time within the same layer. You can also copy and paste keyframes from one layer to another layer. And as well as pasting keyframe values from one property within a layer, to the same property in another layer, you can also copy and paste between different properties, as long as the properties use the same data type.

You can only copy keyframes from one layer at a time, however. After they are pasted to another layer, they will appear in the relevant property. The first of the copied keyframes will begin where the current time marker is at the time of pasting. After pasting the keyframes, they will remain selected so you can move them along the timeline if they require adjustment.

After Effects also allows you to copy and paste more than one property at a time, if they are being copied and pasted between the same of layer properties. This means you could copy and paste the Rotation and Opacity keyframes of one layer, to the Rotation and Opacity properties of another layer. If you're copying from one type of property to another type, for example, from Opacity to Rotation, you can only copy and paste one property at a time.

To select the keyframes you wish to copy, you can click and drag a marquee around them. To select particular keyframes, you can hold SHIFT and click over desired keyframes. Then choose Edit > Copy from the menu, or CTRL+C (Windows) / COMMAND+C (Mac).

Then you just have to select the desired position, or layer, and choose Edit > Paste, or CTRL+V (Windows) / COMMAND+V (Mac), which will paste the keyframe values to the same property at a different time, or within a different layer. To paste to a different property, select the property, and then paste the values in as above.

The ability to copy and paste like this is extremely useful, and can save you a lot of time. For example, say you were animating the text for a title credit sequence for a movie and the animation of the text was to be consistent for every single title card. Once you had perfected the animation to get the first title credit on and off the screen, you could then copy the relevant keyframes of that animation to different text layers, so it is applied to different titles. You wouldn't have to animate every layer of text separately, and desperately try and match the animation of the first title. Simple advertisements would also be easy to change. If your advertisement zipped the latest sales items into frame, and whooshed them off again, instead of having to reanimate the advertisement every time the sales items changed, you could just bring in new layers of the new sales items, and copy over the keyframes of the original animation.

Moving keyframes

Moving keyframes is easy. Drag and select the keyframes you wish to move, or SHIFT and select specific keyframes. Then drag the selected keyframes to the new position on the timeline.

To move keyframes to a particular point in time, move the current time indicator to the desired time. Then hold down SHIFT when dragging the keyframe and it will snap to the current time indicator as you approach it.

To increase or decrease the spread of a group of keyframes, select the group (must be at least three keyframes) and hold down ALT (Windows), or OPTION (Mac), and drag the keyframe at either end of the group to expand or contract the selection.

Deleting keyframes

To delete keyframes, select them as you would to copy them. Then press the DELETE key on the keyboard.

If you click on the stopwatch icon for a layer property, it will delete all keyframes from the property. This is not an on/off switch though. Clicking on the stopwatch again will not bring the keyframes back. To bring the keyframes back, you'd have to choose Edit > Undo.

Now let's take a closer look at the transform options themselves.

Transform options

As we have seen, each layer we add has five Transform options we can set or animate:

- Anchor Point

- Position

- Scale

- Rotation

- Opacity

It is amazing how much you can achieve with just these five options. Let's take a closer look at each.

Anchor point

Under the Transform category, the first property we come to is the Anchor Point. The anchor point for each layer is set to the center by default. When we rotate a layer, it rotates around the anchor point. When we scale a layer, it scales from the anchor point. If we were animating a wheel, the default anchor point should do nicely, as it's fairly common for a wheel to rotate about its center. But if we were animating a monkey swinging on a vine, we would need the vine to rotate at its top, not its center, in which case, changing the anchor point would be a good idea.

Not only can we change the anchor point, but we can animate it over time. However, if we move the anchor point with the normal selection tool the layer's position in respect to the composition will change. You can see this in the image below, where Spacedude's right arm (which is in its own layer) has come away from his body. This happened when we moved his anchor point from his elbow up to his shoulder (we'll be formally introducing Spacedude later on in the chapter!):

 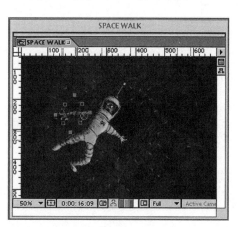

If we want the layer to remain in position while moving the anchor point, we need to use the Pan tool to shift the anchor point. Using the Pan tool allows us to shift the anchor point in the Layer window, without changing the layer positioning in the Composition window:

 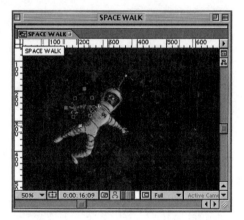

Spacedude keeps his arm, much to Monty Python's dismay. We'll be playing with anchor points in a tutorial towards the end of the chapter.

> When using the Pan tool to change the anchor point, keep in mind that if the layer contains a motion path, the path will be altered, and may then need readjustment.

Position

Each layer starts off at a certain position in the Composition window. If we've dragged the source material into the timeline, After Effects will automatically center the layer. If we've dragged the source material into the Composition window, it will be positioned wherever we dropped it.

To begin animating the position of a layer, move the timeline to the time at which we want the animation to begin, position the layer, and then click the stopwatch icon. That's our first keyframe down.

Then we move the current time marker to the point in time at which we want the next keyframe. One of the easiest ways to set the new Position keyframe, is to click and hold the layer in the Composition window, and move it to the position we desire. As you move the layer in the Composition window, you will notice a series of dots appear between the starting position and wherever you move the layer. You will also see a position keyframe appear on the timeline.

To finish setting the keyframe, drop the layer into the new position you desire. Each dot in the series represents one frame along the composition timeline, and the X symbols represent the keyframes. Dots that are close together indicate slower movement, and dots further apart indicate faster movement. Together, the dots and X's represent a motion path, which we can then adjust (we'll cover motion path adjustment later in this chapter).

Another way to position a layer is by selecting it, and then using the arrow keys to move it one pixel at a time. If you hold down the shift key while using the arrow keys, it will move ten pixels at a time. Should you wish to constrain the movement of a layer to a vertical or horizontal plane, press and hold the shift key after you have started moving the layer within the composition window. You can also have the layer snap to the edge of the compositions frame, by pressing ALT+SHIFT (Windows) or OPTION+SHIFT (Mac) after you start dragging the layer.

You can also change the position using the hot text in the Timeline window.

Scale

When you drag source material onto the composition timeline or Composition window, the image or footage will be set to 100% of its original size. You can change and animate the size of a layer in a number of ways. Keyframes can be set the same as for any of the other properties. You can then change the size by selecting the layer within the Composition window. The layer, when selected, will have four small corner squares and four small side squares around it.

To change the scale, you can select any of the four corner squares and drag them. To change the scale while maintaining the layer's original proportions (its ratio of width to height), drag a corner square while holding down SHIFT. You can scale the layer vertically or horizontally by selecting and dragging one of the squares to the top, bottom or sides of the layer.

You can also change scale in increments. To change a layer's scale in 1% increments, select the layer, hold down ALT (Windows) or OPTION (Mac), and press the + or - keys on the numeric keypad. To change a layer's scale in 10% increments, select the layer and hold down ALT+SHIFT (Windows) or OPTION+SHIFT (Mac) and press the + or - keys on the numeric keypad.

Another handy trick we can use to change the scale is flipping the layer over. We can flip it horizontally, vertically or both. When you play with the selection handles in the Composition window, notice as you change the layer size, the hot text automatically updates the scale values. As you shrink the layer, these values approach zero, and from there continue into negative values. When this occurs, you have flipped the layer.

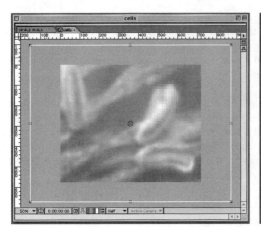 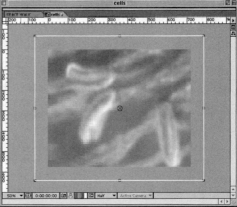

We can also change the scale using the hot text in the Timeline window.

Rotation

A layer can be rotated clockwise or anti-clockwise as many times as you need. You can use the rotation tool in the Composition window to rotate a layer, or you can change the rotation using the hot text in the Timeline window. Looking at the hot text for rotation, you can specify the number of times an object will rotate (the figure on the left), and the number of degrees it will rotate in respect to its starting position (the figure on the right).

Opacity

Opacity can be changed within the Timeline window using the hot text, as described earlier. For existing keyframes, we can double-click the diamond symbol to change opacity values.

Motion

Motion paths

We've already touched on motion paths, when we discussed setting position keyframes in the Composition window. The series of dots (one for each frame) connecting X symbols (keyframes) is an excellent visual guide when animating. Keep in mind that setting fewer keyframes often avoids unnecessarily complicated motion paths, and makes it easier to adjust motion paths if you need to. We'll look at motion paths and how to modify them as we progress through this chapter.

For now, let's put into practice what we've covered so far.

The incredible shrinking vortex

1. Remove all the keyframes from the vortex.jpg layer by selecting them, and then pressing the DELETE key, and remove any property values by clicking the Reset hot text.

2. Before we begin setting any keyframes, use the hot text to reduce the scale of the vortex.jpg layer scale to 10%. Because vortex.jpg was quite large, reducing its size also makes it easier to see what we're doing with the layer.

3. Position the current time marker to three seconds on the timeline, which should be where our vortex makes its entrance to the composition stage.

4. Now drag the vortex to the top left-hand corner of the Composition window so its position is roughly P1 in the image below. Click on the Position stopwatch to place our first keyframe.

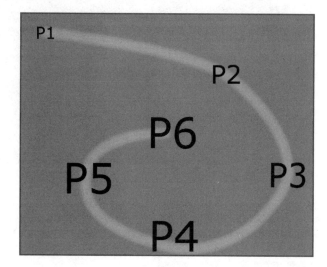

We'll be using this image as a diagram for the movement and growth of the Vortex layer, so you may want to refer back to it throughout this tutorial.

5. Move the current time marker to around eight seconds, and then drag the vortex over to position P2 in the Composition window. Notice a new Position keyframe appears.

6. Move the current time marker to around 11 seconds, and then drag the vortex to position P3.

7. Now move the current time marker to around 12 seconds, and then drag the vortex to position P4.

8. Move the current time marker to 12 seconds and ten frames, and drag the vortex to position P5.

9. Finally, move the current time marker to 13 seconds and then drag the vortex to the center of the Composition window; position P6.

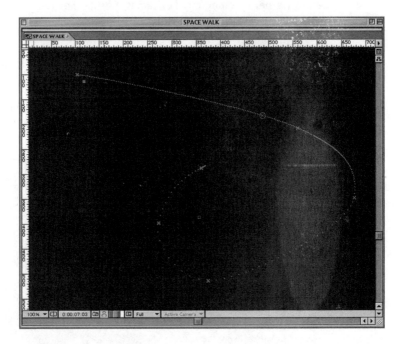

Notice how between P1 and P3, the dots are close together, indicating slower speed. From P3 to P4, the dots are further apart, indicating faster speed. From P4 to P5 the dots indicate the layer is moving at its fastest, and from P5 to P6, it moves a bit slower again.

But we're not done yet!

10. Any decent vortex needs some serious rotation, so return the current time indicator to three seconds and click the rotation stopwatch symbol. Then place the current time indicator at 13 seconds, and set the rotation hot text to the left of the X to 10. We have now set revolutions to 10, which means we should see ten revolutions between our two rotation keyframes.

Next, to add a bit of depth, and to have our vortex emerge from the vast darkness of space, we're going to play around with Scale and Opacity.

11. Return the current time indicator to three seconds. Click the stopwatches for Scale and Opacity. Change Scale to 4% and change Opacity to 0%.

12. Move the current time indicator to 11 seconds, and change the Opacity to 100%. At this point in time, we want our vortex fully visible. However, we still want it to be growing closer, so don't touch the Scale property just yet.

13. Now move the current time indicator to 12 seconds. At this point, we'll make our vortex full size. Use the hot text to set the Scale to 100%.

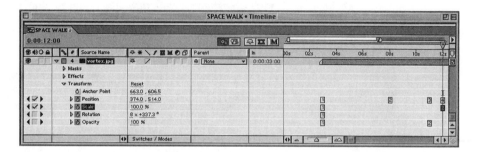

14. Then move the current time marker to 13 seconds.

Notice that the center of our vortex doesn't line up with our final keyframe, which is in the center of the page. That's because the center of our vortex.jpg file is not the center of our actual vortex. To perfect our little sequence, we can change the Anchor point. Because we want the change to apply to the whole animation, there's no need to press the stopwatch to set a keyframe.

15. Double click the vortex.jpg layer name in the Source Name column of the timeline. This will open the Layer window. Click on the dark arrow at the top right-hand side of the Layer window to reveal the Layer window menu, and choose Anchor Point Path.

16. Now drag the circle with the x in the middle (the anchor point), to the center of our vortex and let go.

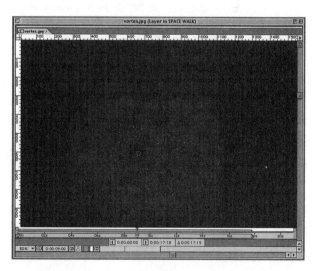

17. Close the Layer window, and in the Composition window, at 13 seconds on the timeline, our vortex should appear roughly at the center of the frame.

18. Now return the current time marker to three seconds in the Timeline window. Hit the space bar or press the play button in the Time Controls window to get a rough preview of our vortex animation in the Composition window. Note that the playback will not be in real time.

Using value and velocity controls between keyframes

When we were looking at adding keyframes, you may have noticed that upon clicking the stopwatch symbol, an arrow appears to the left of the stopwatch, just like the arrows for each of the layer property categories.

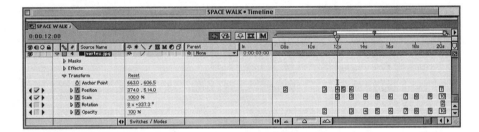

If you click on these arrows, you will reveal different graphs for Value, Velocity or Speed, depending upon which property you are looking at. These graphs can be used to edit, refine and improve our animation.

If you click on the arrow to the left of the Position property, you'll reveal a Speed graph, and if you click on the arrow to the left of the Scale property, you'll reveal a Value graph and a Velocity graph.

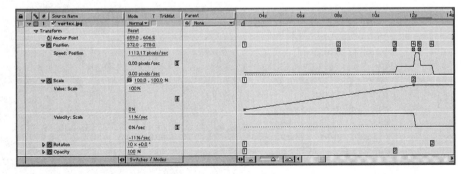

The Value graph displays the value of keyframes for a layer property, and also the interpolated value between keyframes. You can use these graphs to change values, by dragging the square markers (keyframes) up and down. You can also add keyframes to the graph with the Pen tool. If the graph is flat (horizontal), there is no change of value between keyframes. If it slopes up or down, then there is an increase or decrease in the keyframe value.

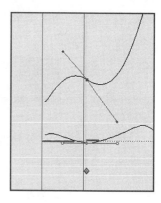

The Speed graph displays, and can be used to change or refine, the value and rate of change for spatial values, such as Position. The Velocity graph displays, and can be used to change or refine, the value and rate of change for non-spatial values such as Opacity.

If you have the Scale property selected, you will notice at the 12-second mark, there is a change in level on the velocity graph, and each level has its own blue adjustment handles. These handles can be dragged up to accelerate, or down to decelerate, entering and leaving the keyframe.

In the real world, where gravity applies, most things accelerate into motion and decelerate to a stop. The ease handles can be used to assist in simulating this type of motion, which is very useful for animating many different types of movement such as that of a bouncing ball.

Let's put these smooth new techniques to the test in our composition.

Smooth animator

1. Select the vortex.jpg layer in the Composition window. Notice that the trail of dots indicates a sudden change of speed at a number of our keyframes, particularly around 11 seconds, 12 seconds, and 12 seconds + 10 frames. We can ease in and ease out of keyframes to make this movement a bit more natural.

2. Within our vortex layer in the timeline, click the triangle next to the Position property to reveal the Speed graph. Click the Position property (the text, not the stopwatch, we don't want to lose our keyframes!). With the Position property selected, the blue ease in / out handles should appear on the graph.

Notice that at the points at which we identified a sudden change of speed in the Composition window, the graph has some steep slopes where it jumps from one level to another.

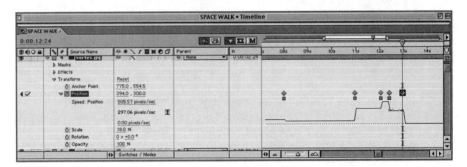

3. Select the Position keyframe at 11 seconds. Note that now only the ease handles around that keyframe are visible. Select the lower ease handle by clicking on the small circle on the end of it, to the left. Drag it to about the halfway point between its starting position and the ease handle that lies above it at the top of the slope.

    As you move it, notice how the slope gets more of a curve. Pay attention to the Composition window as you move the handle around. Ensure the current time marker is positioned on the keyframe you are working on and watch how the dots move closer together or further apart, depending upon which way you're moving the ease handle. We want to see the dots go from being bunched up to more evenly spaced over a number of frames around the keyframe. In the graph window, we want to see the sharp slope joining the two levels become more of a gradual curve.

4. To complete the transition, select the top ease handle, and drag it down to meet the lower handle. The graph should now resemble a gentle curve rather than a steep slope.

5. Now repeat the process for the other keyframes along the Position Speed graph at the 12 second, and 12 second + 10 Frames positions on the timeline. You can also have the vortex ease into its center position by adjusting the ease in handle for the 13-second keyframe. This will make the vortex come to rest in the center more gradually.

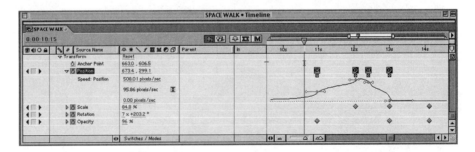

6. If you want to be a real perfectionist, you can do the same for the 8-second mark as well, although the transition there should not be nearly as noticeable.

Motion sketch

Another way to utilize motion paths is to draw one using Motion Sketch. Motion sketch allows you to draw a path, while not affecting keyframes for other properties such as Rotation or Opacity. To use motion sketch, select Window > Motion Sketch. Press the Start Capture button to begin, and then drag the layer around the screen as you want it to move. As you begin dragging, the timeline will begin to record your movements over time, and will stop when you let go. If you move fast, After Effects will record keyframes to reflect fast movement, and vice versa if you want it slow. By default, the playback speed is 100% of the speed at which you sketch, but you can also have it play back faster or slower, as a percentage relative to your sketch speed.

The smoother

After Effects also has a tool which can be used to smooth motion paths, although it can also be used to smooth value and velocity curves. To access the Smoother, select Window > The Smoother.

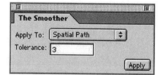

The smoother adds necessary keyframes, and is also useful for removing excess keyframes, which often come with Motion Sketch curves. At least three keyframes of a curve must be selected for the Motion Smoother to work, although you can select all keyframes to apply smoothing to an entire curve. The smoother will automatically decide between Spatial Path or Temporal Graph based upon the type of layer property you selected keyframes for. The tolerance setting specifies the maximum distance between new values and the original curve. The higher the tolerance value, the smoother the curve, but also the further the new curve shape will be from the shape of the original curve. You can use a trial and error approach by relying upon Edit > Undo if you don't like the smoother results.

Using keyframes to balance the motion path

You can also refine a motion curve in the Composition window by selecting a keyframe (X symbols). You will notice one or two small boxes or diamonds near the selected keyframe. Select a box, and begin to drag it, and you will see it's a control handle which can be used to shape and refine the motion path. It acts like a Bezier curve, similar to what you would find in Illustrator or Photoshop.

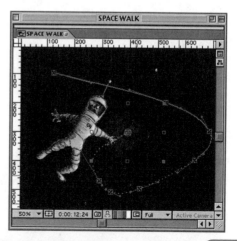

You can also add keyframes to a motion path in the Composition window by using the Pen tool. To do this, you need to select the layer you want to change in the timeline, then select the Pen tool. In the Composition window, the motion path should be visible for the layer you have selected. Move the Pen tool to a position along the motion path where you want to add a keyframe. A + symbol appears next to the Pen tool icon. Click to add a new keyframe at that point in time along the motion path.

Motion tracking and image stabilization

Yet another way to manipulate motion in your After Effects projects is to use the Tracker/Stabilizer. In the Production Bundle of After Effects, you can use the Tracker/Stabilizer to incorporate animation or effects into moving camera shots, as well as stabilize footage where the camerawork is too rough, or has experienced unexpected bumps.

After Effects does this by matching pixels from a selected area of the frame to similar pixels in subsequent frames. You can track position or rotation, which allows you to incorporate elements into hand-held footage that were not originally there. To access the Tracker/Stabilizer, double-click the layer you wish to apply it to, and in the Layer window that opens, use the menu to select the Tracker/Stabilizer controls. A Tracker/Stabilizer panel will then be added to the Layer window.

Say we wanted to put a monkey on someone's back, and we had footage of someone out for a stroll, and footage of a monkey on a branch with the branch removed. You can set a Feature Region which is the area or element of the footage you wish to track from one frame to another, so in this case we would set a region around the walker's shoulders.

As the footage progresses through frames, it will need to look for matching pixels, so by setting up a search region, you are giving After Effects a hint where to look. If the movement of our walker is large between frames, you will naturally need to set up a larger search region. You can then use a Track Point to specify where the initial layer is attached to the second layer. To get the monkey on our walker's back, we can specify the walker's shoulders, and the monkey's feet. You can use the Tracker controls to identify the element you wish to track in one layer, and then use the tracked motion to animate a different layer. Using the Tracker controls, we can use the motion of the walker's shoulders and use it for the motion of the sitting monkey.

The Tracker/Stabilizer is the perfect tool to fake bigfoot sightings, churn out home videos of UFO close encounters, or protect anonymous interviewees from their 15 minutes of fame, via highly pixelated faces.

The Wiggler

The Wiggler tool (again only available with the Production Bundle) almost represents the opposite end of image stabilization: it is used to add randomness to any property as it varies over time. This could be very handy to help us animate a falling leaf, buzzing fly, or spinning top, without having to make all the subtle movements ourselves. The Wiggler will add fluctuations to a property by randomizing interpolations coming into or out of keyframes, and will also add keyframes where necessary.

To use the Wiggler, you need to select a group of keyframes (at least two) and choose Window > The Wiggler. In the Apply To options, select Spatial Path to add deviations to motion, or Temporal Graph to add deviations to velocity. You can also specify the noise type. For smoother deviations with no sudden changes, specify Smooth Noise. For sudden changes specify Jagged Noise.

You then need to decide how many dimensions will be affected by the Wiggler. You can choose between One Dimension, All Dimensions Independently, or All Dimensions The Same. All Dimensions Independently will apply different random deviations to different dimensions, whereas the All Dimensions The Same option will apply the same random deviation to each dimension as they occur.

The Frequency determines how frequent the deviations occur. The higher the frequency, the more often the deviations appear. Magnitude is specified to determine the maximum size of the deviations.

When you're happy with the settings click Apply. If you then need to readjust the settings, choose Edit > Undo The Wiggler to reset the keyframes and try again.

Relative motion

Parenting

Parenting allows us to have the layer properties of a 'parent' layer affect a 'child' layer. For example, we could take a character like Pinocchio, and have his body as the parent layer. We could then set his head, arms and legs as child layers. This would allow us to animate the limbs or head within their own layers, but if we then moved the parent layer (Pinocchio's body) all the other body parts would follow and remain intact, including any animation we had set for those layers.

A parent layer can have as many child layers as you like, but each child layer can never have more than one parent layer. Parenting can be used for all transform properties except Opacity.

The parent column should be to the left of the timeline in the Timeline window. If you can't see it, choose Panels > Parent from the Timeline window menu. For each layer, the parent column has a small spiral-like symbol, called a **pick whip**, and also a drop-down menu that should read None by default. To use parenting, you first select the layer you wish to be the child. Then select the pick whip, and drag it to the layer you wish to become parent, or open the drop-down list and select the parent layer from there. As you drag the pick whip, an extendible line will follow the cursor and prospective parent layers will be highlighted as you roll over them.

By default, a child layer's properties then become relative to the parent layer. However, After Effects changes and manages the keyframe values of the child layer so that its properties appear to remain relative to the composition. After Effects allows you to have a child layer visibly alter its properties relative to the parent layer when a parent is assigned or unassigned. To do so, hold down ALT (Windows) or OPTION (Mac) when you assign or unassign parent layers.

You can also use invisible parent layers by using a **null object**. A null object is an invisible layer that has all the properties of a normal layer except opacity, which means you can animate it like any other layer. This can be useful to control a number of layers with an invisible guide. You could have a group of separately animated layers chase the null point layer, maintaining their positions with respect to the parent, for example.

To use a null object choose Layer > New > Null Object. The null object differs slightly from your usual imported footage, in that its default anchor point is the top left-hand corner. If you need to, you can adjust the anchor point like any other layer.

Let's have a go at putting some of this into practice.

Good parenting

Here's where we formally introduce you to the star of our teaser. You've seen him twice already, once with an arm, and once without: it's Spacedude!

1.   First we need to import the 3 Photoshop layers of spacedude.psd as footage into After Effects. So choose File > Import > File..., select the spacedude.psd file, choose the Import As Footage option, and then bring in each layer as separate footage for body, right_arm, and left_arm.

2.   Drag body/spacedude.psd onto the timeline above the vortex.jpg layer, to begin at 0 seconds. Then drag right_arm/spacedude.psd, and left_arm/spacedude.psd onto the timeline below the new body layer, but above the vortex.jpg layer.

     You should now have 4 layers in this order:

     ■   body/spacedude.psd

     ■   right_arm/spacedude.psd

     ■   left_arm/spacedude.psd

     ■   vortex.jpg

3.   Now open up the 3 new layers for body, right_arm, and left_arm, and set the Scale value to 30% for each layer (don't set a keyframe, just change the value with the hot text).

4.   Now that Spacedude and his arms are each 30%, move to the Composition window, and position Spacedude's arms so they fit to his body.

5. Once the arms are in position, and don't look like they are going to fall off, using the pick whip or the pull-down menu, make the left and right arm layers children to the parent body layer.

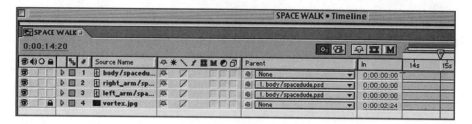

6. Now we can test our work. Select the body layer in the Composition window, and drag it around. The arms should remain attached to the body no matter where you move it.

Expressions

Expressions can be used to create relationships between the value of different layer properties, or to define the value of a property with a mathematical function. They can, for example, be used to make shadows change in relation to the movement of an animated sun, to animate a crowd scene, animate the rain, or animate a swarm of bees.

Expressions are based on the standard JavaScript language, but you don't need to know JavaScript to use them. At the same time, if you can already do amazing things with Flash ActionScript, then you should be able to do amazing things with expressions.

You create and view expressions in the timeline window. To create an expression, select the relevant property in the Timeline window, and choose Animation > Create Expression from the main menu. To remove it, do the same but choose Animation > Remove Expression.

You can also ALT-CLICK (Windows) or OPTION-CLICK (Mac) the stopwatch icon of the relevant property to create an expression. Do the same to remove it.

After either of the above steps, the expression details will open up. From there, you can drag the pick whip to another property to create a relationship, or you can type an expression into the text box.

To the left of the pick whip icon is another icon, which will open up the expression graphs. To the right is an arrow which will activate a pop-up list of commonly used expressions, from which you can choose one you'd like to use.

The = sign next to the stopwatch acts as an on/off switch for the expressions, and looks like an equal (on) or not equal (off) symbol.

Another thing to keep in mind when using and reusing expressions is that some of them rely on particular layer names, so if the layer names change, the expressions reliant upon them will no longer work. To begin to understand the enormous potential of using expressions for animation, let's go to an example.

In space, no one can see your keyframes

Seeing as we have separate layers for Spacedude's arms, let's make them wave about with an expression. We're going to make them rotate, but before we do, we'll need to change the anchor points so they rotate around the shoulders, and not the middle of the layer, which is their current default. Remember we looked at this problem back in the section on anchor points above. Flick back there for a quick refresher if you like.

1.   Double-click on the left_arm layer to bring up the Layer window. In the Layer window menu, ensure that Anchor Point Path is ticked. Now, we already went to the trouble of positioning the arms with the body, so to ensure the positions are maintained, we need to use the Pan Behind tool to change the anchor point.

2.   With the Pan Behind tool, drag the Anchor Point to the center of the top of the arm. In the Composition window, check the arm is still attached to the body. Now do the same with the right_arm layer.

3.   Open up the left_arm layer and ALT-click (Windows), or OPTION-click (Mac), the Rotation stopwatch symbol. This will bring up the expression options for rotation. In the text box on the timeline, it should read Rotation. Change this expression to read rotation.wiggle(0.5,12,3). This will make the arm rotate once every two seconds, about 12 degrees.

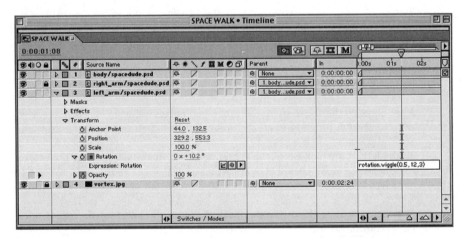

4.   Now do the same for the right_arm layer, but so the arms are different, make the expression rotation.wiggle(0.3,8,3). The right arm will rotate about once every three seconds, about eight degrees.

5. To add a little bit more of a spacy feel, use the rotation expression rotation.wiggle(0.2,5,3) on the rotation property of the body layer.

6. Now click at various places along the timeline, from 0 to 30 seconds, to see the automatic arms and space walk in action.

Setting preview options

There are five different options for previewing your work in After Effects:

- RAM Preview

- Standard Preview

- Manual Preview

- Wireframe Preview

- Video Preview

Which preview you use, and how you use it, depends upon what you are trying to check. If you need to check how a final composite will look, you would tend to look at full quality images to the detriment of speed. If you're checking the motion or movement itself, you would tend to sacrifice image quality for playback speed.

Let's look at each preview option in more detail.

RAM Preview

RAM Preview can be used to preview frames and audio at the composition frame rate, or as fast as your system can handle. The number of frames you can preview depends upon how much contiguous RAM has been allocated and is available to After Effects. If a layer's audio is switched off, it will not be previewed.

RAM Preview can be used for the Timeline, Layer and Footage windows. In the timeline, the time specified within the work area will be previewed, so make sure you adjust your work area to what you need to see. For the Layer and Footage windows, only untrimmed footage will be previewed.

For a RAM preview, click the button on the right-hand side of the time controls, or choose Composition > Preview > RAM Preview from the main menu.

You can also save a RAM Preview as a self-contained movie by selecting Composition > Save RAM Preview... from the main menu.

Standard Preview

Standard Preview will preview all frames within your composition at the fastest speed at which After Effects is able to incorporate layer switches, composition switches and composition settings. This preview is often much slower than real-time play back.

For a Standard Preview, click the regular play button, or press the space bar.

Manual Preview

You can also preview a composition, layer or footage files by manually scrubbing through the timeline with the current time indicator, or using the jog and shuttle controls in the Time Controls window. Again, your ability to do so smoothly will depend upon processor and memory limitations.

Wireframe Preview

Using this option, each layer is represented as a rectangular outline, mask, or alpha channel outline. This is a particularly good option for reviewing the animation or motion of a layer. Choose Composition > Preview > Wireframe Preview. A related option to the Wireframe Preview is the Motion with Trails preview, which you can select from the main menu under Composition > Preview > Motion with Trails.

Motion with Trails is similar to the Wireframe Preview, however After Effects also displays a trail of outlines. Be mindful that this can look very confusing if there is a lot going on within the composition, in which case, it is often advisable to hide some layers, or even preview one layer at a time.

Video Preview

To preview your animation on an external video monitor, choose Edit > Preferences > Video Preview, and then select your display device, and specify relevant preview options.

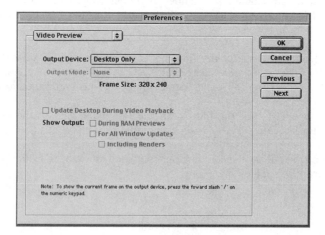

Speeding up your previews

If you need to speed up your previews and reduce waiting time, you can reduce the composition's work area, reduce the composition's resolution, and reduce the composition's size in the Composition window, or in the Time Controls window. You can also choose to skip frames in the Time Controls window.

Well that's pretty much it for this chapter. The only thing left to do is finish off our movie! While we've been busy working on our teaser trailer for our galactic tragedy, our producer has kindly reminded us not to forget the ten seconds of credits and legals to go in the final ten seconds of our 30-second teaser. We'll just have to end with a bang at the 20-second mark.

Open the pod bay doors HAL!

We've animated our vortex layer up to the 13 second mark, so we have seven seconds left to play with. How about we have Spacedude sucked toward the vortex for six seconds, and then have the vortex abduct Spacedude, and hyperspace out of view in one second?

1. Open up the vortex layer, and open the transform properties so we can clearly see and access the key frames. We want to keep up the rotation rate of our vortex. At the moment it is on screen for ten seconds, with one rotation each second. To take us to the 20-second mark, drag the rotation keyframe at 13 seconds to around the 20-second mark.

2. Because the vortex is now on screen from three seconds, up to the 20second mark (17 seconds), to maintain the same rate of rotation, we need to double click the keyframe and change the Revolutions to 17.

3. We want our vortex to keep on rotating in the same position, so ensure the current time indicator is on 20 seconds, and then set a Position Keyframe for our vortex.jpg layer.

4. To give our vortex more life, we'll use Scale and Opacity to have it pulsate, and then zoom into the void of space. To do this, start by moving the current time indicator to 14 seconds, and set a Scale keyframe of 95%, and an Opacity keyframe of 90%.

5. Then move the current time indicator to 15 seconds, and set a Scale keyframe of 100%, and an Opacity keyframe of 100%. Select the four keyframes you have just created, copy them, and then paste them at the 16-second and 18-second points. You should end up with a pair of keyframes at every second mark between 14 and 19 seconds, and a pulsating vortex.

6. Now, move the current time indicator to 20 seconds, and set a Scale keyframe of 2%, and an Opacity keyframe of 10%.

7. Now open up the body/spacedude.psd layer. Move the current time indicator to 15 seconds, and click the Position and Scale stopwatches to set keyframes.

8. Move the current time indicator to 19 seconds, and then drag the body/spacedude.psd layer to the center of the vortex, which should give us another keyframe. Then set a Scale keyframe of 20%, and click on the Opacity stopwatch to set an Opacity keyframe of 100%.

9. Scroll back down to the vortex.jpg layer, and select the Position and Scale keyframes at the 20-second mark. Copy the keyframes. Move back up to the body/spacedude.psd layer, and select it. Make sure the current time indicator is at the 20-second mark, and then paste the keyframes. Spacedude should now zip off with the vortex.

10. Now set the Opacity of body/spacedude.psd to 0%.

   Notice how Spacedude's arms stay bright in that last second. That's because the child layers do not inherit the Opacity values of the parent layer, so we need to change them separately.

11. Move the current time indicator to 19 seconds, and set the Opacity keyframes to 100% for both arm layers. Finally, move the current time indicator to 20 seconds, and set the Opacity keyframes to 0% for both arm layers.

You've now successfully animated spacedude's journey into the vortex, and you're ready to render!

Conclusion

Throughout the chapter, we've covered a lot of After Effects features, including setting keyframes, parenting layers, and using expressions. You should now have a good understanding of the After Effects timeline, and how to animate layer properties over time. We're now ready to go on to look at how best to build up our layers, which is the subject of the next chapter.

6 Building Layers, and Introducing 3D

In this chapter, we'll be looking at how to use After Effects to build layers using different media such as video, audio, stills, animated still sequences, and text.

In traditional cel animation, the artwork is built up in layers. For example, the background layer represents the environment the character is in, the next layer may have the body of the character, the third layer may contain the character's eyes, the fourth its mouth, and so on.

With the advance of computer technology that we're now seeing, this technique can be used to create visual effects for both television and film production. We have seen the results in many of the feature films we watch, though the use of such effects is not always obvious (especially if they are well crafted! – the compositing artist will have used their skills as much to hide the presence of effects, as they have to create and insert them into the scene).

For example, say a client has edited a short item for a television magazine program and presented the finished item to the broadcaster. They then discover that the broadcaster cannot show the video because of some advertising displayed on the T-shirts of some of the contributors. By using Photoshop and After Effects, the advertisements can be removed with a bit of work using keyframes, alpha channels and mattes.

Alternatively, After Effects can be used to build opening title sequences for film, television programs, and corporate videos.

In 3D work, different layers can be rendered out from the 3D animation program and composited together in After Effects to provide more control over how texture-maps are blended with bump maps and lighting textures.

These are just a few examples of the many ways in which After Effects, and the layers that are integral to its process, can be used to develop stunning visuals for your programs.

> *Like most things worth doing, developing and fine-tuning your compositions will take time. You shouldn't expect to see stunning results the first time round. Each piece of work needs to be looked at and reworked over and over again.*

Building layers using different media

Let's start by looking at how we can use layers in After Effects to composite media created in software programs such as Adobe Premiere, Adobe Photoshop, Macromedia Flash and a variety of 3D animation programs.

For the exercises we will look at here, I shot some material using a miniDV camcorder. This material was then digitized into Premiere, ultimately to produce QuickTime movies using the DV codec. Having done this, the final montage can then be exported as a new QuickTime movie that can be used as a layer in After Effects.

One of the advantages of Premiere is that the sequence you edit can be imported into After Effects as a **Project File**. This leaves the edit laid out in the After Effects timeline as it had been in Premiere. For more detail on this, refer to **Chapter 4**, which covers how to prepare and import media generated using other software packages.

Setting up After Effects

Throughout this chapter, we'll be looking at an After Effects project called `Layers Project.aep`. This project, and its associated files, can be found on the accompanying CD-ROM.

1. Copy the `Juggler` folder from the Chapter 6 folder to your hard drive. This will allow the media to play properly. Some of the files are in full DV resolution and will not run smoothly from the CD-ROM, as the data rate is too slow.

2. Open the example file `Layers Project.aep`.

3. Create a new composition, and call it `Comp 6.1`.

The new composition will appear in the project window above a composition titled Juggler. In the composition window, the new composition will appear with the tab titled `Comp 6.1`. At this point, the composition window shows a black rectangle.

For the time being, we'll leave this until after we have looked at the composition entitled Juggler.

Juggler

The Juggler composition was produced on an iMac DV. The arrangement of the screen was set up to accommodate the 15 inch monitor size. For this reason, I found that setting the composition window to 50% allowed me to view all the windows and palettes with relative ease, as well as increasing the speed of playback. The screen resolution was set at 1024 x 768 pixels, 75Hz using millions of colors. Use the Control Panel and Monitors on a Mac or Display on a Windows computer to change these settings if you wish to match the ones I used.

Opening the composition

Double-clicking on the Juggler composition in the project window opens the file in the composition window. Try this now. What you should see is an image of a boy juggling some colored balls, against the backdrop of clouds and blue sky. To the left of the boy is a yellow blurred object which is a text graphic of the title, "The Juggler".

By clicking on the arrow beside the folder Media Cp7 in the Project window, you'll be able to see the three files used to produce the composition:

- Cloudx2002.mov

- Juggle.psd

- Juggle_010.mov

Ignore Brickwall2.psd for now; we don't need to refer to that one yet.

> *The reason why the boy juggling is called* Juggle_010.mov *is because it was the tenth shot taken of the boy during the shoot. Naming the clip this provides me with an easy method of accessing the shot if I need to find it again. When you are preparing your material, you should give your media clips and still images names that will help you easily identify where they were sourced.*

Click on the arrow beside the folder Rendered Movies in the Project window. Then double click on the movie Ex_7_2.mov. This will open a movie window. Now play through the clip.

The clip runs for about six seconds. It consists of fast moving clouds as a background, with the boy juggling three balls, one green, another blue and the last yellow, in the foreground. From the left of the screen the title "The Juggler" flies in, out of focus, and moves around the boy from behind, moving to right of screen. The title then flips around and travels to the foreground, coming to rest in focus. In the last second, the title fades away.

Looking at the composition layout in the timeline

If you now take a look at the timeline for the Juggler composition, you will see that it is made up of four layers:

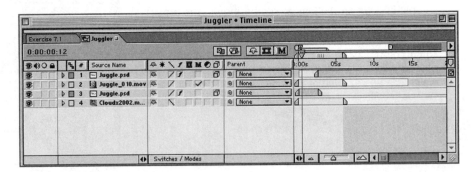

The base layer (layer 4) is `Cloudx2002.mov`. This clip was made from ten minutes of video captured into Final Cut Pro. The speed of the clip was increased by 2002% to create a 30-second clip, which was then rendered out as a QuickTime movie. You can also achieve this effect in After Effects by placing the cloud clip into a new composition, and then selecting Time Stretch from the Layer menu:

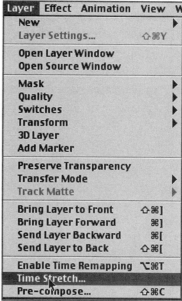

If the Stretch Factor in the Time Stretch window for the original 10:49 cloud clip is changed from 100% to 4.65%, the length of the clip is decreased to approximately 30 seconds:

For ease of use, and to save on processing time, this clip would then need to be rendered out as a QuickTime movie before being used in the Juggler composition.

This clip supplied on the CD-ROM has just over eleven seconds of material, as the 30-second clip was too big to fit on the CD!

Layers 1 and 3 are made up of the same file, `Juggle.psd`, which is the title text, created in Photoshop. The reason it is split across the two layers is to create the illusion of the text flying in from behind the juggler and then moving in front of him. We will look in depth at how this is done a little later on in the chapter.

Now, though, double-click on `Juggle.psd` in the Project window, which will open the file into a Footage window. The tab at the top left-hand corners includes the file's name. The current time field indicates that the footage is a still:

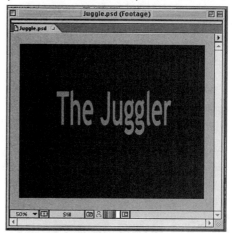

Let's take a look at the settings in the Interpret Footage window. Select File > Interpret Footage > Main.

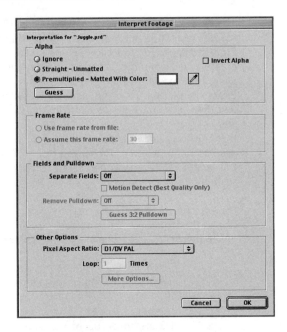

Here we can see that `Juggle.psd` has a Premultiplied – Matted With Color alpha channel. The color selected as the background is white (while it was transparent when in Photoshop). This effectively provides the clip with an alpha channel allowing background image in After Effects to show through with only the title The Juggler remaining opaque. Separate Fields is switched off, as the file did not originate from video. Finally, the Pixel Aspect Ratio is D1/DV PAL. This project was originated using a PAL system.

Close the Footage window for `Juggle.psd` and then double-click on `Juggle_010.mov` in the Project window.

Now, this should be a surprise for you. The boy juggling has not been shot against a blue or green screen, but against a brick wall. Nightmare!!!!!

We did this deliberately to show you how After Effects is a great tool for creating traveling mattes. It took 12 hours to create the one I used here; to generate the splines and move them along with the boy. There are still a few flaws, which with a bit more time we could tidy up, but we've left them for now so that you can explore how the mattes can be easily manipulated, once we have looked into how they have been constructed.

Adding layers to a composition

So let's start building up our own versions of Juggler so you can see how the layers are built up, and ultimately how the traveling mattes work. In the following exercise, we will begin to build up the layers in the composition, and work on the clips to create the same effects used in Juggler.

Ah, yes, 12 hours of moving splines! Well, I won't make you do that, but we'll start as if we were starting from scratch, and then when it comes to the 12 hour spline-athon, I'll pull out the "one I prepared earlier!"

Building a composition

To start with, we're going to look at building the simple composition of the Juggler. Firstly, we need to move the cloud background movie from the Project window into the Composition window.

1.   We will use the composition created earlier, called `Comp 6.1`. If the tab for `Comp 6.1` is still visible in the Composition window, click on it to make it active. If it is not visible in the Composition window, double-click on the Composition icon for `Comp 6.1` in the Project window.

2.   The background movie needs to be placed into the Composition window. To do this, simply click on `Cloudx2002.mov`, and drag it onto the Composition window. As the movie is brought across the Composition window, you will be able to see a white outline of the movie frame as it moves across the gray area surrounding the black frame of the composition view.

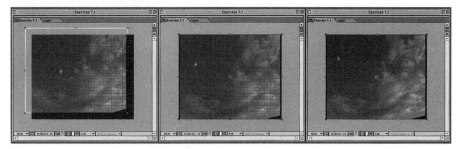

3.   Once the movie has been placed squarely over the composition, the white outline will disappear.

The image of the movie is only visible within the frame of the Composition window. You can fine-tune its position within the window by using the up and down arrows or the left and right arrows on the keyboard. However, you will notice that there are some black edges to the video material being used. Let's get rid of these.

4.   In the Timeline window, click on the arrow beside the source name of the clip, and then click on the Transform arrow. This drop-down menu will reveal:

■   Anchor Point

■   Position

■   Scale

- Rotation

- Opacity

The Scale will now show something like 106.7, 109.0%. If you move the cursor over either of these values, you can increase or decrease them as you like.

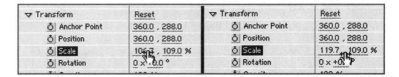

5. Scale up the size of the image until the black edge is concealed behind the gray area. A slightly easier way to do this is to click on one of the corner anchor points of the image within the Composition window, and drag the anchor point out until the black edge disappears.

6. Now Juggle_010.mov can be dragged onto the Composition Window. You will notice that it completely covers the background cloud clip. Save the project.

Traveling mattes

The next step, as we build up the layers of this piece, is to create the traveling matte around the boy and the colored balls. The first task here is to generate a mask, using the Pen tool, around the boy in the first frame of the movie clip.

Creating a mask using the Pen tool

1. By double-clicking on Juggle_010.mov in the Composition window, a layer window is opened. Alternatively, go to Layer > Open Layer Window.

2. Drag the corner of the layer window towards the lower right-hand corner of the screen to enlarge it. Then set the image to 100% using the drop-down menu at the lower left of the window.

3. Select the Pen tool from the Tool palette, and single-click anywhere in the layer window to create the first control point. Click elsewhere to create a second control point and a line is drawn between the two points. By holding the mouse button down and moving it as you create a control point, a Bezier curve is created. The new control point will then have levers, which can be moved using the corner cursor created by the Pen tool as it hovers over them.

4. Select and delete the marks you have just made, and use the Pen tool to trace out the figure of the boy. Join the final control point to the first control point by clicking on the latter.

5. By clicking on the Composition window, we can now see that the boy has a mask, which reveals the background sky. Select the timeline. Layer 1 should be highlighted. Click on the layer 1 triangle to reveal the drop-down list.

When the Mask drop-down list is revealed, it shows the first mask as Mask 1. To the left of this is an arrow and a yellow colored square. If you click on the yellow box, the mask color palette window opens to allow you choose the color of the mask.

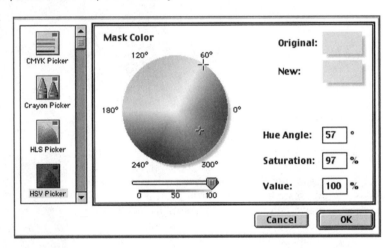

This is especially useful, as we are going to produce three more masks for each of the colored balls. As the balls are at times obscured by the boy's hands as he juggles, the different colored masks allow you to easily identify the position of each ball.

6. Now click on the arrow to the left of the color square beside Mask 1. A drop-down list reveals Mask Shape, Mask Feather, Mask Opacity and Mask Expansion. As the first mask has been created, we need to set a keyframe on the first frame of the clip being used.

> *If you forget to activate a keyframe on the first frame for the mask, when you move along the timeline and change the shape of the mask to make a traveling matte, you will find that the mask does not change as you had intended. By placing a keyframe on the first frame, when you move to change the mask a few frames further on, the changes you make will automatically add a keyframe at this new point on the timeline, and the mask will become animated.*

7.   To add the keyframe, click on the stopwatch icon to the left of Mask Shape. In doing so, a tick appears in the Audio/Video Features panel, an arrow appears beside the stopwatch, the stopwatch icon changes to a watch with hands, and a keyframe is added into the timeline.

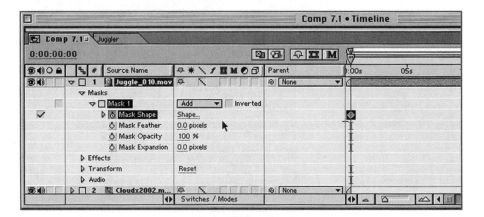

The next step is to produce a mask to reveal each of the colored balls.

8.   Using the same process we used for the boy, create a separate mask for each of the visible colored balls. To do this, you will need to go back into the layer window and move the timeline along so that you can see each of the balls you need to cut out.

9.   In the Timeline window, change the mask color for each of the colored balls. Then save the project.

> There are green, blue and yellow balls.. If you choose a color for the mask that is the same color as the ball you may find it hard to see the mask when you come to change its position, so choose an alternative color for each ball.

Creating traveling mattes

The next stage is to move two frames along the timeline to see how much the boy and the colored balls have moved out of position with the mask. To do this use the Time Control palette, and click on the next frame button.

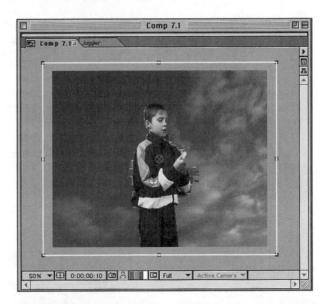

If you are used to using non-linear editing packages, the left and right arrow on the keyboard allows you to move frame by frame. However, if you do this in After Effects, you will be moving the selected elements of the mask, or moving the clip itself, to a different position in the Composition window. To correct this, use the Undo option in the Edit menu. This will also tell you what the last action was to prevent you going back too far.

Using the layer window for Juggle_010.mov, we can adjust the control points of the mask so that none of the brick wall in the background is showing. Once the first control point has been altered, a new keyframe will appear in the Timeline window.

1. Go through the first 25 frames of the composition and adjust the masks to hide the brick wall. Work on each of the masks separately. For the juggling balls, select all of the control points for each of the ball masks and drag the entire mask to the same position as the image of the ball. A new keyframe will be added each time you move the mask. This process will need to be repeated every few frames.

2. Adjust the working area of the Timeline window so that it is 25 frames. Set the Composition window to Third resolution and click on the Play button in the Time Control palette. Then save the project.

Playing through the work area, you should be able to see whether you need to make further adjustments to the composition to hide the brick wall. What you have created is a traveling matte.

3.   Adjust the resolution of the Composition window to Full, and make any necessary adjustments to the traveling matte. Then save your project.

If you feel like it, go ahead and add the keyframes for the remainder of the sequence. Alternatively, just stick with the 25 frames, and let's move on.

Feather-edging the traveling matte

If you play back the work area at full resolution, the playback speed will not be real-time unless you are using a multi-processor computer with a high specification. However, you should be able to see that the mask has a sharp edge and the boy and cloud shot do not sit too well together. After Effects provides a useful tool to soften the edges of the masked area of a clip by a specified number of pixels. Half this number of pixels will be outside the line of the mask, and the other half will be inside the line of the mask. Effectively, the feather-edge changes the opacity of the mask from 100% to 0% across the number of pixels that are chosen. Therefore, if you choose the feather-edge to be tenpixels (five inside the mask line, and five outside the masked line), the pixel closest to the center of the mask will be 100% opaque and the pixel furthest from the center of the mask will be 0% opaque. We used this effect a little back in **Chapter 4**.

Applying a feather-edge will also increase the size of the mask. So if you choose a feather-edge of ten pixels, the circumference of the mask will have increased by five pixels. This may reveal more of the brick wall in Comp 6.1. To reduce the circumference of the mask throughout the entire traveling matte, the mask can be contracted.

Feather-edging

1.   We need to make sure that the first frame of the composition is selected in the timeline. This can be achieved by clicking on the First Frame button on the Time Control palette.

2.   Take a look in the timeline, and you'll see that for Mask 1, under the Juggle_010.mov layer, the Mask Feather is set to 0.0 pixels. To change the value, place the cursor over the pixels' value, and it turns into a white hand with an arrow either side of the index finger. Then just move the cursor left and right. The range of the Mask Feather is between 0.0 and 1000.0 pixels.

If the Mask Feather is set to 200.0 pixels, it is possible to see how the image of the boy blends with the image of the clouds. However, more of the bricks are revealed:

3.   Set the value of the Mask Feather for Mask 1 of the `Juggle_010.mov` layer to 4.0 pixels. Then click on the stopwatch beside Mask Feather in the drop down list. This will add a keyframe on the first frame of the composition. This means that the effect of changing the feather value will be applied to the whole of the timeline, unless you add another keyframe, or change the pixels value.

4.   Next, click on the play button on the Time Control palette. As the composition will play back slower than real-time, you should be able to see any places in which the one second long traveling matte does not hide the brick wall.

As mentioned earlier, we can contract the circumference of the mask so that the feathered edge is within the area of the boy's body. We'll use this technique now to get rid of any stray bits of wall.

5.   Click on the Mask Expansion in the Mask 1 drop-down list for the `Juggle_010.mov` layer. Because we are contracting the mask, we will need to choose a minus number for the pixels value. If the contraction is too great then the image of the boy will begin to disappear, as in the screenshot below:

By giving the value a positive number the brickwork is revealed:

For the composition we are working on, the Mask Expansion can be set at −2.0 pixels. Save the project.

To save us extending our one second mask for another ten seconds, we're going to move onto the "one I made earlier". If you click on composition 6.2 in the Composition window, you'll see that we have just over ten seconds of traveling matte. We'll be working with this composition from here.

Locking the layer

So we don't lose the work that went into producing our traveling matte, it's a good idea to lock the layer so that it isn't adjusted accidentally. This can be achieved by clicking on the Lock switch in the Audio/Video Feature panel of the timeline.

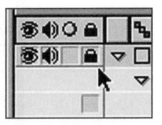

Alternatively, using the menu Layers > Switches > Lock will also lock the layer. Once you've locked your layer, save the project.

By clicking on the lock icon once more, the layer becomes unlocked and the lock icon disappears.

Adding the third layer to the composition

Now we'll add the title of the composition, 'The Juggler'; a piece of text created in Photoshop.

1. Double click on `Juggle.psd` in the Project window to open its Footage window.

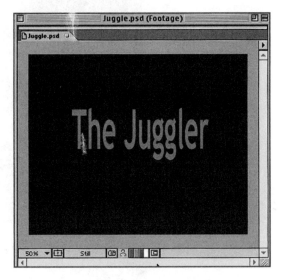

You will notice that the title 'The Juggler' is in orange and the background is black. In this instance, the reason the footage window shows the background as black is that an alpha channel has been applied to the still in Photoshop.

If you look at the footage window you will see red, green, blue and white buttons below the image. These represent the color channels of the 32-bit image.

2.   Click on the white button.

By clicking on the white button, you will be able to see the matte of the title which forms the alpha channel. The alpha channel enables the text to be revealed when it is placed onto the Composition window, and the background to be transparent so that the lower layers can be visible through it.

3.   Set the composition to the First Frame, then select Juggle.psd from the Project window and drag it to the Composition window for Comp 6.2. Then save the project.

At the moment, the text does not stand out too well against the other layers beneath it. To give it more clarity, we'll add a Drop Shadow.

Using the Effect Controls window to develop the text layer

1.   In the timeline, select Juggle.psd by clicking on its source name. The composition should be set at the first frame.

2.   To apply this effect, choose Effect > Perspective > Drop Shadow. This will open the Effect Controls window.

3.   The default starting point determines the shadow color as black. Using the dropper, choose an alternative color from the Composition window, or click on the black rectangle to choose a color from the color picker window.

4.   Set the Opacity to 60%. The arrow beside the control drops down a slider tool to enable you to change this value between 0% and 100% opaque. Alternatively, you can place the cursor over the value number, hold the mouse button down and drag to the left to reduce the percentage or to the right to increase the percentage value.

5.   You can alter the direction control to change the position of the drop shadow in relation to the text itself. You can do this by clicking on the direction wheel, or by

dragging the value number to the left or right as above to change the percentage value. For our project, set it to $0 \times +135.0^{\circ}$

6. You can adjust the distance of the shadow from its source by using the slider from the drop-down icon, or by dragging the value number across, as above. Set the Distance to 10.0.

7. Use the softness value to blur the shadow so that it darkens the background around the edge of the text. Set it to 13.0.

8. Click on all the stopwatches to add a keyframe for each value to the timeline. If you drop down the list for the effects in the Juggle.psd layer, you will see all the settings have been added to the timeline. Now save the project.

> *If you select the* Shadow Only *option, only the shadow appears in the composition. This is useful if you want the text and shadow to be on separate layers.*

Animating the title

The static title currently covers most of the action of the boy juggling. So in the next section, we will look at how we can animate the text so that it travels into shot, moves behind the boy from left to right, flips round and moves in front of him to stop at the lower left of frame. To accomplish this, we will use the Transform features within After Effects.

Using the transform features for animation

To start with, we will position markers on the layer to indicate where certain actions should start and finish. The complete move should last for about three seconds of the six in the work area. The title should remain static for two seconds before fading away.

1. First, select the Juggle.psd layer containing the text file. Then add a Marker by choosing Layer > Add Marker. This will place a marker at the first frame.

2. Now position the current-time marker at the three-second point on the timeline, and add a second marker. This is to indicate where we wish the move to end once we begin to animate the text.

3. Repeat this process to add a marker midway between the fourth and fifth second mark, and another at about half a second before the end of the composition. These last two markers indicate the beginning of the fade we will apply to the text. Save the project.

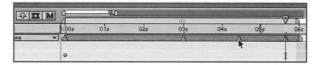

These markers can be adjusted as need be, by simply dragging them along the timeline to a more suitable position as seen fit. They can be deleted by simply right-clicking (Windows) or COMMAND + CLICK (Mac OS) on the marker on the timeline.

We are now ready to move the layer so that it can be animated. We'll work from the end position, as the current size of the text is suitable to finish on.

4. To do this, move the time marker to the second marker position in the Juggle.psd layer, as this is the point at which the title will settle before fading.

5. As this layer is selected in the timeline, it can be dragged to a new position in the Composition window. Drag the text to the bottom left-hand corner of the composition.

6. As the position has been changed, we must click on the Position transform stopwatch to create a keyframe at this point.

7. Here, the Opacity level should be set to 100%. This is achieved by simply clicking on the Opacity transform stopwatch. This adds another keyframe to the timeline. Now position the current frame marker at the third marker on the layer.

8. At this marker point, the title will not be moved from its current position, but the Opacity will be maintained at a constant 100%. To enable this to happen, add another keyframe to the timeline for the Opacity transform. This time don't click on the stopwatch, as this would remove the previous keyframe for the Opacity. Instead, click on the gray square to the left of the Opacity stopwatch to mark a keyframe at current position.

The gray square represents After Effects Keyframe Navigator. It is activated as soon as a keyframe is applied for a particular feature or effects filter. A tick in the Keyframe Navigator indicates there is a keyframe at the Time Marker position. When there is not a gray square present it indicates that no keyframes have been used for a particular feature or effect.

9. We now move to the fourth marker position, the current frame. This time, we need to change the Opacity value to 0% so that the title is no longer visible. To do this, move the cursor over the Opacity value, hold down the mouse button and drag it to the left. Alternatively, single-click on the value, type 0, and hit ENTER. In the Composition window, you will see the title disappear.

10. Set the Composition window resolution to Third, and play your composition through to see the effect generated. Then save the project.

Creating a motion path for the title layer

The next step is to create the motion path for the Juggle.psd layer to travel along.

1. Set the time marker to the second marker position. From this point until the end of the timeline, the `Juggle.psd` layer needs to remain scaled at 100%. To make sure this happens, click on the Scale stopwatch to mark a keyframe and activate the Keyframe Navigator for this transform element.

2. Now position the time marker midway between the first and second markers. In the Composition window, you will see a circle with an X inside it at the center of the layer. You can use this to reposition the layer. As this is done a motion path is created.

3. Move the `Juggle.psd` layer to the right of the boy. The illusion we are trying to create is that this layer flies around the boy to the front of the screen. At this position, then, the scale of the layer should be smaller than the end frame size of the layer.

4. Click and drag the Scale value to about 62%. A keyframe marker has appeared on the timeline, and a tick is now present in the Keyframe Navigator.

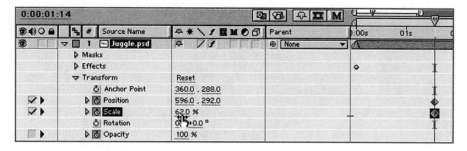

5. Now position the time marker on the first frame. Once again, reposition the layer, this time so that the title is just out of frame to the left of the boy. As the layer is moved, the motion path becomes a Bezier curve. A keyframe is added to indicate a position value change.

6. We want to give the impression that the title is zooming in from a distance, so scale the layer down once more to about 8.0%. Once the Scale value has been changed, a keyframe appears in the timeline as before.

7. Now play the sequence through and save the project.

3D – using the 3D layer, cameras and lights

So far, everything we've been doing to the composition has consisted of a two-dimensional treatment of each layer. After Effects 5.0 and onwards offers the additional feature of allowing layers to be treated in three-dimensional space to create even more dynamic effects. You can open out a layer to 3D options by using the 3D switch in the switch panel of the timeline:

The layer we're going to be manipulating in 3D is the Juggle.psd layer.

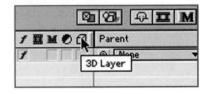

Applying 3D effects to Juggle.psd

Before we manipulate anything in 3D, we need to look at the Juggle.psd layer independently of the other layers in the composition. This can be achieved by using the Solo switch in the Audio/Video Features panel of the Timeline window, which allows you to see just the layer that you are working on.

1. Set the time marker to the first frame and play the composition sequence. You will notice how uninspiring the movement is. This is a job for 3D! Select the 3D layer from the switch panel.

When the 3D layer is selected, four more Transforms appear, replacing the Rotation transform of the previous 2D layer. Manipulating these transforms enables you to move the layer in a similar way to the way you can move a three-dimensional object in a 3D animation package. To see how this can improve the movement of the title in the Juggle.psd layer, we shall change some of the values of the X, Y and Z Rotation Transforms. We'll begin, once more, at the end of the movie so that we can see how the final title will end up.

2.   Position the time marker at the second layer marker. Now change the X rotation value to −30.0°, the Y rotation value to +8.0°, and leave the Z rotation at +19.0°. Again, these values can be changed by typing in the new value and hitting ENTER, or dragging the value number with the mouse to the new value number. Hit the stopwatch icon to add a keyframe to the timeline as each value is changed.

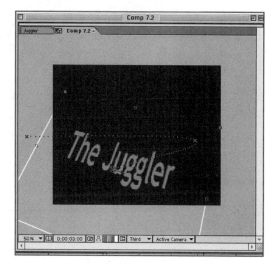

3.   Now we have the new finishing position for our title. Next, move the time marker to the midway point between the first two layer markers, in line with the other keyframes at that point.

4.   Here, change the Z rotation value to -46.0°, the Y rotation value to +25.0°, and leave the X rotation at −30.0°.

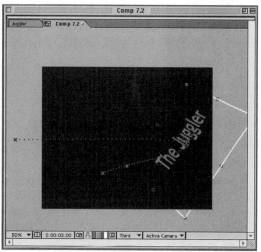

5. Next, move the time marker to the first frame. This time, change the Z rotation value to -186.0°, the Y rotation value to +136.0°, and the X rotation to −161.0°.

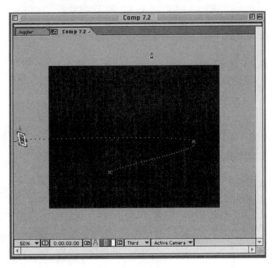

6. Now play the composition through, with the resolution set at a Third, and the Juggle.psd layer set to Solo. Save the project.

   You should be able to see the title spin round and then come to a stop. However, the last movement appears to be slower than the first section of the animation, and requires adjustment. This can be done by selecting the five keyframes, midway between the first two layer markers, and moving them closer to the three-second mark.

7. Select the five keyframes associated with Position, Scale, X Rotation, Y Rotation and Z Rotation in the Juggle.psd layer, and move them to the two-second position in the timeline. The composition should once again be viewed to see what changes have been made. Once again, save the project when finished.

   You should now see Bezier control levers along the motion path at the keyframe point. The motion is still a little erratic as the title moves around the sharp curve. The Bezier control levers can be used to alter the shape of the motion path and make this motion smoother. We can also make the movement smoother by using the value graphs in the timeline.

Smoothing out movement using the value graphs

If we look at the scale value graphs in the timeline, by clicking on the arrow beside the Scale option name, we can see that the lines relating to the Scale Value and Velocity are pretty straight.

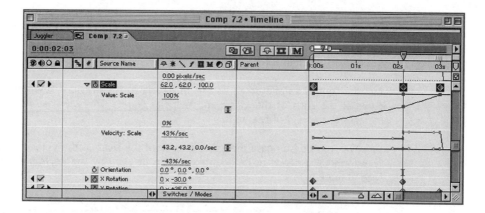

Because we moved the keyframe that was two-thirds of the way along the titles path, closer to the end to balance its speed, there is now a steeper value change at this keyframe. However, we want the scale of the title to increase at a more constant rate, so we can remove the keyframe here to end up with keyframes for the Scale change only at the start and finish of the motion path.

1. Remove the keyframe by simply placing the time marker over the keyframe to be removed and then clicking on the tick in the keyframe navigator.

    The line between the first and last keyframe relating to the Scale Value is now straight and constant.

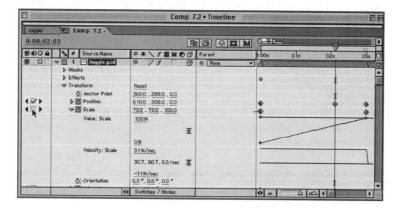

2. Play through the composition to see the effect. Then save the project.

    You should be able to see that the scale increase is now smooth. The only problem left is that the scale movement comes to an abrupt stop once it reaches the end of the motion path. We can ease the final part of the scaling so that it finishes more gently. To do this, we need to look at the Scale Velocity graph just below the Value graph.

3. By clicking on the control lever in the Velocity graph (make sure that Scale is highlighted so you can see the lever), the keyframe icon changes from an icon representing linear movement, to an icon that indicates a mix between a continuous Bezier path and a linear path.

4. Pull the control handle down and slightly towards the previous keyframe, to create a curve at the ends of the Value and Velocity graphs. This will ease in the final scale increase at the end of the path.

   However, this doesn't ease the entire motion of the layer, as the Velocity for four more Transforms also needs to be adapted, as can be seen by the keyframes at the three-second mark below:

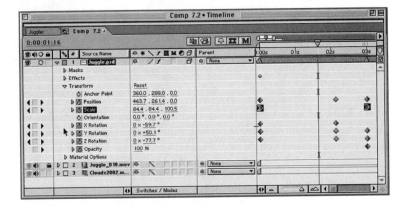

You can see that the four other Transforms also have keyframes around the two-second point on the timeline. Unlike the scale value keyframe, which was unnecessary, these other Transforms are required to layer the move around the boy juggling (which we will look at in the final stage of this composition), so we need to keep them.

5. Play through the composition, and work on the Velocity graphs for the other keyframes at the third layer marker until you're happy that the movement is smooth. Practice makes perfect with the Bezier curves! Save the project.

Fine-tuning the title move

It's now time to look at the whole composition to see if the title successfully navigates around the boy as he juggles.

1. Deselect the Solo switch in the Audio/Video Features panel in the timeline for layer Juggle.psd. Set the time marker to the first frame and play the composition through.

You'll notice that the rotation of the layer doesn't allow the title to fully clear the boy's hands, which will spoil the illusion of the title passing behind, and then moving in front of the boy.

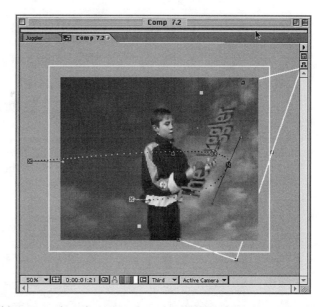

To correct this, we need to change to the value of the Z Rotation to give the title a little more room on the right. This will then allow us to move the position of the Juggle.psd layer across a little.

2.   Set the time marker on the keyframes around the two-second point on the timeline. Select the Z Rotation transform and adjust the value from 0 x -46.0° to –94.0°.

3.   Select the Position transforms, and change the first of the three values to 640.0. Now play the composition through once more. Remember to save the project once you're happy with the results.

Splitting Juggle.psd across two layers

Now we're ready to create the illusion of the title moving from behind the boy to the front. To do this, we need to split the layer across two tracks and sandwich the layer with the boy in it between the two.

1.   Start by setting the time marker to the first frame of the composition. Then select the Juggle.psd layer.

2.   Use Edit > Duplicate from the menu to duplicate the Juggle.psd layer. A new version of the layer will then appear in the timeline.

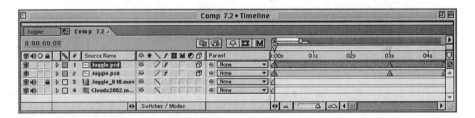

3.   Use the mouse to drag one of the Juggle.psd layers so that it becomes layer 3 in the timeline. A black line will appear as the layer is being moved, indicating where its new position will be if the mouse button is released. Once the mouse is released, the second Juggle.psd should be located in the third layer.

4.   Move the time marker to the point on the timeline where you feel it's most suitable for the title to switch from behind the boy to the front of the composition (this is the point at which we will move from layer 3 to layer 1 in the composition). I found the best point to be just after the two-second mark.

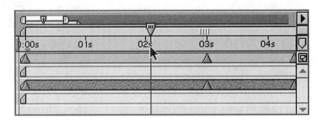

5.   Now select `Juggle.psd` in layer 1, and drag the In tab to the time marker. Then select `Juggle.psd` in layer 3 and move the Out tab to the time marker position.

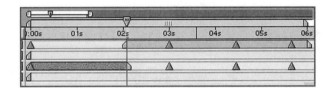

6.   Play the composition. When the composition is played through from the first frame, the title will be behind the boy as it travels from left to right. It will then turn and move from right to left in front of the boy until it reaches its final resting point.

`Exercise_7_2.mov` is a rendered version of the exercise just completed. The only difference between your version and this one is that in `Exercise_7_2.mov`, a Gaussian Blur filter has been added to the title. View this file to see if what you have created is similar. If you like the blurring effect, why not add a Gaussian Blur filter to your own composition?

`Comp 6.2` is now complete, well done!!

In the second half of the creation of this composition, we were able to manipulate one of our layers in 3D. However, there are more exciting 3D effects you can apply to layers, so let's take a look at some now.

3D lighting effects

One of the great features introduced to After Effects 5.0, and still present in After Effects 5.5 are 3D lights. These allow you to shine a pool of light onto a layer, change the diameter of the light, its color, and the amount of fall-off. By default, when a light is added to a layer, it's aimed along a vector towards the center of the composition. This location is called the 'point of interest'. There are four types of lights to choose from, each of which can be individually modified.

■   The Parallel light is unconstrained, and emitted from a distant source such as the sun.

■   The Spot light is constrained by a cone shape, and emits light in a similar manner to a theatrical spotlight.

■   The Point light is omnidirectional and unconstrained, with qualities similar to a light bulb.

■   An Ambient light affects the overall brightness of a scene, casting no shadow, as it has no light source.

The controls for the lights are very similar to the 3D layer controls, and can be animated in the same way as layers.

If you look at the Comp 6.3 composition in Layers Project.aep, you'll see that Light 1 has been added as another layer above the Brickwall2.psd layer. Over the six seconds, a motion path has been created for the angle of the light, and the direction it's pointing in. To replicate this composition, follow the tutorial below.

A little light

1.   Create a new composition. Add Cloudx2002.mov to the composition to create the background layer.

2.   Then add Brickwall2.psd, click the 3D Layer box, and copy and paste the traveling matte (all four masks) from Juggle_010.mov used in Comp 6.1 into it.

3.   Add the Light 1 layer by accessing the menu Layer > New > Light. Accept the default options and move the time marker to the first frame.

4.   In the Options drop-down list in the Light 1 layer, change the color of the light to orange, and click the Color stopwatch to add a keyframe.

5.   Now place the time marker at the end of the timeline, and change the light color to blue.

6.   Expand the transform menu for Light 1 in the timeline, and click the stopwatches for each of the controls and alter the values of the controls until you have a scene you're happy with.

7.   Now move the time marker to the end of the timeline and readjust the controls to a new position. You'll notice that a line is drawn across the composition window, representing the paths of the lights position and point of interest you have chosen. If you click on the control points at the end of these lines, you can apply Bezier curves to the lines. Create a more three-dimensional path for the light using Bezier curves.

8.   Now play the composition to see the lighting effect.

9. Now try making the Cloudx2002.mov layer a 3D layer and play the composition again to see the effect.

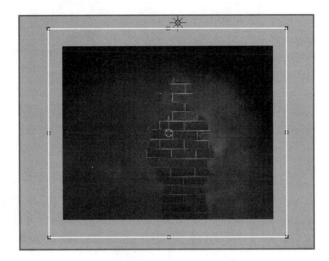

By making the cloud layer a 3D layer, the light now affects the background as well.

3D cameras

In addition to adding 3D lights, you can also add 3D cameras to create more dynamic effects. When a new camera is created, it becomes a new layer in the Timeline window, and its name appears in the 3D View pop-up menu.

To demonstrate the use of 3D cameras, let's create a new composition based around the Brickwall2.psd and the Cloudx2002.mov used in Comp 6.3.

Working the camera

1. Create a new composition and follow the first two steps of 'A little light', above.

2. Add the camera to the composition by selecting Layer > New > Camera

The Camera Settings window appears.

Let's just take a moment to look at the Camera Settings window in a little more detail, as it's an important one.

- By default, After Effects names each camera in sequential order as they're added to a composition, starting with Camera 1. However, if you wish to change the name to say, Top, Right, Medium, or Close-Up, you can label each camera according to the setup you wish to use.

- Each camera can also be assigned a Preset. By default this is 50mm, representing the standard lens used on a 35mm stills camera. The presets range from15mm to 200mm, with seven alternatives in between. If you wish, you can specify a custom setting.

- Zoom indicates the distance the location of the camera is from the image plane.

- Enable Depth of Field allows the camera to be controlled in a more realistic manner by allowing the Focus Distance (the point at which the camera focuses, which could be across the entire plane, or a single point immediately before the camera lens), to be changed.

- On a stills camera the Aperture, or iris size, is controlled by a ring on the lens marked with F-Stop numbers. F-22 is the smallest aperture, and provides the greatest depth of field. F1.8 sets the widest aperture, and creates the shallowest depth of field. Depth of field represents the distance in focus either side of the focal plane. At F-22 anything from 2 meters to infinity will be in focus. At F-1.8, only a few inches either side of the focal plane remain in focus. You can choose to use the traditional F-Stop method to adjust the aperture, or adjust the aperture itself.

- In the screenshot on the previous page, the Units are expressed in pixels, therefore the Focus Distance is set at 1067 pixels. Similarly, with an F-Stop at F-5.6 the aperture would be set at 25.31 pixels.

- With the Blur Level set at 100%, the blur is consistent with the natural blur associated with the camera settings. Anything less than 100% reduces the amount of blur.

- Finally, the Measure Film Size option allows you to measure it horizontally, vertically, or diagonally.

We haven't discussed the whole window in a great deal of detail here because you'll probably know most of this already. Let's return to the tutorial!

3. Accept the default options in the Camera Settings window, and press the Solo button on Layer 2 to help us focus on the camerawork.

4. We're going to use the camera to circle 360° around the image of the juggler. To do this, set the time marker to the first frame, and add a keyframe to the camera Position transform in the Timeline window.

5. Now move the time marker to the three-second point in the timeline. After Effects allows you to change the views in the Composition window, which can make it easier to alter the camera's position and point of focus. Change the view to Top by selecting the 3D View Popup, to the right of the Resolution menu in the Composition window.

6. Alter the magnification ratio in the Composition window to 12.5%, and use the Position controls to position the camera at the twelve o'clock position (the starting point being six o'clock). This action creates a second keyframe in the Position transform. You can also see that we have now produced a Bezier curve motion path.

7. Next, move the time marker to the end of the timeline and move the camera another 180° clockwise, back to the six o'clock position. This creates a third keyframe in the Position transform of the Camera 1 layer. Now use the control levers on the Bezier curves to create a circular shape for the motion path.

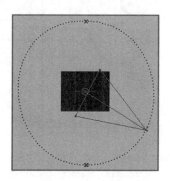

8. Check that the resolution of the Composition window is set to a Third and play your movie. You should be able to see the camera move around in a circle.

9. Now set the Composition window to Active Camera view, deselect the Solo icon in layer 2, and press the play button again. This time you should be able to see the effect of the camera move.

Synchronizing animation to audio

In After Effects, you can also add audio layers. For track laying and actually adding audio effects, it's easier to work in other non-linear editing packages more suited to this kind of work, such as Adobe Premiere and Final Cut Pro. However, the audio capabilities of After Effects come into their own when you need to animate to audio, such as when synchronizing speech to a character, or keeping in time with music.

In the following example, we'll look at how to use some dialog to lip sync a drawn character animation.

Are you talking to me?

The character we're using here was originally hand-drawn, and then scanned into the computer. In Photoshop, I added various layers for some eye movements, and eight further layers for mouth movements.

1. On the CD-ROM you'll find a Photoshop file entitled character.psd and an audio file called Announcer.aif. Transfer these to your hard drive.

2.   After opening After Effects, use Import > Multiple Files... to import the two files into the project. Import character.psd as a composition, as this will retain the settings based on the dimensions of the Photoshop file. Import the audio file Announcer.aif as a Footage file. Name the new project Sync1 Project.aep.

3.   Double-click character.psd in the project window to open up its 14 layers. We can't see the outline of the character's hair, so add a Solid layer to highlight it by selecting Layer > New > Solid from the menu. Choose a color for the Solid layer, then click OK.

4.   The Solid layer will appear above all the other layers, but needs to be dragged to below the lowest level in the timeline so it doesn't obscure the other layers. Once this is done, the character and his hair will appear in front of your background.

5.   Select the eye icon for each of the eight mouth layers. This may make the character look like he's suddenly grown a beard, but we'll shave him bald again in a minute.

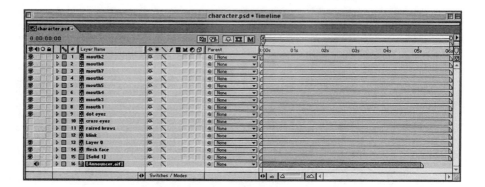

6.   Select the first mouth layer and click the triangle beside the layer name, followed by the triangle for its Transform options. Click the stopwatch for the Opacity control to add a keyframe, and set the Opacity value to 0%. Now repeat this process for each of the mouth layers except for mouth1 (found in layer 8), it is set at 100% opacity. This is the closed mouth.

7.   Next, drag the Announcer.aif file from the Project window, so that it is positioned in layer 16 of the timeline. At this point, it will be obvious that the audio layer is shorter than the rest of the material in the timeline. To solve this problem, select Composition > Composition Settings... from the menu, and adjust the duration to 00:00:05:03.

8.   On the Time Controls palette, select the speaker icon, and click the RAM Preview button, on the top right of the palette, to have a listen to the audio. Click on the Audio tab to reveal the audio palette. This displays the VU meter and the levels controls, with the values set below them. To see the VU meter in action, choose Composition > Preview > Audio Preview (Here Forward) from the menu.

9. Click on the triangle in layer 16. This makes the waveform visible. By holding down the CTRL (Windows) or COMMAND (Mac OS) keys, the timeline marker can be dragged along the timeline, allowing you to hear the changes in sound. Using the Zoom tool at the base of the timeline to zoom in as close as possible, it is possible to see how the waveform changes from one frame to another. This is enough detailed sound information for you to animate our character's mouth to.

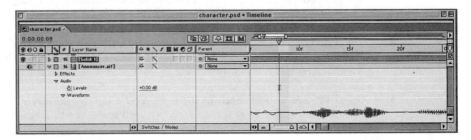

10. Select each frame, and give the appropriate mouth shape 100% opacity, as needed. Give the non-corresponding mouth shapes 0% opacity. Each time the opacity is changed, a keyframe will appear in the timeline.

> *To help you work out how to use each mouth position,*
>
> mouth1 *can be used for the phonetic sounds 'bu', 'mu' and 'pu'*
>
> mouth2 *can be used for the phonetic sounds 'ku', 'du', 'gu', 'nu', 'ru', 'su', 'thu', 'yu' and 'zu'.*
>
> mouth3 *can be used for the phonetic sounds 'ah', ay', 'i' and 'eye'*
>
> mouth4 *can be used for 'ee', 'see', 'kay' and 'en'*
>
> mouth5 *can be used for 'o'*
>
> mouth6 *can be used for 'ooh' and 'u'*
>
> mouth7 *can be used for 'ell', 'dee' and 'thu'*
>
> *Finally,* mouth8 *can be used for 'fu' and 'vu'.*

11. Once you have worked through the timeline to change each mouth shape so that it relates to the audio clip, do a RAM preview to review your work.

Conclusion

This has been quite a long chapter covering the building of layers in various compositions. By the time you get to this point, you should have a good understanding of how to manipulate each layer using keyframes, value and velocity graphs. You've looked at 3D layers, 3D lights, 3D cameras and also created traveling mattes.

You'll discover there's even more to layering as you get more familiar with After Effects, but we've covered all the central concepts and techniques here to enable you to hit the ground running and start producing great After Effects!

Once you've mastered how to use the layering system in After Effects, the only limitation is your imagination. Now you should probably take a break.

In the next chapter, we'll be looking at the various filters and effects you can apply to layers in After Effects.

7 Filters and Effects

After Effects filters really are right at the heart of what the package is about. So much so that we couldn't possibly have gotten this far through a book on After Effects without having used them already. Some are there to alter the tonal qualities of an image, some to distort it. Others are there to create completely new picture elements, like lens flares, laser beams, or text effects. There are even filters designed to create and alter sounds.

In this chapter, we'll be learning how to place, animate and combine filters. We'll look at each filter present in the After Effects library, and discover how to add more filters produced by other companies to expand the package.

In this chapter we hope to expand on what you have already learnt about effects, and quickly describe the filters provided. By the end of the chapter, you'll be able to:

- Locate effects filters

- Add filters to layers

- Alter the parameters of filters to create different looks

- Animate them to produce changing effects

- Combine filters on a single on-screen element

Applying filters

Placing a filter onto an image or video clip is as easy as selecting the clip and choosing the filter from the menu. When an effect is applied to a layer, the Effect Controls window opens. This is the window where the settings of the various effects are defined. In order to make use of the filter, you'll need to specify these settings on the timeline (if you want to animate the filter), and sometimes on the canvas itself.

A layer can have as many filters as you like applied to it. The Effect Controls window and the Timeline window both list all the filters you've placed, and all the animation functions of each (in the Timeline window, the filters are listed in the Effects section under the layer name). To the left of each animation function, you'll find a stopwatch icon. This appears in both the Effect Controls window, and the Timeline. When left blank, adjustments to the function are applied along the whole length of the clip. When the stopwatch is turned on, a keyframe is produced in the current frame, and the value of the function is changed smoothly between this, and a second keyframe, which is created in the frame at which you want the animation to stop.

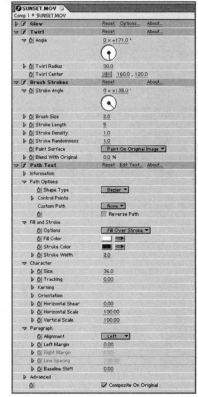

The order in which effects are applied to a layer is of great importance, because effects are rendered; in order from top to bottom, in the filters list. For example, if you have a video clip and you add a text filter to it, and then drop in a blur filter, you'll get a blurred screen with blurred text on it. If you place the blur first, then the text, you'll get sharp text on a blurred backdrop:

You can change the order of effects in the Effect Controls window by simply dragging effects up and down in the list.

The filters that come with After Effects are pretty wide ranging, but you're not limited just to them. You can buy extra filters designed for After Effects (or for other effects packages like Combustion, Commotion, and even Adobe Premiere and Photoshop) which all use the After Effects plug-in format.

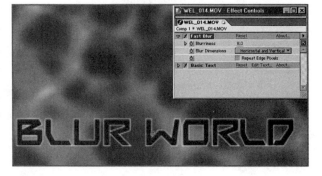

There is a massive range of third party effects filters out there. There are plug-ins to simulate the effect of cine-film on video images, those aimed at producing graceful slow motion shots, and others designed for creating rain and snow effects.

Here are a few useful websites:

- http://www.msp.sfsu.edu/instructors/rey/aepage/aeportal.html - great resource for AE users including info about plug-ins and where to get them.

- http://www.adobe.com/products/aftereffects - Adobe's own site. A good set of links to other sites, plus downloads of free plug-ins (foam, caustics, wave world, card-dance, card wipe – all of which we've detailed later in this chapter)

You can also purchase plug-ins from many commercial sites around the net. Here are a few:

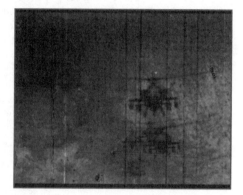

- http://www.thepluginsite.com

- http://www.alienskin.com

- http://www.digieffects.com

- http://revisionfx.com

- http://www.aliaswavefront.com/pfx_zone

There are even filters available to turn After Effects into a morphing studio, or a video painting package.

> *Some third party plug-ins are not compatible with Mac OS X and so won't appear in the effects menu or palette if you try to install them. To avoid these problems you should check the compatibility with the plug-in developer, alternatively you could just use them in OS 9x.*

Additionally, Photoshop compatible filters can be easily copied into the After Effect's plug-in directory, and will automatically appear when After Effects is loaded. These often work successfully and have the ability to be animated – although some may have reduced features.

With all the effects filters available in After Effects, there's a strong temptation when you first get hold of the package, to go crazy with them, throwing dozens of filters at every layer in your composition. The results are plain to see in overblown logo animations and unconvincing special effects the world over. Only experience will teach you where an effect will work and where it won't. Over 90 filters are included as standard in the package, and each one is capable of producing many very different effects, so even before you start combining filters, the possibilities are almost limitless.

The only way to get to grips with After Effects filters is to just start experimenting with them. So let's go!

Basic filters

As we mentioned above, adding an effects filter is pretty easy, but once added, you'll want to start animating with it. In this exercise, we've got an easy job. We've got a text image, and we want to make it move around the screen, and surround it with neon. To do this:

1. Create a new composition, right click in the timeline and select New. Then choose to add a new solid from the pop up menu that appears, and you will see a blank box appear in the composition window (alternatively, you can hit CTRL + Y on a PC and COMMAND + Y on a Mac to add a new solid). Next, select Effect > Text > Path Text, and type in the text, selecting an appropriate font.

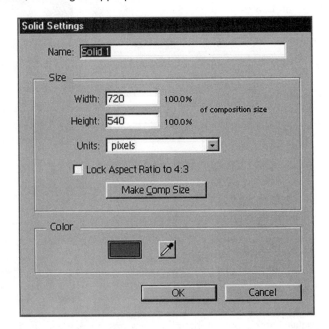

The text appears in our composition, which means we've added our first filter! It's worth taking a look right now at the way that filter has manifested itself in our production. The most obvious place we can see its effect is in the monitor window where your composition is displayed; as it will look when rendered.

2. Open the window and take a look.

You'll see that the solid is transparent now, and the text has been written in a line across the screen. The start and end points of the line are shown, along with handles with which they can be controlled.

3.　Try dragging the points around until you get an idea of how the text can be manipulated. You'll see that it's a bit like controlling bezier curves.

The second, and in some ways most important set of adjusters for the filter appear in the Effect Controls window, and under Effects in the solid layer's menu. If you can't see it, you can bring it up from the Effect menu, or by right-clicking the timeline.

Here, a bewildering array of controls are shown, each with an arrow to its left. Every filter has its own controls, and each time you add one to the track, all its attributes will be added to the window.

4. Right now, why not use these controls to alter any attribute of the text you like. We changed the color to white, and used horizontal sheer to slope the characters backwards:

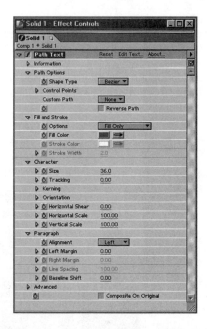

5. Lets get animating! Open the Paragraph attribute, and click the stopwatch icon next to the Left Margin item.

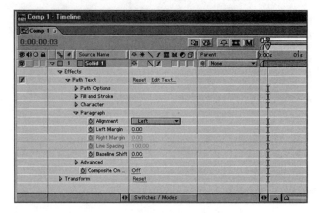

This sets our Left Margin attribute into animation mode (you can turn on animation in the Effect Controls window in the same way), and creates a new keyframe.

6. Now, move the playback head to the end of your animation, and set the Left Margin to 200. The text moves to the end of the path and another keyframe appears. Whenever we change the Left Margin setting, we're changing it to the new value only at the point in time where the playback head is placed.

7. Sit back and watch your marvelous creation.

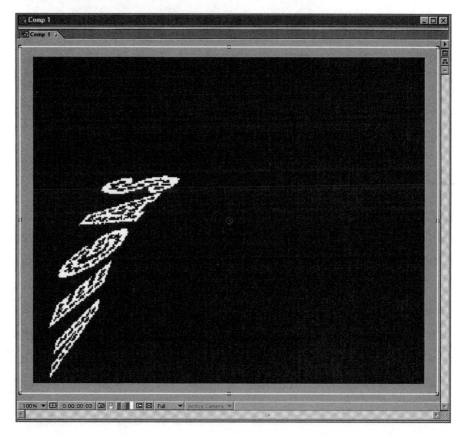

With our input, After Effects automatically creates an animation that moves the value smoothly between the keyframes, so now when we play the animation, or scrub through the timeline, we can see our lettering move. You can click on keyframes and drag them around to change the speed of your animation, and you can add or delete them just as easily.

Try adding a couple more filters and animating them to create a more impressive look. Here, we've dropped in a Glow filter, and animated its color using just the same techniques. You can take a look for yourself by loading the file vegas.mov from the CD (note the Glow filter is only available on the Production Bundle version of After Effects).

Effects filters

After Effects comes with 90 or so effects included. Some are quite straightforward, others are more complex and involved. Some (marked with an "*" in our list below) are available only with the Production Bundle version of the software. Here's a complete listing of the various effects, along with a description of what each one does:

3D Channel *

This set of effects integrates 3D scenes into 2D composites, and alters 3D scenes. They are effects designed to let you work with the 3D channel. The 3D channel is a grayscale image embedded in some files (specifically RLA format images) produced by 3D packages. If an object is close to the camera it will appear white, if far away, it will be black. Thus, the 3D channel lets you alter the effect of a filter based on the distance an object is from the camera. By telling AE to increase the blur on an object for darker 3D channel values, you get a depth of field effect. By telling it to make dark 3D channel values decrease the contrast in the image, you get 3D fog.

Here are the effects themselves:

3D channel extract *

This effect makes the 3D channel in a layer visible, if it has one. Use this filter to create a track matte for the animation you've extracted it from, and objects in the distance will be made more transparent. You can then place another track containing the same animation on the timeline behind, and add other filters to create effects for more distant objects.

Depth matte *

This lets you use a 3D channel to remove everything behind a given point along the z axis. This effect is used to matte everything in front of or behind the value specified. This is useful for placing other layers between foreground and background objects in a 3D image or animation.

Depth of field *

This effect allows you to use the 3D channel in a shot to create depth of field. You can alter the focal range and the extremes of blurring to make distant or close-up objects in a scene go into or out of focus while other objects remain sharp.

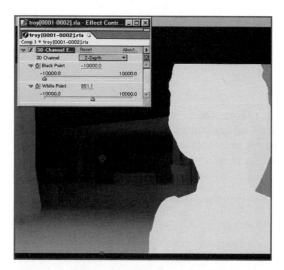

Fog 3D *

Add 3D fog to your shot with this effect. The fog will increase with distance because this effect applies fog along the z axis, so that the distant parts of a 3D scene look hazier or disappear behind the fog. Objects at the front of the shot, therefore, will be clear, those in the distance will be foggy. Effects like fog can take a long time to render in 3D packages. Use After Effects for a short-cut.

ID matte *

This effect isolates elements in a 3D channel image. Image files with extra information (such as RLA files – image files which contain extra channels giving information about objects in the scene) can give different elements in a picture different ID numbers, in other words, they can differentiate between different objects in an image. ID Matte lets you select an object from an image (as long as it's been rendered in the right way – exactly how you do this will depend on your 3D animation package) and separate it from its scene, allowing you to add extra effects to it without affecting its background.

Adjust effect

These are a collection of effects for altering the tonal balance of your image. Color and brightness levels can be altered and animated with these filters.

Brightness and contrast

Two simple controls let you slide the brightness and contrast in an image up and down. If you need a more subtle filter, try the Levels filter (see below).

Channel mixer

This is a difficult filter to master, and the results will vary a lot depending on the image you're using it on, so the only way to really get to grips with it is to experiment. Basically, it lets you alter the red, green, and blue balance of your shot, based on contributions from the other color channels. In other words, you can make the strength of the blue in each part of the image dependent on the strength of the red.

With it, you can make complex adjustments to color, or produce black and white images that keep the definition which is sometimes lost when original color images don't vary in brightness.

Color balance

This effect adjusts the amount of red, blue, or green in your shot. With this filter, you can adjust the highlights, mid-tones, and shadows separately for a more interesting effect. For example, in a green landscape shot, you could make the highlights more yellow to make the day appear sunnier and give a greater range of color throughout the shot.

Color stabilizer *

This filter is new in AE 5.5. In the same way that an **image stabilizer** goes through a shot frame by frame, removing any small camera motions, the color stabilizer lets you smooth out changes in brightness or color temperature. This is useful for compositing shots where changes in exposure would destroy the illusion, or for exterior shots where clouds have obscured the sun for a moment.

Curves

This lets you alter the brightness of all the pixels (of a given brightness) in your shot very finely. By altering the slope of the graph, you can, for example, make just the darkest areas lighter (to bring out detail in the shadows). Different graphs for the red, green, and blue channels let you be even more specific about the contrast in your shot.

Hue and Saturation

Here you can change the hue, saturation, and lightness of the whole image, or of certain colors. With this effect, you can bring out a certain color by increasing its saturation, whilst decreasing that of other colors. For example, you could make a portrait shot monochrome except for the blue eyes, or change the color of a team's strip in a sports event.

Levels

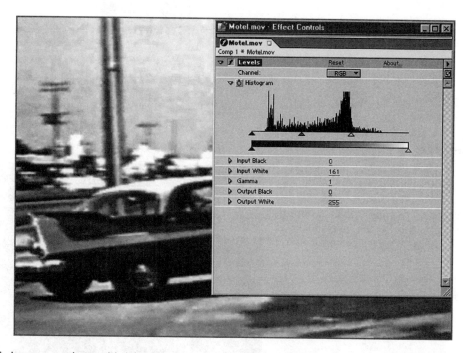

This is a more advanced brightness and contrast adjuster. The graph presented shows how many pixels of each brightness exist in your shot. The sliders underneath let you compress the graph to change the contrast of different parts of the image. You can adjust the red, blue, and green levels separately if you wish.

Levels (individual controls)

A new levels control for After Effects 5.5. It's basically the same as the Levels control, however, the Levels (Individual Controls) effect simultaneously displays all the adjustable tracks for each channel. This effect lets you be more specific about the different color channels.

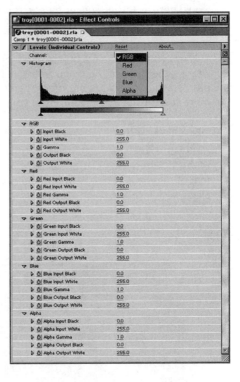

Posterize

Use this to reduce the number of colors in the shot. The result is to create flat areas and contours of color rather than smooth gradients, so the image looks as though it's been painted.

Threshold

This effect reduces all colors in an image to either pure black or pure white. The single control lets you choose the level at which the change from black to white occurs. Use this effect to convert grayscale or color images to high-contrast, black and white images.

Audio effects

After Effects isn't really designed as an audio tool, but for your general audio requirements, some filters are supplied which let you create and edit sound effects. To this end, the audio effects can be very useful. And they can be really good fun to play with as well!

Backwards

This filter plays the audio of your layer backwards.

Bass and treble

This adjusts the bass and treble of the audio to make it stronger and deeper, or lighter and more 'tinny'.

Delay

This is a simple echo effect. You can adjust the length of the delay, and the sound of the echo.

Flange and chorus

This combines two separate audio effects, Flange and Chorus, into a single effect. It lets you add multiple copies of a sound together, modulating and de-tuning them. The result, depending on the settings, can sound like a choir where there was one voice, or a discordant jarring effect, if you should need one. A good one to experiment with.

High-low pass

This filter sets a limit above or below which frequencies should pass. It lets you remove high or low frequencies from your sound.

Modulator

This creates warbling and swooping sounds of variable depth, and wavelength. You can also change the type of wave from sine to triangle for more abrupt and distorted modulation.

Parametric equalizer

This is a very sophisticated tool for boosting or reducing sounds from different frequency ranges. The filter offers three identical parametric equalizers in one shot, and each offers a graph letting you choose the frequency and range of the sound you're singling out, and allows you to boost, or cut it.

With this effect, you can cut out traffic noise from a shot, or increase the level of the voice in a badly recorded interview.

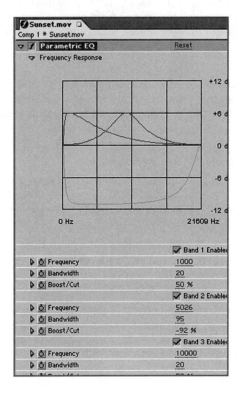

Reverb

This is a more complex and subtle echo effect than the simple delay. This tool offers the best way to produce the effect of the resonance a real environment has.

Stereo mixer

This filter provides four controls to let you adjust and animate the stereo position of any sound, moving it from one speaker to the other, or just bringing the left and right levels up or down to fill out the sound. With this tool, you can add a significant level of credibility and impact to your animations by matching the sound movement to the image movement. An object moving from left to right across screen will instantly seem more convincing if the sound moves left to right also.

Tone

This filter creates a simple tone using a sine triangle, saw or square wave. You can add in up to five different tones, and alter their volumes. Use this as the basis for a sound effect, and add other filters to build a more interesting sound.

Blur and sharpen

These include various effects to blur (or soften) and sharpen your layer. There are many different types of blur, and each has its own unique properties. Some are much slower to render than others, but create a more natural effect. It's often useful to use a slight blur effect when you want to integrate new elements into an image. By applying a small amount of blur to the whole image, you can usually smooth over the subtle differences between the image quality of its new elements.

Channel blur

This effect lets you change the focus of the red, blue, and green layers of an image individually. This can add a slightly dreamy, or glowing quality to your image.

Compound blur

This blurs the layer based on the brightness values of another layer. For example, you can blur out a certain shape in your shot by creating a black and white map of that shape, and using it as the blur layer. If the blur layer is animated, you can move the blurred (or sharp focused area) around the screen.

Directional blur

This effect creates the illusion of movement by smearing the image in a given direction.

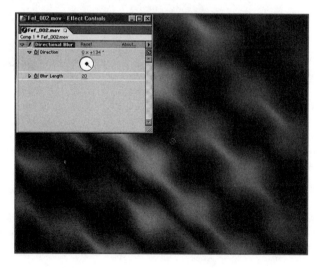

Gaussian blur

This is a high quality blur, but one which can take a lot of processing. The higher the blur setting, the longer each frame will take to draw.

Fast blur

This produces a pretty decent bog-standard blur effect, which lets you choose horizontal, or vertical blurring, or both, and works much faster than Gaussian blurring.

Radial blur

Used most for zooming or spinning effects. The center of the effect is left sharp, but the outside becomes more and more de-focused. It is very good for "tunnel vision" type effects.

Sharpen

This is an effect that increases the contrast of each pixel, sharpening the image. At low values, this brings out the detail in a shot. At high values, it starts to emphasize any JPEG compression and makes the image more pixilated.

Unsharp mask

This filter brings out the detail in the most contrasting areas of an image (generally the edges of objects). This makes an image stronger without making it harsh. Detail is enhanced, but the soft areas remain soft.

Channel

These are filters for working with color, brightness, and transparency aspects of the image. These can include the red, blue or green parts of the image, the luminance, saturation, and alpha channels.

Alpha levels

This is an effect which is used with images and videos that have transparency built in (such as TGA files, and some QuickTime videos). This filter alters the contrast of the matte, making semi-transparent areas more, or less transparent.

Arithmetic

This is a rarely used filter, which lets you perform mathematical functions on the red, green and blue channels of the image. The result is to enhance or suppress the relevant color over the image.

Blend

This effect lets you mix from one track to another using a range of modes. It can be useful for creating transitions, or bringing the texture (or color) of one object through another.

Cineon converter

This effect provides a high degree of control over color conversions of Cineon frames. It is useful only if you're using Cineon files (a format used for transferring film sequences into your computer). Cineon images store color in a different way to After Effects. This filter adjusts the colors and intensities in your image so you can get an accurate reproduction of your original image.

Compound arithmetic

There's actually no point in using this filter. It's just there to allow you to import old After Effects files from previous releases that use this filter. It can't do anything you won't be able to do better using layer modes.

Invert

This filter turns your image into a negative. You can invert the whole RGB image, or reverse any of 12 different channels separately. There's also a blend slider so you can combine the negative and positive image. A useful note here is that you can invert the alpha channel of an image – making everything that was transparent visible and vice-versa.

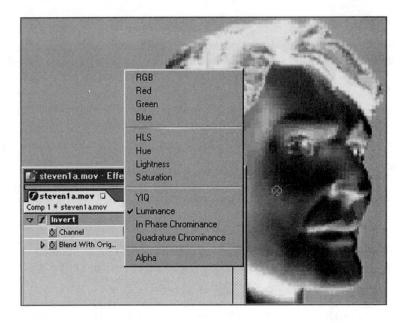

Minimax

This effect expands or contracts the alpha channel. For example, if you've got an image on a transparent background, you can erode its edges or give it a border. Using Minimax on color channels produces a blocky kind of blur, or painterly effect.

Remove color matting

This just removes the colored fringing around objects, which can appear when transparent backgrounds aren't perfectly removed.

Set channels

This filter copies information from any channel of one layer to any channel of another. You can, for example, use the luminance information from one shot as the transparency layer of another.

Set matte

Again, there's no need to use this filter. It's just there to allow you to import old After Effects files from previous releases that use this filter. Nowadays, we'd use the track matte functions on the timeline.

Shift channels

This effectively lets you swap the channels around. For example, making the amount of red in an image dependent on its alpha channel, or making the brighter areas transparent.

Distort effects

These are effects designed to distort and geometrically manipulate the image itself.

Bezier warp

Imagine your image is attached to a rubber sheet. This filter lets you distort the sheet by dragging the corners around and curving the edges. The result is that you can twist the rectangular image to conform to any shape you like.

Bulge

This effect distorts an image around a specific point. It makes the image bulge outwards or inwards. You can place and animate the position, size and shape of the bulge either in the Effect Controls window, or interactively on the composition itself.

Corner pin

With this effect, you can take each corner of your image and move it wherever you like to distort the image. Useful for perspective effects like turning a video clip into a moving poster placed on a wall in another shot, or turning scrolling text into a Star Wars style opening sequence.

Displacement map

This moves pixels in an image to the left, right, up or down based on the color of pixels in another layer. With this, you can create the effect of looking through frosted or etched glass, or just shift a section of one image horizontally or vertically.

Mesh warp

This filter covers your image with a grid. Each vertex of the grid can be dragged to distort the image in very complex and controlled ways. You can use this to create warp and morphing effects (although if you do a lot of morphing, you'll probably use a dedicated package or plug-in for greater control).

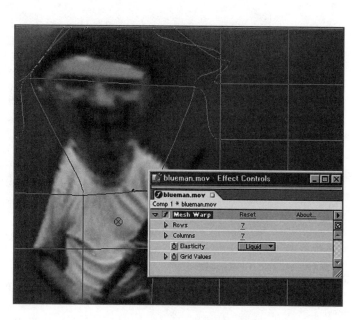

Mirror

This effect creates a mirror image of your shot. You can control the center, and angle of the reflection. You can use multiple instances of this filter to create kaleidoscope effects.

Offset

Here you can roll the image left, right, up, or down without moving the layer itself. You place the center of the image, and everything else is shifted to compensate. Any pixels which get shoved off one side of the layer roll back in on the other side.

Optics compensation

This artificially creates lens distortion, producing fish-eye, or stretched shots. It can be useful for creating weird camera effects, or for removing them from already shot footage! It can also be used to match the distortion when you're trying to superimpose an object into a scene shot with a wide angle, or extreme zoom lens.

Polar co-ordinates

This filter produces strange, rippling and curved distortions by changing the way the co-ordinates of each pixel is calculated. If you want a strange, hall-of-mirrors type effect, try this one.

PS (Photoshop) Pinch

This is a Photoshop filter, which pinches the image inwards towards the center of the shot.

> *Photoshop filters are disabled by default in AE 5.5. So if you open a project up which uses them it will inform you that these filters will be removed if you click* OK. *To enable them you need to exit After Effects without saving, and locate the folder which contains them on your hard drive. This will be inside* After Effects 5.5/Plug-ins/Standard/ *and called* (PSFilter) *on PCs and* (PhotoShop Filter) *on Macs. You should now remove the brackets from the folder name, and restart After Effects.*
>
> *However, you should also note that these filters are not carbonized (compatible with OS X), and Adobe has no intention of making them compatible. Your only recourse is to either run AE 5.5 in OS 9x, or try to replace the effects with equivalents in AE.*

PS (Photoshop) Ripple

This creates ripples as though the image is reflected in water (however, you can't animate the ripples).

PS (Photoshop) Spherize

This is the opposite of the Pinch filter, it bulges the shot outwards. If you need to animate the position of the bulge, try the Bulge filter instead.

PS (Photoshop) Twirl

This effect spins the image as though it's in a whirlpool. The middle spins furthest, smearing the image around in a vortex. Use Twirl rather than PS Twirl for a more controlled effect.

PS (Photoshop) Wave

This is a complex wave generator that distorts your image in a controlled ripple.

PS (Photoshop) Zig-zag

Here we have a Photoshop filter that creates ripples as though from a pebble dropped into a pond. However, if you have the Production Bundle, it's usually better to use the Ripple filter.

Reshape *

This filter distorts an image from one mask shape to another. By drawing masks onto a shot, you can define the way the image distorts from one shape to the other. It is useful for morphing and warping transitions.

Ripple *

This creates concentric ripples as though in water. It is very easy to animate (with or without keyframes).

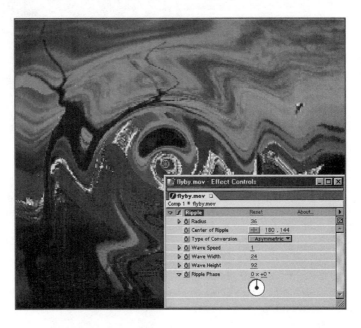

Smear

This filter creates a mask shape, and then moves just that part of the image, smearing everything around it. Processing time can be long for this filter.

Spherize

This creates a bulge, which can be animated both in size and position. If you have the Production Bundle, Bulge is usually a better choice.

Transform

Move, rotate, scale and skew the layer in 2D with this effect. You can also change the opacity. Use this filter if you need more control than you can get from the relevant options on the timeline. Specifically, note that the transform functions use the layers anchor point – so if you move that, you'll change the way it rotates, scales and moves.

Twirl *

This creates a spinning vortex effect. You can alter the size, strength and position of the swirl.

Wave Warp *

A sophisticated ripple and wave generator which can be animated without keyframes, and which offers a good range of different wave types.

Expressions

These are new in AE 5.5 and are not strictly filters. After Effects allows you to script your own tools using expressions. The controls available in this compartment are just dummies of the various sliders, angle controls, and color pickers used in AE filters. They don't actually do anything, but once loaded into a layer, they can be wired to expressions and events which you can make them control.

Image control effects

These are a set of filters, which allow you to change the color values in an image. Let's look at the range of effects available.

Change Color

This effect alters the hue, saturation, or lightness of a range of colors in your image. For example, if you're altering a landscape, you can pick the blue of the sky. You can then increase the saturation to turn up the strength of the sky without affecting any other colors in the picture.

Color Balance (HLS)

This is a primitive version of the hue / saturation filter. There's no need to use this filter, as it's only being kept on to retain compatibility with earlier versions of After Effects.

Colorama

This cycles the colors in your image through the color palette. It is mainly used for creating psychedelic effects.

Equalize

This filter automatically adjusts the image to get a good range of contrast over the whole picture. It brightens dark images, and darkens overexposed ones. It can be a good starting point for color correction, or levels adjustment.

Gamma/Pedestal/Gain

This adjusts the strength and brightness of the red, green, and blue channels in a way which can be good for creating lighting effects (like making scenes filmed during the day look like night shots), or producing extreme color changes.

Median

This effect makes each pixel closer in color to those that surround it. The result is a smoothing effect which removes slight grain and imperfections at a low level, and as you increase the effect, gives the image a watercolor look.

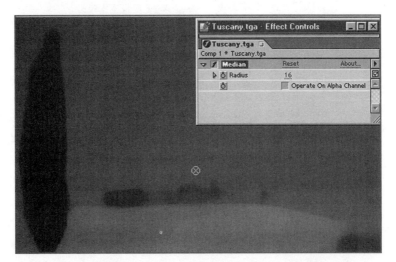

PS (Photoshop) Arbitrary Map

This is just an out of date version of the Curves effect. It is only retained to maintain compatibility with files produced using earlier AE versions.

Tint

This tints your image, allowing you to set a different color for the dark and light areas. More complex effects of this kind can be created with the Colorama filter.

Keying

These are filters which let you make parts of your image transparent based on their color or brightness.

Color Difference Key

Imagine you've shot a figure against a blue backdrop, which you want to replace with another image. Color difference gives you sophisticated control over which colors to make transparent and which to leave opaque. This gives more control than the standard color key by allow you to select color ranges you want to keep rather than just those you want to make transparent, and lets you work well with difficult objects like glass, fire, or hair.

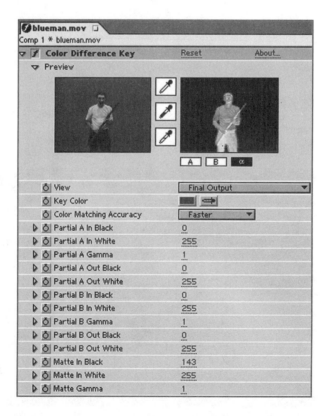

Color Key

Here is the standard chromakey (bluescreen) filter. This is good for well lit bluescreen work, and lets you thin and feather the edges of a shot to improve the effect, removing fringes around superimposed objects.

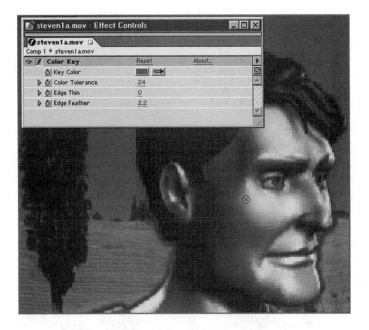

Color Range Key

This is a color keyer designed for poorly lit backdrops. You can keep adding colors to your selection with the eyedropper until you're happy with the result.

Difference Matte

When working with two images, this filter makes all the pixels that are the same in both shots transparent. Say, for example, you've filmed a car driving down a street with a locked off camera, and you want to remove everything but the car. With this filter, you can use a frame of the empty street as the difference layer, and you should be able to do it. In practice, this tends to produce rather dirty mattes which need further work, however.

Extract

This effect creates transparency by keying out (or extracting) a specified brightness range, based on a histogram of a specified channel. It is used for keying out the dark or light areas of a shot (if you wanted to remove a shadow, for example). It's a little like Luma Key (see below), but more sophisticated in its control.

Inner Outer

Use this tool where you'd normally have to draw a complex mask. Draw two rough masks - one defining the inside of the object, and one defining the outside, then use the Inner Outer filter. This uses various methods to locate the exact edge of your object, and key accordingly.

For example, say you're working on a movie, and you want to produce an explosion going off behind your main character. You'll need to draw a mask around them as they run from it so you can drop the explosion between the character and the background. The actor is quite a complex shape, and getting a good quality mask as he moves and his outline changes is very tough. Using an Inner Outer mask, you draw two rough masks, one inside and one outside his shape, and AE will intelligently look at the boundary between the two, try to decide what pixels are background and what are your actor, and separate the two accordingly.

Linear Color Key

This is another color keyer with which you can add or subtract specific shades from the key. It's different from the others because if you apply the filter twice, you can select "keep this color" to bring back colors lost in the last keying operation. This means that you can be more specific about exactly which colors you want to make transparent and which you want to keep.

Luma Key

This filter is used to key out the brighter or darker parts of the image. It is useful for replacing overexposed skies in exterior shots, or removing the background from objects shot against darkness (like pyrotechnics, or other bright objects). It's also good for text and drawing effects where you don't have transparency built into the shot, like scans of line drawings or bold graphics.

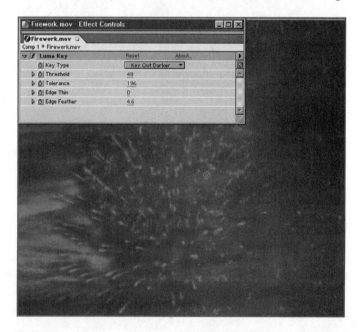

Spill Suppressor

The Spill Suppressor is used to remove key color spills from the edges of an image. Color keying often leaves fringes of your background color around objects especially when they have indistinct edges. The spill suppressor de-saturates these colors making them gray, and therefore less visible.

Matte tools

These tools can improve the quality of mattes (typically those created with the keying tools above). Matte tools are used to remove traces of key color and create clean edges. They work on the edges of the matte, closing holes, or removing fringing.

Simple Choker

This effect lets you shrink, or expand the border of a matte, cutting down on fringing, or restoring edges that have been matted out.

Matte Choker

This is a much more sophisticated version of the Simple Choker. Using this tool requires practice. It performs the expansion and contraction of the matte as above, but repeats the process several times, refining your matte even further as it does so.

Paint effects

Only one effect here – and only for Production Bundle owners I'm afraid.

Vector Paint *

This filter lets you paint onto the layer using various types of brush. It's a little like a primitive painting program, but here your paint strokes are recorded in real time, so you can animate them to paint onto the screen (for example, to write freehand text over time).

Perspective

These filters let you manipulate your layer in 3D, creating perspective effects.

Basic 3D

This lets you create the illusion of twisting and tipping the layer in 3D.

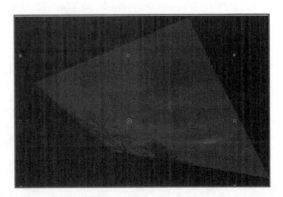

This isn't actually "real 3D", as you'd get using the 3D layers tool on the timeline. Your shot is still flat on to the camera; it's just distorted to look as though it's in 3D. Generally, if you want 3D in After Effects, you should use the 3D layers tool rather than this filter.

Bevel Alpha

This effect gives a chiseled and 'angle-lit' appearance to the alpha boundaries of an image, often giving 2D elements a 3D appearance. It is a rather nice tool for creating the effect of beveled edges. The bevel works on the image's alpha channel, so if you use it on a standard video shot, you'll just get a square image with beveling on the edges. If you use it on an image with alpha information (like a text layer), you'll get rounded, 3D looking text:

Bevel Edges

This is a less useful bevel tool than Bevel Alpha as it only works with rectangular images.

Drop Shadow

This creates a shadow behind the layer. If the shot has no transparency, the shadow will be rectangular (as the layer is). If there's transparency, the shadow will be the shape of the visible area.

Render effects

These are filters for rendering graphical images and fills onto your image. They're useful for creating backdrops, and other graphics effects – you can also draw masks to define the shape of the rendered image.

4-Colour Gradient

This filter is a new one in AE 5.5, and produces four spots of color. The colors blend into each other to produce a color gradient over the image. You can move or animate the positions of the colors, the hues themselves, and the way the color blends. You can also use different overlay methods to produce lighting and shading effects for an image.

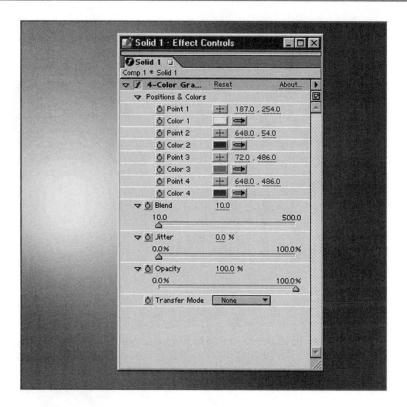

Advanced Lightning

This is also new to AE 5.5. It creates very sophisticated lightning effects. You can animate all aspects of the lightning, and also use the Alpha Obstacle control to make attract the lightning to objects in your scene. Let's pause for a minute to try out the Advanced Lightning feature.

Working with Advanced Lightning

The Advanced Lightning filter has just been added in After Effects 5.5 (Production Bundle). This signals the downgrading of the original Lightning effect to AE Standard version. Here we'll use the Advanced lightning filter to create a backdrop to a title screen.

1. We start by setting up a composition, and right clicking in the timeline to add a solid. We now add the basic text filter to this, and type our caption. The solid is made transparent apart from the words.

2. Next, we add the Advanced Lightning filter. We check the add to original box so the lightning appears over the lettering. The origin button is then clicked, and we position the start point of the lightning at the top of the composition.

3. Next, we turn on animation for the direction button by clicking the stopwatch icon next to it, and, with the playback head at the start of the composition, we place the crosshairs at the start of our text. Moving to the end of the timeline, we place the direction crosshairs at the end of the lettering. The lightning strike now animates across the text.

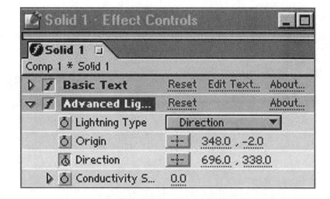

4. Now to add a special function of Advanced Lightning. Open the Forking control, and drag the slider up to 100 percent. This creates much more feathery lightning which will let us see our effect more clearly. We now click on the Alpha Obstacle section, and type in a value of 100.

5. Rendering our shot, we can see the effect. The lightning is still animated, but it's now 'sticking' to the lettering.

The alpha channel is acting as a conductor, attracting the lightning! Creative use of masks and transparency allow you to make your lightning appear to interact with objects in your scene.

Lightning

This is a standard lightning generator with dozens of animation options. It lets you create lightning strikes from one object to another, or more general forking strikes as you might see in the sky. It animates automatically without keyframes.

Audio Spectrum

This filter displays lots of controls. Apply it to a clip with audio, and it will create an animated graph from the noise. You can produce a range of looks from the audio file, and animate its color and style.

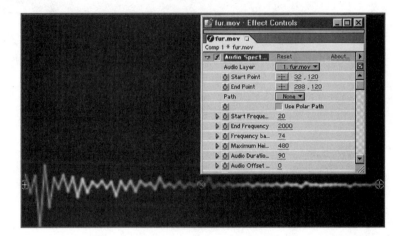

Audio Waveform

This is a slightly different form of the Audio Spectrum filter in that it produces a waveform based on the volume of the sound. These kind of effects are often found on dance music videos, and sci-fi video screens. But part of the fun with After Effects is using its tools to make your work stand out, so just because these effects may seem limited in their application, it's probably just because no-one has used them in another way yet. Cue you!

Beam

This is a filter designed specifically for creating laser battles. It produces a laser beam which animates between two points over a given time. You can add perspective effects by animating the beam's thickness. Try adding motion blur to the beam for a great effect.

Cell pattern

Here is another filter new to AE 5.5. It creates a cell pattern, which can resemble anything from the skin of a lizard to a mosaic. It's useful for creating backdrops, but also for abstract mattes.

Ellipse

This draws an ellipse. That's all there is to it!

Fill

This effect fills the layer, or more usefully, a selected mask on that layer with a solid color. It's good for censoring out unwanted portions of an image, such as a trademark accidentally caught on a video production.

Fractal

This creates fractal patterns on which you can animate the colors and parameters. If you have a degree in fractal mathematics, the variables will make sense to you – for everyone else, the best thing to do is just play around with them until you get a pattern you like.

Fractal Noise

This effect produces fractal noise patterns. These patterns are great for producing smoke, liquid, flame, and other nebulous flowing effects. Just animate the Evolution spinner.

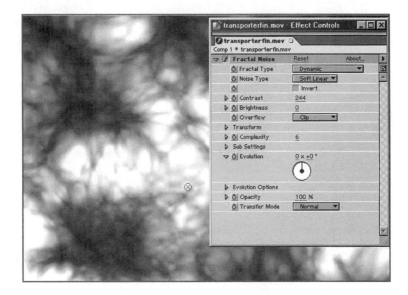

Grid

This filter draws a grid. You can alter the size and shape of the grid significantly to create different effects.

Lens Flare

With this effect you can render a lens flare onto your image. You can create three different types of lens flare, and alter the brightness and position of each. It is used in all kinds of ways to brighten up a shot, or highlight objects on a text screen. It is also great for obscuring poor composites!

Radio Waves

This filter generates concentric shapes moving outwards from a center point. These are automatically animated, but you can control their shape, color, fading rate, speed, and many other attributes. It's a useful filter, but mainly reserved for graphical, rather than realistic shots.

Ramp

This is a color gradient generator. It's not as flexible as the new 4-colour gradient filter, but it is able to produce simple backgrounds which fade from one color to another. Use the Ramp Scattering slider to avoid color banding on broadcast (and internet) outputs.

> **Color banding** *is when, instead of getting a smooth blend between one color and another, you get horizontal lines of different shades because the system can't generate enough shades to make the change appear smooth.*

Roughen Edges

This filter is new in AE 5.5. It roughens the edges of an alpha channel. This can create an eroded or decayed look for text or images.

Stroke

This filter draws a line along any mask or bezier path. It can be useful for animating a brushstroke onto the screen. Try drawing text with a bezier path, then animating a stroke along it to write the text onto the screen.

Time Difference

Another new effect here. This compares the color information on two layers over time, then uses that information for color correction jobs (such as color correction on images whose lighting conditions change), or to add to other effects.

Vegas

This effect creates glows, which can resemble pulsing lights around an object. It's generally more successful on clean graphical images (like text) than on video clips, but you can attach the lights to a bezier path and control them in that way.

Simulation effects

These effects create quite sophisticated simulations of specific events. Use these effects to simulate real-world occurrences such as reflections of light, bubbles, explosions, and waves.

Card Dance – free download from http://www.adobe.com/products/aftereffects/

This is essentially a transition effect. The layer is divided into rectangles, and each rectangle can be animated to move or spin. The result is that the layer can be broken up, or assembled using cards, where each card contains a portion of the image.

Caustics – free download from http://www.adobe.com/products/aftereffects/

This creates a realistic water surface effect complete with reflections of the sky, waves and ripples, and reflections and refractions caused by the water, which distort and alter the bottom of the liquid.

Foam – free download from http://www.adobe.com/products/aftereffects/

This filter creates bubbles. The motion of the bubbles can be controlled using wind, stickiness, and a range of other parameters, and you can texture and color the bubbles using layers or presets. The bubbles even wobble and pop realistically, and you can define a layer as a flow map to make them react to objects in your scene.

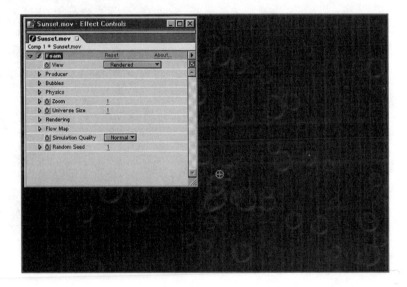

Particle Playground

Use this effect to create animations in which a large number of similar objects must be animated independently. This is a sophisticated and important filter whereby an emitter is created which produces large numbers of particles whose size, life-span, gravity, and so on, can be controlled. Particles can be replaced by layers of video, or still imagery, so you can create a flock of birds, a meteor shower, or a starburst. You can even draw masks or import maps which define the motion of particles, so you can make them bounce off objects, or flow around them.

Shatter

Smash your layer into many pieces which fly, or fall out of the frame with this filter. You can choose from a variety of fragment shapes, from jigsaw pieces to shattered glass, and you can alter the explosion to produce a tailored effect.

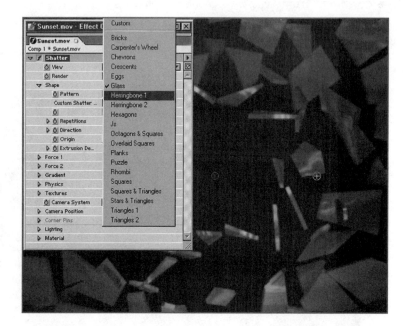

Wave World – free download from http://www.adobe.com/products/aftereffects

This filter produces realistic waves and ripples which spread, collide, and interact with the edges of the layer. It's not much use on its own, but the grayscale map the filter produces can be used with great effect by the caustics filter to create incredibly realistic ripples, or by any other filter that looks for matte images for more unusual effects.

Stylize effects

These filters produce abstract or impressionistic images. Painterly effects, film grain, mosaics and glows are all covered here.

Brush Strokes

This produces a painted effect produced by smearing and splodging parts of the image. The larger the brush size, the less distinct your shot will be. It adds 'roughly painted' looks to an image.

Color Emboss

This filter makes the image appear to be embossed by creating highlights and shadows at points where the contrast between colors is high (usually at the edges of objects in your image).

Emboss

This creates the same raised effect as the Color Emboss filter, but removes the detail of the image itself. The result is just the relief of the image against a gray surface.

Find Edges

This effect scans the image for the boundaries between high contrast areas, and emphasizes them, removing everything else. This creates outlines almost, but not quite as though the object has been sketched.

Glow

This effect creates a glow around either the alpha channel of a layer, or around any bright points of an image. The filter can be used to great effect in many different ways. It's useful for defusing and lighting an image when used subtly, but can also create explosive, burnout and magical effects when used at high intensity.

Leave Color

This is a quick way to take out all color from an image, except for a given color range. Remember the girl in the red coat in Schindler's List? That's the effect.

Mosaic

This turns the image into colored blocks. Use it on a masked section to blur out the face of someone who doesn't want to appear in your production, or on the whole screen to create a pixilated, low resolution display.

Motion Tile

This filter creates multiple copies of the image, and uses them to tile the layer. The position and scale of the tiles can be altered, or animated.

Noise

This creates random animated grain on the image. It's useful at low levels for simulating the effect of film grain, and at high levels for simulating video static. Applying some grain to a composition can help to make it look more like a single image.

PS (Photoshop) Extrude

This effect places the layer on 3D blocks of various heights. The result is to disrupt the image and make it appear to be on multiple raised levels. Quite why you'd want to do that, though, is beyond me. Also, you should note that there is no AE 5.5 equivalent for this filter.

Scatter

This filter takes the pixels in your image and scatters them, the greater the scatter value, the more indistinct your image becomes. Animated, the effect can look like a layer being painted onto sand which is then blown away.

Strobe Light

With this effect, the clip is interrupted every few frames. By default, the interruption is a pure white frame, but other effects like inverting the colors, or making the layer transparent, are also possible.

Texturize

This is a filter which works on two layers. The first is used as the image, the second as a relief texture for that image. Useful for creating canvas or paper type effects, or for giving one object the texture of another.

We're going to take another pause here for an exercise. Here, we'll use the Texturize filter, along with Posterize and Median (Production Bundle), to turn a video image into a painting.

Painterly effects

Here, we want to take a video clip and make it look as though it was painted onto canvas. We'll use three filters to try to create the impression of a painted scene.

1. Open up a new composition and drag in any old bit of footage to play around on.

2. The first filter to drop in is the Posterize filter. This reduces the number of colors in the image. The result is to create ridges of flat color rather than completely smooth gradients.

3. Next, we add a Median filter. This blurs the image by making adjacent pixels the same color. The filter gives us a much more painted look – the detail of the video has now been replaced with blobs of color.

4. Finally, we add a Texturize filter. This does nothing initially, until we place another layer into our composition. This second layer is a simple black and white image of a piece of canvas. We created the canvas in PhotoShop, but you can get from the CD. We set it as the texture layer, and it starts to show through our initial shot. We can change the balance between canvas and image with the texture contrast slider.

Write-on

This lets you animate the position of a brush over time, and will paint using that brush. This allows you to achieve sophisticated effects, but the Stroke filter is often quicker (Production Bundle users will probably find the Vector Paint tool superior).

Text

Here we have a collection of effects to create text and numbers for overlays, credit scrolls, titles, and other text.

Basic Text

This is a filter for creating simple text. There are a number of parameters dealing with the size, color, and position of the text, but if you're generating text in After Effects, you'll probably find working on it with other filters produces a more interesting result (as we saw in the first tutorial in this chapter).

Numbers

This filter is not only for formatting numbers into date, timecode, or a range of other conventions. It also lets you generate random or sequential numbers. For example, you can quickly put a countdown at the bottom of the screen, or produce a randomly changing readout on a computer screen.

Path Text

This filter produces text that can be placed and animated along a curved path. You control the text's motion, and the shape of its movement. Random movement can be introduced to make the text a little less predictable.

Time

This is a set of effects that allow you to manipulate the timing of a layer.

> If you've applied other filters to the layer, they'll be ignored by time effects. To solve this, place other effects after the Time filter.

Echo

This filter overlays images from a few frames before or after the current frame, accentuating movement, and leaving echoes of a moving object trailing across the screen. The more echoes that are overlaid, the more bleached out your shot will be. To solve this, change the echo operator, or reduce the starting intensity.

Posterize Time

This effect gives the clip a defined frame-rate. It's useful for creating jerky motion, or giving interlaced video a filmic look.

Time Displacement

This allows you to create some very weird effects by using another layer as a map to define which parts of the image are taken from which point in time. Imagine a map where a black circle was placed on a white background. Apply this as a time displacement to an action scene, and the action within the circle would lag behind that going on outside of the 'time bubble'.

Transition effects

This is a set of effects which destroy or assemble the layer, revealing, or obscuring the one beneath. They are useful for wiping between one shot and the next. Use the transition completion slider to animate the effect.

Block dissolve

In this effect, random blocks are removed from the layer until it has completely gone.

Card Wipe – free download from http://www.adobe.com/products/aftereffects/

This is a transition version of the Card Dance filter. You can control exactly how the blocks making up the screen are translated or rotated over time to dismantle or assemble the image.

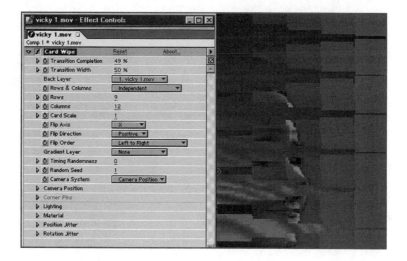

Gradient Wipe

This is the most powerful transition of all. Here you use a second layer as a map to define which pixels vanish first. For example, a map in which a black center spot smudges out towards a white border will produce a transition where the center of the image vanishes first, and the erosion creeps out towards the edge. By producing a good set of maps, you can produce a huge range of transitions with this filter.

Iris Wipe

This filter produces a hole in your image, which becomes wider until the image completely vanishes.

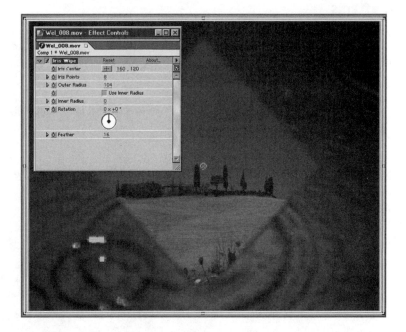

Linear Wipe

This filter is a standard wipe from one side of the screen to the other (as seen on Star Wars).

Radial Wipe

This is the bog standard clock-face wipe, where the image is replaced by a line sweeping around the center point of the screen.

Venetian Blinds

Using this effect, parallel lines appear on your image, getting wider and wider until the shot is completely erased.

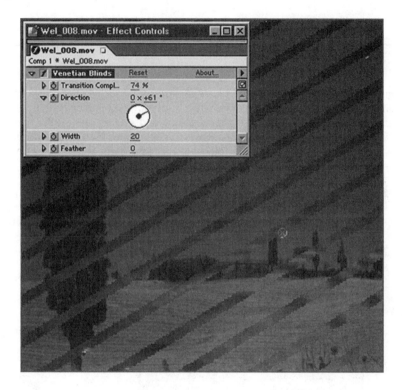

Video effects

A selection of effects designed for interlaced video productions.

Broadcast Colors

TVs can't display the range of colors that After Effects can produce (high saturation colors are especially vulnerable). This filter lets you see what your shot will look like on a standard TV. If you play your video out to a TV, the colors will be adjusted anyway – this filter just lets you get in and take a look first.

Reduce Interlace Flicker

If you've got an image with a lot of fine lines – especially horizontal ones – this filter will stop them from flickering when they're sent out to a TV.

Timecode

This effect displays timecode or frame number information within a layer. This is only really useful as a reference for test renders.

Well, that's all the effects covered, now we can play a little!

Inventing a teleport transporter

Imagine we had an assignment to produce a matter transporter effect for a sci-fi show. The brief is quite loose, so we can combine a few filters to produce something neat. In addition, the director has shot the scene using a locked off camera shot, and a bluescreen studio, and given us an empty frame with which we can freely and easily work. All the files used in this tutorial are on the CD in the chapter 7 teleport transporter folder, just import them from there, or copy them into a convenient directory on your own computer.

1. Creating the composition, we drop in the background, and place our bluescreen figure on top of it. A quick application of the Color Difference key and the spill suppresser makes fast work of the blue background. Our character is ready to be beamed out.

2. Our first addition to the image is that of a Glow filter. Drop this onto our figure, and base it on the alpha channel rather than the color channel, so that the glow surrounds the figure rather than highlighting its bright spots. Choose some warm colors for the glow.

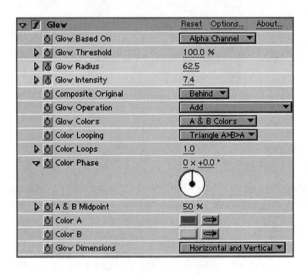

> **Standard Version**: *If you're using the standard version use a Color Balance HLS filter instead.*

3. Next, we need to animate the glow. Placing the playback head about half way through the animation, click the stopwatches to turn on animation for the glow's radius and intensity. Start both at zero. Moving to the point at which the figure vanishes (about 3 seconds into the animation) take both parameters up to 100.

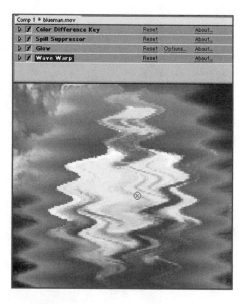

Playing back, the character starts to glow, and the glow spreads to completely cover him by the time he vanishes.

> **Standard Version**: *Instead, click the stopwatches to turn on animation for the filter's hue, saturation and lightness. Start them at zero. Moving to the point at which the figure vanishes, take the lightness and saturation up until the character is completely white. We can also move the hue knob so that the actor changes color as he vanishes.*

4. Next, we add some distortion in the form of a wave warp filter. On this, we animate the wave height and width parameters. The figure begins with no warping, and ends as he vanishes looking like a badly tuned TV.

> **Standard Version**: *Instead use a PS wave filter. On this, we turn the vertical scale down to zero, set the max amplitude at 38, then animate the wavelength down from 999 to 0 over the course of the animation.*

5. The effect looks nice, but it would be nicer if the glow didn't distort with the figure. All we need to do to get around this is change the order of the filters in the Effect Controls window by dragging the wave warp filter up above the glow filter.

> **Standard Version**: *Ignore this step.*

6.   The shot's beginning to look very nice, but our character's final disappearance is a little abrupt. Look under Transform in the timeline, and animate the character's opacity so he fades out over his last half-second of existence. See how it looks. When we were devising this example, we didn't think that was enough, so we also added a Scatter filter, and animated the scatter amount from 0 to 1000 over about a second, so our character shatters into pixels as he fades.

> **Standard Version**: *Instead of the scatter, use a blur filter, and animate the horizontal blur amount from 0 to 100 over about a second, so our character looses focus as he fades.*

7.   We dragged this filter up between the wave warp and the glow filter so the shape of the glow is retained as the figure breaks up.

> **Standard Version**: *Ignore this step.*

8.   Finally, switch to the background layer. After the character has vanished, we want to leave a little echo. Drop in a lens flare filter, and animate its size. Make it grow from nothing just before the figure vanishes to a bright star just after he's gone, then slowly fade out. You can also animate its position so that it floats slowly towards the top of the screen.

9.   Playing back, the effect is nice, but let's try having the flare starting to rise slowly, and speeding up. Click the down-arrow to the left of the flare center parameter on the timeline to reveal the speed graph for the parameter.

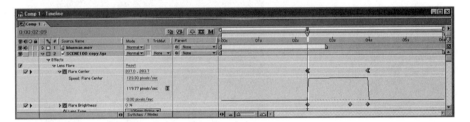

10. This controls the way After Effects moves between keyframed values. The current state of the graph indicates that the lens-flare moves at a constant speed. Select the first keyframe, a blue control appears on the graph.

11. You can drag this to change the slope of the graph so that our flare starts slowly, and then accelerates. Using these graphs gives you far greater control over the way animation takes place between your keyframes.

Our teleportation effect now looks positively Star-Trek-worthy.

Summary

Obviously you're not going to need all these effects in any one project, but given that this is After Effects after all, these filters are a core feature, and one you'll come back to time and time again when you're looking for something to jazz up your projects.

After reading this chapter you should be getting a better idea of which kind of filters are effective where, and some might even have stuck out as being appropriate to a particular project you have in mind. Hopefully you're no longer quite so daunted and better equipped to navigate through the sometimes dizzying variety of filters at your command with After Effects 5.5.

8 Render it Right

After Effects has the capability of exporting a wide variety of file types, which vary in their usefulness from general purpose QuickTime and AVI movies, through high quality but hard disk guzzling still sequences, to very specific file types suitable only for one or two uses (like the filmstrip format used to take short sequences into Photoshop).

How you output your finished movie will be determined by what you expect to do with it. Is it being prepared for television, film, DVD, the Internet? In most cases, a good rule of thumb is to output your work at the highest quality you ever think you may need, and then create any lower resolution versions from that. That way, you'll always be able to go back to your original if you need to create a better version later.

For example, if you're producing a video for the Internet, you could just render it out in RealMedia format straight from After Effects. But what happens if you're asked to produce a TV version of it later on? Or if you need to combine your project into a longer sequence (like your showreel for example) using a non linear editor? If you render your shot at full DV quality, then create the Internet version from that it'll take a little longer initially, but you'll have a high quality master from which future copies can be made at any resolution. At the end of the day, it will be the producer's choice, but they're likely to be guided by your advice.

In this chapter, we'll learn how to render a variety of file types, videos, still sequences, and even Flash movies. We'll also take a look at how After Effects is used in different ways throughout the production process, and how this determines the way you'll export your files.

Previews

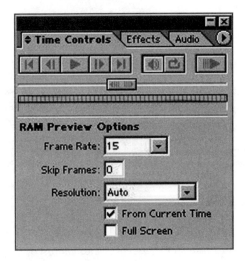

After Effects is very good at allowing you to preview and scrub through your work as you're going along. RAM preview, along with the ability to turn layers and effects on or off and vary the resolution and quality of previews, means you can get a very good idea of the way projects will look, and animations will behave when they are rendered.

The simplest method is to simply drag the playback head, and watch as the composition window is updated. This is called a "manual" preview. It gives you an idea of what the screen will look like, but isn't much good at letting you judge the speed of animations. RAM preview is good for displaying a few seconds of your project at a time, but can only hold as many frames as your memory will allow. Wireframe preview (Composition > Preview > Wireframe Preview) removes the images from your project, showing only their frames. This is not very interesting to look at, but it does show the speed of your animations.

That said, the only way you can really find out how your finished video is going to look is to actually render it. Test renders are renders featuring either a portion of your project or the whole project at reduced quality, or with certain effects turned off; and are an important part of using any effects package. The ability to know when to go for a test render and when not to can save you a lot of time!

To enable you to produce a quick test render of a portion of your timeline, at a variety of resolutions, it's well worth setting up a range of presets in the Render Queue. That way, you have less distraction from the business of building your projects. This is a subject we'll look at later in this chapter.

Fields

Just before we dive into the main body of the chapter, we're going to look in a little more depth at fields.

As we saw in **Chapter 4**, interlaced video, such as television content, contains fields. Each frame you see is made up of two fields. The two fields are essentially two images, which are laid a fraction of a second (1/50th for PAL TV or 1/60th for NTSC) apart onto your TV screen, one horizontal line at a time. The cathode ray tube of your TV fires first one image onto the screen from top to bottom, leaving alternate blank lines. It then goes back and fills in the gaps with the second field as the light from the first is fading. The result is a steady looking image in which fields are interlaced to produce a single image. This is called interlaced video.

So when we say that PAL plays at 25 *frames* per second, we could also say that it plays at 50 *fields* per second. The equivalent applies to NTSC.

Interlaced images were initially used in television because the cathode ray tubes could not create a good enough quality image in a single field, therefore two images were combined to create one frame. In the US 60Hz is used so 60 fields are generated to produce 30 fps (approx). In the UK 50Hz is used so 50 fields are generated to create 25fps. If you are new to After Effects, fields can seem like another annoying obstacle, but for projects destined for the TV screen, it's important you understand how to deal with them. Luckily, After Effects makes this a lot less painful than you first might think.

When you import interlaced video into your system, each frame is made up of alternate horizontal lines taken at slightly different times. If you have not separated the fields you will notice when you look at an image of a fast moving object – there are often horizontal stripes across the image, particularly at the edges. This is because the motion has occurred between the first and second field, so the images from the two fields are very different.

When you separate the fields in After Effects the stripes vanish and the image looks clearer.

The two fields that make up the frame of interlaced video appear on the screen in a particular order: either upper field first, or lower field first (in other words, the cathode ray tube has to place one field onto the screen before the other). Unfortunately, field orders in footage vary. Separating the fields allows us to use footage from different sources that can have different field orders, and composite them for a high quality final result when we render. If the fields are not separated, particularly for different footage sources in the one project, the final result will be stripy and of poor quality.

The decision you have to make is which field comes first? After you have imported your interlaced footage, highlight it in the project window, and then choose File > Interpret Footage > Main…

In the Separate Fields pop-up list, select Upper Field First for Avid video or Electric Image. Select Lower Field First for DV footage, or footage captured from an IEEE 1394 FireWire / iLink.

We can leave Separate Fields off if we have film, or footage which uses progressive scan, as this is non-interlaced. Progressive scan is where each frame is displayed in its entirety from top to bottom. Much like a film projector displays each frame of film, one after the other. A computer monitor uses progressive scan, as do some of the more expensive DV cameras.

Which field first?

1. If you are unsure of which field is flashed first, then we can test the footage.

2. Select Upper Field First, and then open the footage from the project window by holding down ALT (Windows) or OPTION (Mac) and double-clicking the footage. This will open the footage in the Footage window.

3. Make sure the time controls are visible (Window > Show Time Controls) and then find a segment of the footage that contains some moving elements.

4. Step forward through 6 or so frames and observe that the moving elements do in fact move consistently in one direction. If they do, we made the right selection.

5. If the moving areas move back every second frame, then open the Interpret Footage window again and select Lower Field First instead.

That about covers it for footage we're bringing into the project. But we still need to make a decision about rendering fields when it comes time to output. If our project is to be output to computer or film, or perhaps to another post production facility for input into a Flame compositing system or the like, then we can render whole frames. On the other hand, if your project is destined to go directly to TV, or DV which does not use progressive scan, then you will need to render it to fields. Just like any inputs to our project, you need to determine the field order for your output. You can then render the project to fields.

In the Render Queue window, if you click on the Current Settings hot text, a Render Settings dialog box will open. Within the Time Sampling section, there is a Field Render menu you can use to specify the field order for your render. Use this to set the Field Rendering to the same field order as your video equipment.

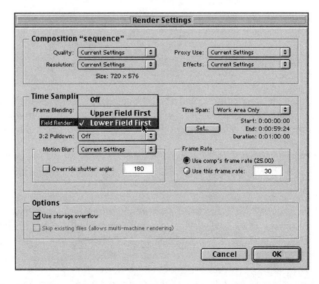

If your final render is not sharp, jitters or looks distorted, when you play it on video, chances are you have rendered with the wrong field order. If you do not know the field order your video equipment requires, you can perform another test. Some video equipment displays the upper interlaced field first, and some displays the lower one first. What you need to remember is that the field order that you require to record to video can change with changes to your hardware or software, such as using a different video card or VCR. So if this happens you need to perform the test again. You basically need to render out a simple animation of a block of color with horizontal movement on a contrasting background. The animation should be rendered twice, once for each field order. When played on video, the correct field order will appear clear and crisp with smooth movement, the incorrect field order render will have distortions and jerks.

The test is simple and further details can be found in the After Effects user guide or Help menu under the topic Testing the field-rendering order.

The rendering process

Creating or making a movie from a final composition is the last step of the After Effects process, and it could take a few minutes, to many hours, depending upon the size and complexity of the composition. To render a movie, you must first place the composition in the Render Queue. Here, it becomes a Render item and renders according to the settings given to it. While After Effects is rendering something, you cannot use it to do anything else.

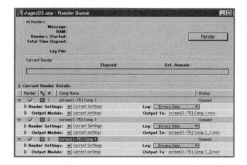

The first step to take once you're ready to render then, is to hit Make Movie on the Composition menu. This brings up the Render Queue window, where you can see and manipulate a list of current and previous renders, and watch the progress of your rendering as the movie is created.

> *Unfortunately, the* Render Queue *has its roots in a time when After Effects was only used by a few companies who needed to be able to automate and batch-process large numbers of very slowly rendering effects. The result of this today is an output system which is very good at allowing you to organize and queue multiple renders, and can quite happily produce a dozen different movies while you're off on holiday, but which becomes a little annoying when it's asked to do the normal day to day work of quickly knocking up test renders of a single project. The* Render Queue *requires strict management if it's not to turn into a massive list of "dead" instructions, and details of renders done way back in the history of the project, which are now completely irrelevant.*

The Render Queue window

Once the Render Queue window is open, you can set up a render by just dragging the composition into it from the Project Window. A new item will then appear in the queue with all the default settings. Let's take a look at the queue in detail, and discover what each of these settings is about...

The Render Queue isn't quite as daunting as it may first appear. Each new composition you've selected for rendering appears as an item in the list. It can be opened, or folded neatly away with the triangle to the left of the composition name. Just next to this is a tick box. This will be checked initially, and indicates whether the shot will be rendered or not when you click the render button (at the top right of the window).

Next to this is a colored square. This is purely a way to color code your list (you can give all your test renders a blue box, all your pre-composition renders a green one, for example). You can change the color by simply clicking on the square box.

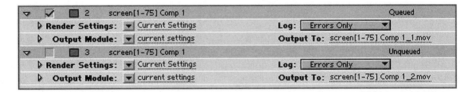

This is followed by a label indicating the name of the composition to be rendered. Double click this to open the composition itself. Next up is the status of the render – to start with, this will read queued to indicate that the item is waiting to render. If you uncheck the tick box at the left, the item will become unqueued, and once it's rendered, the message will change again.

The final two items in the row indicate when the render was started, and how long it took to complete (this information is only filled in after the render is done, of course!).

Underneath the label row, four more items let you choose the way your project is set up, and the kind of file it will produce. Let's look at each of them briefly.

Render settings

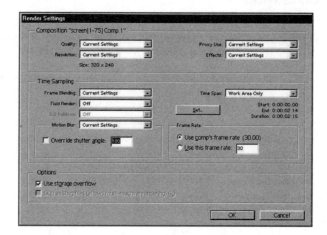

Render Settings is the first option in the Render Queue window below the colored square label box. Click the Current Settings label to bring up the Settings window. This deals with the overall quality and resolution of your image, the way fields are rendered, the effects, the frame rate, and the portion of your timeline that you want rendered.

The quality selector defines whether you're using best, draft quality, or wireframe (a rarely used setting which leaves out the actual images, just displaying the rectangular frames as boxes). **Draft quality** saves rendering time by doing quick and dirty versions of some filters. For example, blur filters end up being rendered more quickly, but can look pixelated. The resolution lets you change the degree of detail in the rendered image as a fraction of the composition size. Use this when creating test renders to make things move more quickly, but don't use it to set the resolution for your final movie – because you can be a lot more specific about resolution in the output module (see later).

The Proxy Use drop-down box lets you choose whether to render using the original files or proxies. Proxies are low resolution identical versions of the original footage, but need less processing, because they're smaller files, and so speed up your work. If you've created proxies for your footage you can choose to keep them – for a low resolution test render – or automatically replace them with the full quality versions – for a final render.

The Effects drop-down lets you choose to have effects filters included, or turned off during rendering. Removing the effects can be useful in speeding up a test render, but of course, isn't a lot of use in a final version.

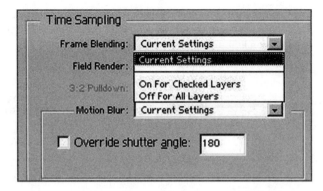

Under Time Sampling, the Frame Blending selector lets you choose superior quality for fast and slow motion sections of your work. Normally, slowing a piece of footage down, simply involves repeating certain frames. This can lead to a jerky effect. With frame blending enabled, new frames are created by blending the "before" and "after" frames together. This creates a much smoother look.

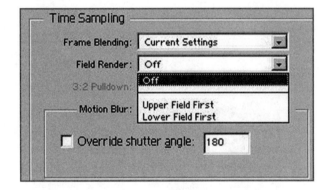

The Field Rendering control lets you choose field dominance for interlaced video. This setting is used for TV work, and its setting will depend on the equipment you're using. See above for a detailed explanation of field rendering. If field rendering is enabled, the 3:2 pull-down box also becomes active.

The 3:2 pulldown control is only useful for work, which was originally on film, effects which are to end up on film, or animations which you want to look more filmic. It alters the apparent framerate of your composition to a film framerate (24fps), but leaves the real frame rate unaltered (using 3:2 pulldown on 30 frames per second video creates a video which still has 30 frames per second, but only 24 *different* frames per second). For more information on 3:2 pull-down, see **Chapter 3**.

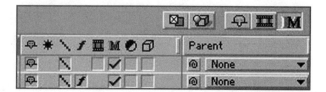

The Motion Blur selector lets you turn motion blur on or off (but only for animations you've created – you can't create or remove motion blur within a captured video without special software). Motion blur also has an override shutter angle box so you can render output with different amounts of motion blur. It's important to note that none of these controls will actually do anything on their own. You need to turn on the relevant functions on the timeline too (see image).

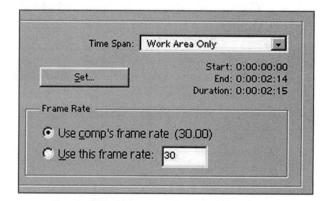

The frame rate setting lets you choose your own frame-rate, or keep the composition's frame-rate. The time span section lets you decide what portion of your timeline you're going to render. You can render just the work area, the whole composition, or type in values for the exact portion of the timeline you want to see reproduced.

The Use storage overflow button allows After Effects to carry on rendering even when it runs out of disk space. The remaining files are placed on the next drive in your overflow list (specified on the Edit > Settings > Overflow dialog). Of course, you can only do this if you've got more than one hard disk in your machine!

Finally, the skip existing files checkbox forces After Effects to search the directory in which your production is being rendered for similarly named files, missing out any which have already been rendered. This is useful when you're creating your output as a sequence of still images, and either you interrupt rendering and then restart it, or use more than one computer to render files to a networked drive for faster results.

> *Default settings for the* Output Module, *and* Render Settings *will depend on the settings you've used in the composition window whilst working on your project. Watch out for this because if you're working on a complex project, you tend to turn down the quality settings on the* Composition *window to a quarter, or even a third, and use the zoom to reduce the resolution so you get decent playback. If you forget to change the settings for your render, it will appear at the same scale, but at reduced quality, and you might not become aware of this until you've finished your render (or worse, until your entire finished production gets played out to video!).*

Output Module

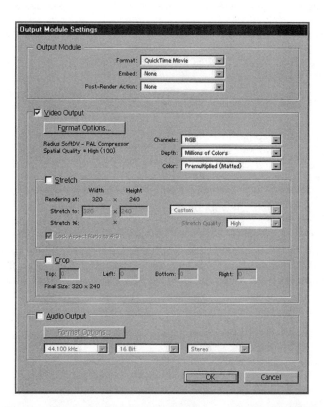

The Output Module is the second option under the render queue. This brings up a window which allows you to choose the way the images, once rendered, will be placed on disk.

The first is the Format type. You can choose from a vast range of output types, but the most commonly used for each medium are:

- **Movies** – Video For Windows, or QuickTime, although Realmedia movies for the net can also be rendered;

- **Still image sequences** – TGAs, BMPs, PNGs, and Photoshop images;

- **Internet animations** can be exported as Animated GIF although you'll need to be very careful about the file-size of images produced if you want to keep download time realistic;

- MP3 can be used for **audio** only export,

- and Filmstrip files are useful because they can be imported into **Photoshop** and further altered there..

For each output file type there are different format options (see below).

> *Flash (SWF) files are exported in an entirely different way, and aren't available through the* Render Queue *(more on this later).*

The Embed selector comes just below the format selector. This is rarely used, but is quite neat, especially if you're working with Adobe Premiere as your editing package. The selector lets you embed either a pointer to the After Effects project file, or the whole file itself inside the movie. That way, editing packages with the edit original function will let you click on the finished file in the editor's timeline, and instead of opening the rendered movie, you'll open After Effects with the project in it, so you can work on the composition some more.

This means that you don't have to leave your effects work to the end of your production, and you can keep tweaking it throughout the process. Just select project link to force your editor to load your original AE file, or project link and copy to include the actual AE file itself inside your movie file. Only QuickTime and Video for Windows files allow this kind of embedding.

In AE 5.5, a new Post-Render Action selector has been added. Post-render actions allow you to instruct After Effects to perform certain duties after it has finished rendering a composition. For example, you can tell After Effects to automatically import the finished render back into the project, or use it as a Proxy or a replacement for another file. If your project is made up of several pre-compositions, you could set AE to render these, and automatically replace the un-rendered originals in your final composition, ready for easier editing.

For example - say you're producing a title sequence for a series. Each episode has different contents, and you want a clip from the episode in its title sequence, but the same effects have to be applied for each episode.

You'd use the Render Queue to produce a render of the clip from episode 1 with a post-render action to load that clip into the final title effect composition. You'd then put another item in the render Queue to render the finished sequence. You could then include another Render Queue item for the clip in episode 2 and so on...

Next in the Output Module, comes the video and audio settings. Each has a tick box, so you can render just audio, just video, or both. Of course depending on your choice of output file type, you may not be able to render both sound and vision – there's no audio track on a JPG file!

The video section has a Format Option button to allow you to choose compression settings for your video or image file. These will depend on your own system, and the file type you're creating, but it's worth noting a couple of compression codecs for video productions:

- Cinepack, Sorenson, and Indeo codecs are good as standards for video material, they're present on most people's computers, so almost anyone will be able to play files compressed in this way. In addition, they're all good at compressing video to a bandwidth that will work well for CD ROM distribution and playback on computers.

- DV software codecs give you TV quality images, which will always be 3.6mb per second. They're good for general purpose video work. Just make sure you use the correct codec for your TV system (PAL or NTSC) and for the aspect ratio you're producing (4:3 for normal work, or 16:9 for widescreen work).

In general, try to output your movies at a quality at least as high as your source material. That way you'll always be working from the best quality "master" clips.

The channels, depth, and color selectors are usually defined by your choices of format and compression. However, they do allow you to choose whether to render an alpha channel with your video (so transparent areas are maintained, and you can superimpose the video later).

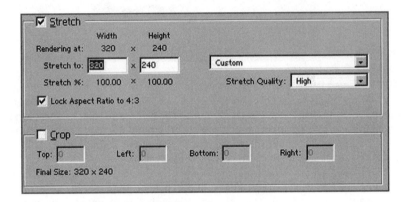

The Stretch and Crop sections let you define the size (in pixels) of your image if you want it to be different from that of your composition. Stretch expands or contracts the movie to whatever output size you want, without loosing any of the edges of the composition (there are a range of presets for commonly used resolutions). Crop slices off the edges to give you a cut-down version of your composition (useful if you're creating a widescreen version of a TV shaped composition).

Lastly, the audio section lets you choose the quality and stereo settings of your sound. If you don't tick this box then the audio that you went to so much trouble with won't be rendered, so make sure you remember to arrange the audio settings. You can choose to use an audio compression codec, although unless you're creating work for the Internet, there's really not a lot of point. You can pick the audio sample rate, unless you're working on DV in which case it's fixed at 44 or 48kHz, giving higher or lower sound quality. 22kHz is usually fine for CD ROM productions, and 8khz is good for Internet movies. The mono/stereo choice will depend on your own preference - stereo sound uses twice the bandwidth of mono. 16 bit sound is higher quality than 8 bit, but also uses twice the file space.

Log

When After Effects renders your movie, it generates a log file. This is a text file, which lets you know how the render went, and whether there were any problems. You can choose whether the log file is generated only in the case of an error, or whether every render produces a log – indicating the settings of the render, and details of the render time for each frame.

If your scene has been created correctly, and you're happy with the result, there's no reason to even look at the log. If anything abnormal happens during rendering, however, a note of the event should be recorded in the log file, and you can load it up in any text editor to find out more.

The log will tell you if the render has been terminated, and give an explanation as to why. It will also let you know if you've filled up the disk, and After Effects has used an overflow volume (if you've set one up) to store the remainder of your renders.

Output To

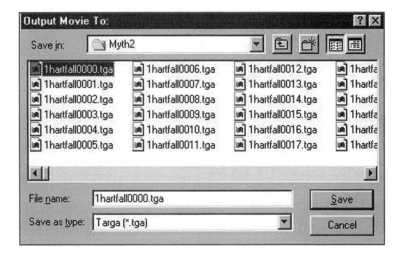

The final item in the Render Queue is the Output to option. This is simply the filename your movie or sequence will be given, and the folder it will be saved to. If you're creating an image sequence, the name will be followed by several hash signs, indicating that your shots will be sequentially numbered.

Presets

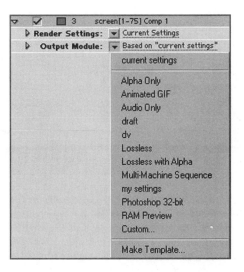

Both the Render Settings and the Output Module can be given presets to save you time in setting up your render. The down-arrow to the left of the label gives you access to a dropdown list of presets. Those included with After Effects are based on the needs of a range of users, but you're likely to need to create your own to suit your style of working. Just select the Make Template item at the bottom of the list then use the Edit button on the window that appears, to create your own template (see "Rendering for real" walkthrough).

Once created, a template will remain in the Render Queue forever. It will be available to you instantly in any future project you create until you decide to delete it (which you also do with the Make Template option). If your template is something you use all the time, you can make it the default when a new item is added to the Render Queue by selecting Movie Default in the Make Template window.

Do the render!

Once you've decided on just how you're going to export your project, and set up all the rendering parameters you can start your rendering. It's easy enough - just hit the Render button at the top right of the Render Queue.

You can then leave the computer to get on with it, while you make a cup of coffee, or go on holiday – depending on the complexity of your project.

Rendering obviously takes up as much of the capacity of your computer as it can, so if you're doing other tasks with it while the rendering is going on, this will slow down all applications (including the rendering itself). If you've got simple tasks to do, like word processing, emailing, or general admin stuff, you'll be fine, and although there'll be some impact on rendering times and the performance of your other packages, you should be able to get on without too much trouble. However, don't try doing other video work like editing, 3D animation, or running another copy of AE because you'll almost certainly find it's more trouble than it's worth. And, of course, playing videogames is, unfortunately, right out!

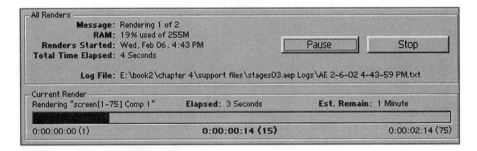

If you're going to be multi-tasking with After Effects, it's worth knowing when to use the Render Pause button which appears next to the Render button whilst rendering is taking place. It's worth hitting pause if you've got another processor or disk intensive job to do. If you're loading or saving a big document, opening an application, or even just playing a video or sound file, hit pause on your rendering before you do it, and life will be a lot smoother.

While rendering is going on, there are a few ways you can check on its progress. The progress bar appears at the top of the Render Queue displaying the progress of the job, the time taken so far, the frame number currently being rendered and the estimated time for the entire render.

Below this, further information about the render can be accessed with the Current Render Details section. To open this, just click the triangle next to the label. This reveals detailed information about the render and how it is progressing.

The rendering section tells you the composition, layer and stage currently being rendered - so you can see if your render is being slowed down inordinately by one particular filter, or compositing job. This is useful because there are often alternative ways of working in After Effects, and a different method might give faster rendering with the same results (for example, using fast-blur instead of camera blur filters, or not using extremely high resolution images when they're not needed).

Next to this is the Frame Times section. This lets you know how long the last frame took to render, how this compares with the time taken for the preceding frame, and what the average frame time is. Look out for massive jumps in frame times caused by the introduction of complex effects, or particle emitters.

Below this section is the Output Modules group. Here you can keep an eye on file sizes, and easily see from the estimated file size and free disk space indicator whether your render is going to fit or whether it will flow over into another disk (if you have one set up). If you're using uncompressed image files, or DV footage, the disk space estimate will be perfectly accurate because the file size for each frame of video is known from the start. If you're using some other forms of compression, the final file size is less certain, and will be determined by the amount of movement and color change in your shot, and the type of compression you're using.

Well, we've spent a lot of time in this chapter looking at the various render options, what they mean, and how to use them, but let's get a bit more practical now, and do a render for real.

Rendering for real

Here we've got a project that we've been working on for a while. We've done RAM previews as we've worked on the shot, and this has given us a fair idea of how the shot will look, but we need to do a quick low resolution output, before we can commit to a long full quality render. We'll use the Render Queue and duplicate our settings to re-use when we re-render later.

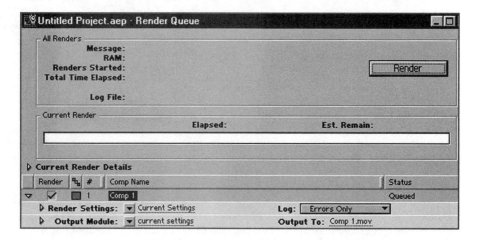

1. We think we've got the scene pretty well put together, so we'll go for a practice render right away. Select the timeline, then choose Composition > Make Movie.... The Render Queue opens with our composition as the only entry in it.

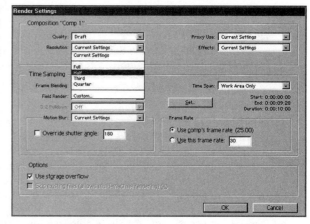

2. We can't just render the shot – the set up needs tweaking a little first. Let's start with the render settings. Click on the Current Settings label to bring up the settings window. Current settings are taken from the settings of your composition, and the crucial ones are the quality and resolution controls. Choose draft for quality, and half for resolution to get a reasonably sized image which will render quite quickly.

3. Choose length of comp from the Time Span selector so we can render the entire production. Everything else we can leave as it is.

4. Next we choose the output module. The current one, Lossless, isn't particularly useful, so we'll prepare our own output module which we can use in future productions. Click the down arrow beside the Lossless label, and select Make Template.

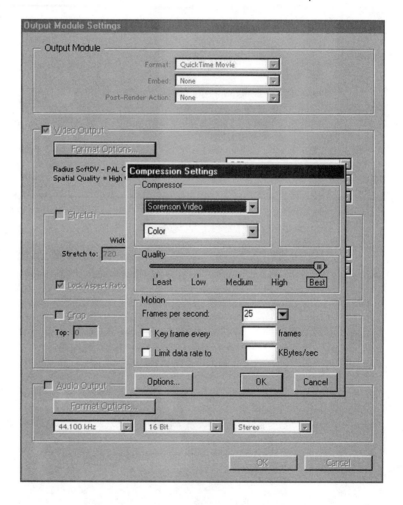

5. In the dialog that appears, give the template a name, and select Edit to set it up. This gives us all the usual controls over the compression and sizing of our video. In this case, we're setting up a template for low quality test renders, so for format, pick QuickTime, and in the format options set up, pick Sorenson Video as the compression codec. Click OK, then OK again to return to the Render Queue.

6. Our Output Module is now set up, and we can use it on any project just by selecting it from the drop-down list. The only other thing to change is the movie title (just click the Output to label, and choose where you want to place your file).

7. Finally, click Render, and the scene is produced and saved. Loading it up, we take a look at our test. It's OK, and we can go ahead and render the final version.

    Each time you want to do a test render, you'll need to go through and set up all the parameters again. This can be time consuming and annoying – especially as you'll often need to create several tests before you're happy to render a finished movie. However, there is a way around it. Select your last render, then go to the Edit menu, and pick Duplicate.

    A new render appears in the queue containing all the settings of your previous test. The only thing that changes is the name of the output file (which is given a "_1" suffix). If you want to overwrite the previous file, just pick duplicate with Filename. In this case, we're happy with our test render, but selecting Duplicate will still save us a bit of time with our settings, so let's use it. This is quicker than using presets and lets you set up a new render of your project with a single click.

8. Select the render you have just completed from the Render Queue and choose Edit > Duplicate. A new item appears in the list. It has exactly the same output settings as the test render, so we need to change a few things.

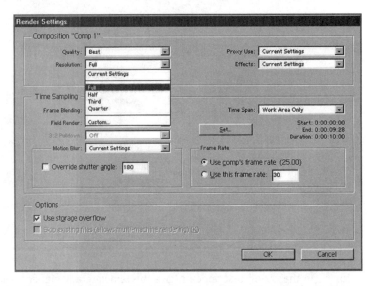

9. In Render Settings, choose best and full for the quality and resolution settings, and turn on motion blur, and frame blending. Changing the Time Span to Custom. allows us to feed in our own start and stop points, but this is not necessary here as we're rendering our whole movie.

10. Returning to the Render Queue, select the output module. Set the system to produce a Targa sequence instead of the QuickTime movie we produced the first time. This renders our production as a series of numbered stills, which take up a lot of disk space, but retain the full quality of our original shot. Make sure you create a folder somewhere on your hard drive for these files. If you just go around rendering out still sequences all over the place, you'll quickly find your disk is full. Manage your disks!

11. Hit Render. Because of the greater quality and resolution, the project takes a lot longer to produce, but it is our final version.

In this example, we first produced a test render to check that our material would look the way we wanted it to, before rendering it for real. If we just want to do a test render, though, there is another way to render out a sequence in After Effects. It's pretty straight forward and easily explained in a tutorial.

Outputting a test movie using Export

The Render Queue is a little long winded, so if you just want to run off a test render, or if you don't need to set up detailed output settings, you can use the Export function to set up your render.

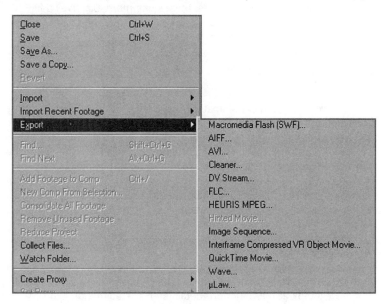

1. Select the composition you want to render, and go to File > Export. You can do a quick render using a range of different formats including AVI, MPEG, QuickTime, and Shockwave Flash, as well as audio formats and still image sequences.

2. Pick your format, and the file selector box lets you choose where to render to. We're creating a quick QuickTime movie – just to see how our work in progress is going.

3. The settings box now appears. This will vary for different movie types, but in our case it lets us choose a compression setting, including the frame-rate and compression codec, a filter and an image size, the pixel size of the finished piece. There's very little point in applying filters to After Effects output – you might as well do it on the timeline where you can control the effect, so you're unlikely to use the filter setting. The image size defaults to the size of your composition, but it can be set manually.

4. For sound, we can pick our compression and bit-rates. When you hit OK, the movie is rendered. You get a basic progress bar to show you how the render is going, but it's not as detailed as the Render Queue one, and isn't updated for every frame.

This quick method has the advantage that you don't have to keep setting up items in the Render Queue. However, it doesn't let you change motion blur, quality settings, or any of the other details the Render Queue gives you control over. It doesn't allow you to choose which portions of the movie you render, and, of course, you can't stack up multiple renders to be performed while you're away from your computer.

Just before we finish looking at rendering, there's one more exercise I'd like to guide you through, and that is rendering a project into a Flash movie. Rendering for the Web is very different to rendering for video, and the difference is worth observing.

Create a Flash movie!

Here, imagine we've created an animation for video, and our client has decided they want the same animation on their website. It's not a complex animation– just a piece of text which slides onto the screen and then fades away while a graphic moves in, animates around, and zooms away again. We need to produce this animation as a Macromedia Flash file. Before After Effects 5.5, this would have meant going back to the original images, and starting again from scratch; re-producing an animation designed in one medium using a completely different tool-set, and re-building it for a new medium. In After Effects 5.5, it's not exactly a snap, but it is at least feasible! So open up a composition containing a text effect, a graphic and some filters, and give it a go.

1. With the composition selected, choose File > Export > Macromedia Flash, and decide on a filename.

2. The SWF settings window appears, offering various choices, just dismiss them for now – we'll look at them in more detail later. The animation is now rendered as a Flash file. It's as easy as that!

3. Only it's not quite... When you load the Flash file, you'll realize it hasn't worked. The text element of our shot hasn't come out at all, and neither have any of the other filters that were applied. This is an important lesson. Flash as a medium can do some useful things, but it doesn't have anything like the range of techniques found in After Effects.

4. We can still reproduce these effects in Flash, but at a cost. Go back and attempt to save your Flash animation again. This time, at the SWF settings window, select the Unsupported Features option, and change its setting from Ignore to Rasterize.

5. Now when you hit OK, the movie takes a lot longer to render. This is because whenever it comes across an effect not available in Flash, it rasterizes it. In other words, it renders a series of still images of that effect, and embeds them into the Flash file.

6. Playback is now perfect. The moving text has been reproduced with bitmaps, and the viewer is none the wiser. Unfortunately, as we've mentioned, there is a cost. Our little animation is now about 1mb in size, and that's unacceptable for a graphic on a web page.

7. We're going to need to compromise. After Effects Text filters are the first things to go. Go into Photoshop (or Photoshop Elements), and create a single graphic of the text. Then import this into After Effects using the replace footage function. Now you can junk the Text filter.

8. Our text can still be moved around in the same way as before, and it looks identical - only now, it's just a graphic, not a filter. It doesn't need to be rasterized, and will take up far less bandwidth.

9. Before we re-render, there's one more thing we can do. Our graphic has a couple of filters applied to it. They may look nice, especially on the TV version, but we have to think very carefully about every effect on the Web. Is it really worth the extra time people will spend downloading the rasterized version? Probably not. Let's junk the filter.

10. Now, when we produce the SWF file, our final Flash animation is much smaller.

Reducing the file size of a Flash animation is a real art, and if you produce a lot of them, you'll learn just how to squeeze the most from very small animations. However, it's unfortunately not a skill After Effects can help you with very much. There's currently no way to find out, without rendering, how big your Flash animation files will be, and what effect your cutting down on filters and effects is having. Perhaps in After Effects 6...

And finally...

By now, you should be able to render out a project, or a series of projects in any format you like. You should be familiar with the different formats After Effects offers, and be able to decide which are appropriate to your projects. You should be able to create presets for the Render Queue, and know how to render test versions of your compositions at reduced quality.

In the final chapter you will learn how to manage all the skills you've picked up in the earlier chapters in order to efficiently complete your projects.

9 Managing Projects

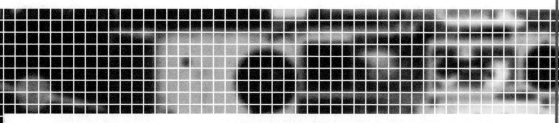

By now you should have a pretty solid understanding of After Effects. You're ready to put it, and your own imagination, to good use. However, before you rush into your own project, it's a good idea to spend a bit of time learning how best to structure your development process. By managing your project properly you can avoid potential pitfalls, and wasted time.

Project lifecycle

Over the course of the following chapter, we'll be looking more closely at how to build layers within a composition. Preparation is the key to success here, as it is always useful to define any potential pitfalls before engaging with After Effects.

The diagram opposite indicates the workflow that can often be taken to bring a project to fruition.

INTERPRET SCRIPT

STORYBOARD

DESIGN WORK

BREAKDOWN ELEMENTS
INTO LAYERS

DETERMINE TOOLS TO USE
SOFTWARE AND HARDWARE

PREPARE COMPUTER
FOR WORKFLOW

CREATE ELEMENTS IN
2D, 3D & VIDEO
EDITING PACKAGE

BRING COMPONENTS
INTO AFTER EFFECTS

RENDER

ADD TO DISTRIBUTION MEDIUM

Interpret the script

Usually the first step is to interpret the script to get an idea of what is being requested of you and your team, if you have one. The best method for interpreting a script is to break the scene you'll be working on into the various shots. Hopefully this will be looked at during pre-production, so that the entire team from production design, cinematography, sound, editing and graphics will get an opportunity to air their views on the best method to tackle the task at hand. Of course, on a lower budget you may find that you are all of these departments yourself but you should make sure that you have a good discussion and spend time with the producer and client to work out the design of the sequence.

Storyboard

Once this has been worked out, a storyboard can be sketched out and a further meeting held to evaluate whether the storyboard conveys the message desired and promotes the development of the storyline. What is also important at this point is that the client or producer signs off each stage of negotiation so that you don't find yourself undertaking unnecessary work, which the client feels they shouldn't have to pay for. At this stage of the production the only costs are your time sketching out ideas until the client has approved them and signed them off.

Design work

With the storyboard approved and signed off, the next task is to design the individual shots in greater detail. This may include illustrating the objects seen in the scene. For example, later on we will be looking at creating a 3D animated copper clock. The illustration may include a colored pencil sketch of how the clock should look, and how its surface may reflect it surroundings. An idea for the background images should be formed. For the example with the 3D clock, live-action footage will be used. The clock itself is to be based on an alarm clock, which has long since stopped working but has an interesting shape and form.

Breakdown into layers

By this point you have a good design laid out, and you need to start thinking about the technical implications of implementing this design. Each layer in the project is likely to be produced in a different way, with varying technical implications. So it's a good idea now to try and split the project up into layers.

In our project, the image of the clock face can be brought to life by animating the image so that the hands rotate. At this stage, the idea of using a star field behind some clouds is also considered. As you can see, this process gradually helps us to break down the components of the images into layers. We can begin to decide what approach we could take to produce the images and determine the software and hardware we will need to use to accomplish this.

Determine the tools to use

With regards to the background we will need to use either time-lapse photography with a film camera, or we could use a digital video camera recording ten minutes of cloud moving and then use a non-linear editing package to speed the images up. The choice is usually determined by cost. To shoot film would cost the hire of a camera, probably 16mm at a cost of nearly $600 a day plus a camera operator at $375 a day, film stock, processing and transfer to video for editing $375 per 400ft of film. A total cost of $1350. To shoot on digital video, say miniDV. Well, the camera, a CanonXL-1, can cost $120 a day, camera operator at $375 a day, tape stock $7.50 and editing with a non-linear editing package on my desktop $52.50 per hour. Total cost using digital video $581.25. So if the determining fact were based on cost then the background shot would be produced on digital video. If however, aesthetic ideals are required and the producer has the money then perhaps film would be used. The point here is that you will need to determine how best to provide the necessary images to accomplish the finished composition and this is one way to determine which approach to take.

Following this hardware discussion we need to determine which software programs should be used to create the 3D animation and how much time will be necessary to create the clock. By creating an illustration of the clock first and getting the producer or client to sign it off then the time spent using the 3D program is reduced, as you will already be fully confident that the design will be used once it is finished. Don't be tempted to rush into using the 3D package before the client is happy with the design, as again, you will find yourself producing work which the client will not want to pay for.

At some point, Photoshop or an equivalent image editing package will usually be used either to tidy up a scanned image, or to resize and shape photographs. For the tutorial explored later Photoshop Elements, a cut down (and cheaper) version of Photoshop, is used to create layers for the clock face and hands. This will then be taken into After Effects to animate the hands as a composition file. The star field used for the tutorial is hand-drawn, scanned, and then further manipulated in Photoshop Elements to simulate the intensity of the stars based on a star chart.

So far, we can determine that there will eventually be four main layers within the final composition. These will include the background star field drawing, the sped up cloud video clip, the animated clock face based on a single image broken down into layers in Photoshop Elements, and a 3D animated clock.

Prepare your computer for the workflow

An essential aspect of preparing to begin working with After Effects and the various media that will be used is to prepare your computer. Video production, animation and graphics can all take up a lot of space on your hard drives. Therefore, space needs to be allocated on the hard drive so that you will be able to tackle the project without having to worry about where to put everything. After each job, you should either back up the entire project onto CD-ROM or go through all the relevant files and decide if everything would actually be needed if the job was ever to be resurrected. In many cases once the material has been backed up on to CD-ROM or even DVD-ROM you may find that you have room for many gigabytes of material. However, you're still not ready to begin working. Hard drives can become fragmented if a lot of material has been stored and deleted on a continuous basis. This can slow down the computer and at times even cause it to crash. To help the system run more smoothly, it is a good idea to defrag the hard drives.

Defragging

To get an idea of how a hard drive becomes fragmented, imagine a sheet of graph paper. Each block is filled with part of a file. With a new computer, the files can be added continuously one after the other, until the system is full. At this point some files may become redundant and can be deleted. There maybe several files to delete, unless you are simply deleting the last files added, this will leave gaps between the remaining files. When a new file is saved it will fill up the gaps that are available around the existing files, breaking the new file into fragments.

If this process is continued over a period of time the whole hard drive can be full of files that are broken up into fragments. This means that when trying to read a file, the head reading the hard drive has to physically move all over the disc picking up the various parts of a specific file, which wastes a lot of time. Defragmenting the hard drive reorders the files so that the various number of blocks that make up the file are contained together.

In the diagram below, the top image shows a visual interpretation of a hard drive which is not fragmented. Each gray area represents a separate file with each segment blocked together. Files can be easily processed. In the lower image, each file is broken up because many files have been created and deleted over and over, making it harder for the processor to locate each segment. If this continues then files can become corrupted due to the fact the processor cannot find all of the segments or blocks that make up the file.

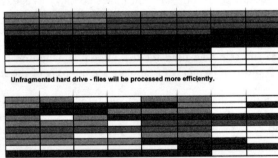

Unfragmented hard drive - files will be processed more efficiently.

Fragmented hard drive - will be inefficient making the processor work harder.

Each operating system has tools which will allow you to defrag your computer. You should find some very easy to follow information on this in the operating system's Help file.

Filing

At this point, a folder should be created on the hard drive for all the components to be kept in. Inside this folder, it is a good idea to create a sub-folder for all of the PICT files that will be generated by the 3D animation package. A second sub-folder can be created to hold any Photoshop images created. A third sub-folder should be created to contain test renders, and a fourth sub-folder for master renders.

In the first folder, you can also store the After Effects project file. By organizing the folders at this point you will be able to easily locate and access material once you are in After Effects. It is a good idea to have the main folder for the project in the sub-directory of the hard drive you intend to use, and to place all other folders into a second folder to limit the number of folders you need to access to find your material.

Create the required elements and bring them into A E

The next stage in the process is to create all of the components using the relevant software packages, and save the images within the project folder and sub-folders as necessary. Once these components have been created, they can then be imported into After Effects and easily accessed via the folders they are contained within.

Render and distribute

The final stage of the process is rendering and adding the material to the appropriate distribution medium; inserting the material into a non-linear editing program as part of an edited sequence, uploading an internet streaming file for a web page or even encoding the rendered animation so it can be included on a DVD package.

From here we will take a more in-depth look at managing this process, by working through an example After Effects project.

The process in practice

As we saw earlier, a sequence has to be determined and storyboarded from a script. With a pencil, I sketched out a series of cube shaped clocks with different perspectives. This developed into the idea of having the clock rotate as it moved towards the camera view. The backdrop to the clock had been inspired by a short film I had seen shot on Super 8mm. In this film, there were fast moving clouds, which appear to have been shot in daylight, but had stars breaking through the bluish black sky. This shot had intrigued me and I felt it would be a good challenge to recreate it in After Effects.

Clocks spinning thru time.
Fast moving clouds with stars
in the background.
1. Create clocks in 3D.
2. Use live-action clouds.
3. Create stars in 3D.
4. Create clock face in Photoshop.
5. Create clock hands in Photoshop.

When it comes to designing images I find it quite useful to be aware of what is around me, whether it's bits of old material, broken mechanical objects, the sky, or the woods and mountain close by. Often my wife and I would go for long walks up the mountain and when I come home I find I am full of ideas, and often problems I may have had trying to design something will have been solved due to the visual impact of what I have seen. Another source of inspiration are films seen at the cinema or on television, but it's often the simplest things that generate the greatest results. Initially, I had remembered that we had a rectangular shaped brass clock but was unable to find it in the cupboards. What I did find was an old copper clock, which had a more interesting shape. Not only that, I realized that I could use the image of the clock face and, with a little bit of work in Photoshop Elements, could create the layers for the interestingly shaped hands to be animated in After Effects.

The biggest drawback with the clock though, was that it wasn't going to be easy to animate it through space. So the obvious solution was to recreate the shape of the clock as an object in a 3D animation and modeling package.

For the sky shot, all I needed was a day with no rain, plenty of sun and some reasonably quick moving clouds, which I could speed up even more using a non-linear editing package or After Effects. When the day arrived, I simply locked off a Canon XL-1 miniDV camcorder on a tripod, pointed it towards the heavens, and recorded fifteen minutes worth of tape. To speed the sequence up, it was necessary to capture the entire fifteen minutes, which required at least four gigabytes of hard drive space to contain at full DV quality. This is one of the reasons why it is essential to prepare your hardware in advance of every project; so that you know you will be able to complete the task without having to lose valuable material or precious time. For the purpose of the following tutorial you will find a file called `Cloudx2002.mov` on the CD-ROM.

To create the star field, I located a star chart in a child's encyclopedia to use as my main source for creating the star field image.

By this stage, it had been determined that four layers would be required to create the composition. The base layer would consist of the image created from using the star chart, the third layer would require video footage of clouds, the second layer would be created from a still image of the clock face and the top layer would be created using a 3D animation package to recreate the copper clock.

The next step is to create the images necessary for compositing in After Effects. We will begin by looking at building the clock in a 3D animation package.

Preparing material using a 3D animation package

As we saw in **Chapters 3** and **4**, by using other software programs, we can produce image sequences that After Effects will recognize and play back as though they were a single movie file. By creating an image sequence in another program, you can use the characteristics of that program to help in the processes of building a composition in After Effects. One such characteristic, common to 3D animation packages, is the use of alpha channels. Many movie type files are unable to use alpha channels, which means that color keys have to be used so that the background can be cut out. And as we saw in **Chapter 4**, if the color is not constant, trying to cut it out can be quite difficult. The use of an alpha channel in a series of images makes this process far easier.

As the 3D clock for our final composition will need to fly through the air (or rather, in front of a background), we need to render our clock image with alpha channels. So we decide to use the 3D animation package Pixels3D to create the brass clock.

The body consisted of a shallow cylinder with both ends closed to form a solid shape. The two alarm bells comprised of creating one hemisphere, which was then duplicated. Each bell was then positioned to make the clock look a little like a certain cartoon mouse. The hammer was made from two further cylinders, as were the two legs. By extruding a spline shape and adding a thin cylinder I create the two wing key-winders. To link the object to the body, each object was selected individually before selecting the body shape, then using a link command the body became the parent to all the other child elements. This is achieved differently in different 3D programs. Some simple methods include using an object manager and dragging the child object over the parent object to link them together. You will need to understand your own 3D program to see which method it uses. Unfortunately, it is beyond the scope of this chapter to explore the different methods used in 3D animation packages to link objects.

The animation of the clock consisted of two elements. The first involved rotating one of the winders on the back of the clock, and the second involved creating a path for the camera to travel along in the shape of a shallow spiral to give the impression of the clock spinning from the background into the foreground.

Finally, I created a copper color to use as a highly reflective texturemap. A still image was taken from the fast moving cloud movie to be used as an environment map giving the impression of what was being reflected on the shiny surface of the clock. This would become visible only in the final rendered image.

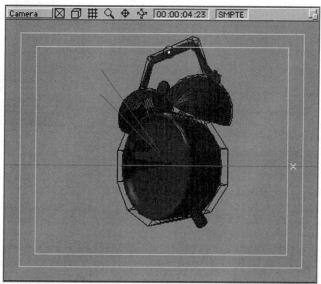

The animation was then rendered out as a PICT file sequence.

Although the images of the clock are provided on the CD-ROM, if you have a favorite 3D modeling and animation package, try to build your own version of the rotating clock to use later in the After Effects exercise. I used a brass clock, but if you have a different type of clock, why not try to build that?

Preparing material for a pre-composed file

The next stage is to produce an image that would represent the clock's face and the hands. The old copper clock that the 3D model was based on also had a great face, which I thought would work very well in this project. The approach I took to capture the image of the clock face is a little bit unusual, but a useful technique to use.

I basically placed the alarm clock face down in my scanner, and hit the preview button to check the clock looked okay. Unfortunately, there isn't a setting in the software for 'clock bunged into scanner' so I used the glossy photograph setting instead. I selected Photoshop Elements as the destination software.

The next step was to make sure the image was scanned in color, and set the dpi to 150. All I needed to do once the image was opened in Photoshop Elements was to adjust the Contrast slider in the Brightness/Contrast option to make the face look whiter, and my clock face was done!

If you produced your own 3D clock, scan your own clock face to use in the composition. Alternatively, you can find the clock face I used on the CD.

The next phase of our preparation stage is to cut out the clock face in Photoshop Elements, then separate the four hands into different layers. If you don't use Photoshop, you can open the finished article from the CD and refer to step 16 below, but it would be worth reading through the tutorial anyway, so you can see how it was put together.

Building layers in Photoshop Elements

1. First of all, choose the Crop tool from the Tool palette, and select and crop a square area just a little larger than the clock face.

2. Select the clock face using the Circular Select tool, and choose Layer > New > Background From Layer from the menu to convert the image into a layer.

3. Invert the selection by choosing Select > Inverse from the menu. Then press the BACKSPACE key to delete the selected part of the image, leaving the clock face and a transparent background. This will later act as an alpha channel when it is saved as a PSD (Photoshop) file.

The next stage is to cut out each hand and place them individually into separate layers.

4. With Magnetic Lasso used as the selection tool, begin creating a mask of the hour hand.

5. Once you have made the selection, choose Edit > Copy, then Edit > Paste from the menu to create a new layer. Repeat this process until each hand has its own layer.

6. Save the image as a Photoshop PSD file so that the layers are retained. This also allows you to keep the TIF file version that was originally scanned which can be reopened to use the Rubber Stamp tool for any adjustments that may be need for each of the hand layers in the PSD file.

7. Next, click the background layer eye icon in the Layers menu to hide the background. This leaves just the four hands visible. These can then be checked to make sure that all the detail is included. If it's not, then the TIF file can be used, with the Clone Stamp tool to add the missing detail to the PSD file. To achieve this:

   1. First make sure the two files are open in Photoshop, and select the Clone Stamp Tool from the Tool palette.

   2. Place the mouse cursor over the area of the image you wish to clone from, in this case the TIF file while holding down the ALT key.

   3. Then once you are happy that the correct area is selected, click and hold the mouse button and let go of the ALT button.

   4. Move the cursor to the area of the PSD image that you wish to change, making sure that the correct layer is chosen.

   5. By holding down the mouse button and dragging the mouse, a replica of the TIF image, the size and shape of the brush being used, is drawn onto the PSD image.

8. Once the hands are complete, remove the original hands in the background image. To do this, select the layer containing the full face in the Layers window. Make sure that the brush icon is only visible on the clock face layer, and deselect the eye icon in the layers containing each hand to hide these layers.

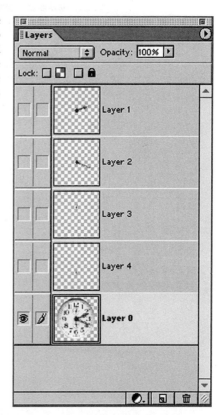

9. Now we can remove the hands on the clock face using the Clone Stamp Tool.

Once the hands are removed, the only other changes we need to make to this clock face are to rebuild the 4, and modify the second-hand time-markers just below the center of the face.

10. To reconstruct the second-hand time-markers, select five seconds either side of the 30 second mark, and copy and paste them to create a new layer, layer 5.

11. Hide the clock face layer so that only the new layer showing the pasted ten seconds marks is visible. Rotate this image 180°, then select Edit > Cut. The layer is now empty and can be dragged to the bin on the Layer window.

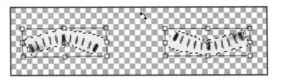

12. Select the clock face layer and click the eye icon so it is visible. Then choose File > From Clipboard from the menu to create a new file containing the ten second marker cut from Layer 5.

13. Use the Clone Stamp Tool from this file, with a brush size of about three, to rebuild the second-hand time-markers around the 60-second marker point. You can 'rubber-stamp' some color from the face of the clock to fine-tune the detail between the markers.

14. Use the Clone Stamp Tool once more to repair the figure 4 on the clock face, by cloning one of the figure 1s from number 11. You will notice that here, the figure 1 is damaged: that's okay – it adds character!

15. To tidy things up around the edges, use some color from around the 4. Also, the shading of the 4 itself can be used to blend the slightly lighter gray of the 1 used for the rebuild.

At this point, the face of the clock should be made up of the clock face image with no hands and a transparent background, plus four additional layers, one each for each hand.

The clock face is now ready to be imported into After Effects as a Photoshop composition.

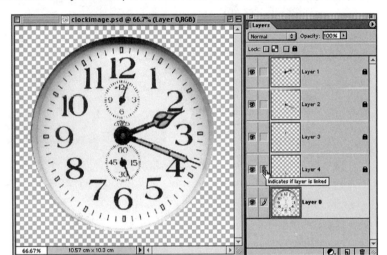

16. Save this image as `clockimage.psd` in a folder created on your hard drive. Use this folder to store all the elements needed to build the After Effects compositions, and transfer the necessary files from the CD to this folder so that you can undertake the following series of exercises. These include:

    ■ the folder `Rendered Clock`, containing all the PICT images of the 3D clock;

    ■ `clockimage.psd`, containing all the layers which build up the clock face;

    ■ `Cloudx2002.mov`, which is the background cloud movie;

    ■ and `nightsky.psd`, which is the star field drawing.

Organizing media and preparing After Effects to begin compositing

All the elements are ready to be imported into After Effects, so the next step is to create a new project, save the file, and create a new composition.

Assembling the elements in After Effects

1. Open After Effects and save the project as `Clock Project.aep`. Then create a new composition.

2. In the Composition Settings window, change the name of the composition to Spinning Clock; set the preset to PAL D1/DV, 720 x 576 (the format the material was shot in), and change the duration to '0:00:05:00'. Click OK.

3. Next, we need to import the footage. Import the clockimage.psd file as a composition so that we can work with it in After Effects.

4. Import the rendered images from the 3D package as a PICT sequence. In the Interpret Footage window, choose either Straight – Unmatted or Premultiplied – Matted With Color, then click OK. Either of these two choices will allow you to use the alpha channel created during the rendering of the 3D clock. If Ignore is selected the PICT sequence will have no alpha channel and you'll need to use a Luma Key filter to see the lower layers in the composition. Using the alpha channel is a cleaner and more effective way to make the 3D clock layer background transparent.

5. Import the Cloudx2002.mov file we used in **Chapter 6** as a footage file.

6. By clicking on the clockimage.psd folder, we are able to see the five layers that had been created in Photoshop Elements.

Making the clock hands move

The next section deals with building the clock face from the Photoshop file we imported as a composition. In it, we're going to use **expressions** as an alternative to using multiple keyframes to animate the clock hands.

Using expressions in After Effects

Expressions can be created in After Effects using JavaScript 1.2, which allows a great latitude in developing sophisticated effects and motion paths (using mathematical functions instead of keyframes to define property values for masks, effects and transforms). But don't worry if you're not keen on creating programming language scripts, because expressions can also be defined using the library provided in After Effects, once the expression has been added to a layer. Yet another alternative is to use the Pick-whip tool, whereby two properties can be connected together and some simple values can be given to the automatic expressions added to the Expression Field in the timeline.

The After Effects manual has a complete chapter exploring expressions, which is worth looking at if you want to dive further into this wonderful wonderland. And if you really want to go for it, it will be worth consulting a JavaScript reference guide, such as Beginning JavaScript by Paul Wilton or Instant JavaScript by Nigel McFarlane , published by Wrox Press (www.wrox.com)

Using expressions to animate the clock hands

1. Create a new composition and name it Clock Express. Keep the settings we used in the previous composition.

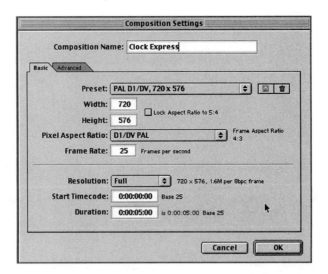

2. The new composition appears in the Project window. The clockimage.psd folder contains the five Photoshop Element layers, which make up the clockimage.psd composition used earlier. Click on the triangle beside the folder to reveal the files.

3. Select all five layer files and drag them into the Composition window.

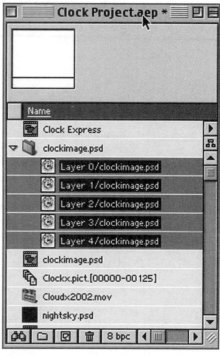

4. When they appear in the Composition window, the clock face is in Layer 1 of the timeline, and is named Layer 0/clockimage.psd. Drag this file down to Layer 5.

5. Reposition the hands into their normal place on the clock face. You may want to turn the grid on to make the exact positioning of the hands more precise.

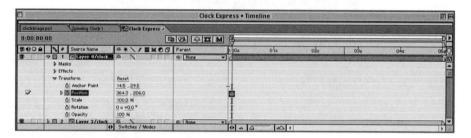

To show time passing in the final composition, the hands of the clock need to turn around. Over our five second timeline, the hour clock needs to move from one number to the next, the minute hand needs to rotate around the clock face one full rotation, and the second hand needs to rotate 60 times.

If you select Layer 1 in the timeline this will activate the layer in the Composition window, where a rectangular shape appears, made up of eight layer handles, one in each corner and one between each of the corner handles. These eight layer handles indicate the size of the layer in relation to the Composition window. If the layer is larger than the Composition window then a white rectangular box connects each of the handles. If the layer is smaller than the Composition window then only the eight handles are visible. By double clicking within the eight handles for Layer 1, the Layer window opens and you will see that the hour hand is not using a frame size that fills the Composition window.

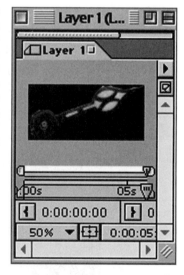

If we were to attempt to rotate the hour hand as it currently is, the rotation axis will fall at the center of Layer 1 and not around the rotation axis of the hand, which is towards the lower left of Layer 1. The hand is positioned correctly within the face of the clock and needs to rotate around the center axis of the clock face. To do this, we need to add an adjustment layer, and make it a parent of the hour hand. Next, we add two adjustment layers to assign the minute and second hands a parent.

An adjustment layer is a transparent layer that can have effects applied to it in the same way as any other layer. Adjustment layer enable effects to exist independently. For example, if a blur effect is required, to appear across the whole of a composition, instead of adding the blur to every single layer, by adding the blur to a single adjustment layer, each layer below the adjustment layer appears blurred. Our purpose for using the adjustment layer is to enable the hour and minute hands to rotate independently around the axis of the clock face instead of the layer that contains them. This is achieved by making a separate adjustment layer the parent for each of the hands. The second hand is offset below the axis of the clock face requiring the adjustment layer assigned as its parent to be offset so that its central axis point is aligned to the point where the second hand's axis point should be, as opposed to the axis point of the layer containing the second hand.

6. First, Layer 1 containing the hour hand is selected and an adjustable layer is added by choosing Layer > New > Adjustment Layer. Adjustment Layer 1 appears above Layer 1 in the timeline. Make sure that the center of this layer is positioned at the center of the clock, where the hand should rotate about.

7. To make Adjustment Layer 1 the parent of Layer 1, we go to the Parent panel of the timeline, click on Layer 1 parent menu, and select Adjustment Layer 1.

8. Next, add an adjustment layer to the minute and second hand, in the same way you just did for the hour hand.

9. Layer 4/clockimage.psd is the timer hand for setting the alarm, so doesn't need to be animated. Move this to Layer 7, just above the clock face. Each of the adjustment layers can then be positioned just above each of the hand layers.

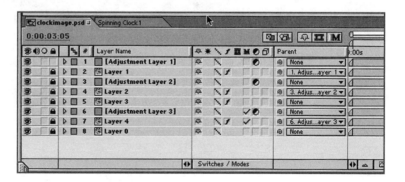

10. The hour and minute hands rotate around the center of the Composition window, so when they're assigned to their respective parent adjustment layers, they'll rotate correctly. However, the second hand is offset below the center of the frame. Therefore, Adjustment Layer 3, which will become the parent for the second hand, needs to be repositioned so that its center matches the point where the second hand needs to rotate from.

The hands of the clock still look flat, so we need to add some depth. This will be achieved by adding a drop shadow to each hand.

11. Check that the timeline marker is set at the first frame, and then select Layer 2. Choose Effect > Perspective > Drop Shadow from the menu.

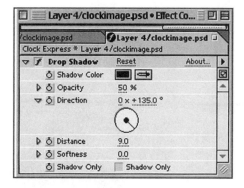

12. In the Effect Controls palette, set Distance to 9.0, then click on the stopwatch. This provides a shadow that has a depth similar to the edge of the clock.

13. Repeat this process for Layer 4, Layer 6, and Layer 7.

14. Layer 5 contains the adjustment layer associated with the Hour Hand. At the First Frame, click the stopwatch for the Rotation transform to add a keyframe to the timeline, and set the value at 0 x +0.00.

15. Then move the timeline marker to the end of the timeline. The hour hand is pointing to roughly the 12 minute marker, just after the figure 2. To give the impression that an hour has passed, the hand needs to rotate 30 degrees since there are 360 degrees in a full circle and 360/12 = 30. To do this, set the Rotation transform to 0 x +30.00.

> *Remember, at this point we are dealing with the hour hand so when sixty minutes have passed the hand only travels from one number on the clock face to the next. Also, the minute hand is set just after the seventeen-minute mark. An hour later the minute hand should rotate 360 degrees,, to rest at the same position.*

16. Once again, set the timeline marker to the first frame. In Layer 3, which contains Adjustment Layer 2, select the Rotation transform.

17. Next, choose Animation > Add Expression from the menu. This will add a  switch between the stopwatch and the Rotation transform, the value will turn red, three expression switches appear, and the Expression field will appear in the timeline with the word rotation. You've now created an expression for the Rotation transform. At the moment it doesn't do anything, so now you'll need to link the expression to another layer so that it performs a function or operation. What we'll do next is link the expression in Adjustment Layer 2 to the rotation values of Adjustment Layer 1.

> *The switch enables you to turn the expression on or off as you need. When the switch is off then the icon changes to *

18. Now expand the Timeline window so that both the Transform lists for Adjustment Layer 1, parent to the hour hand, and Adjustment Layer 2, parent to the minute hand, are visible. Drag the pick-whip from the rotation expression of Adjustment Layer 2 to the Rotation transform of Adjustment Layer 1.

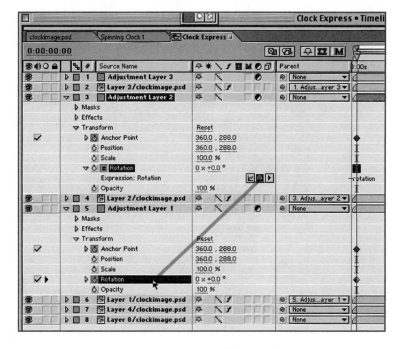

In the expression field in Adjustment Layer 2 the following expression is added:

```
this_comp.layer("Adjustment Layer 1").rotation
```

The expression now indicates that Adjustment Layer 2 will rotate in the same way as Adjustment Layer 1.

19. At this point, both the hour and minute hands will rotate together. In reality, though, the minute hand rotates around the clock face twelve times faster than the hour hand. To implement this, we need to modify the expression to:

```
this_comp.layer("Adjustment Layer 1").rotation *12
```

20. The next step is to add an expression to Adjustment Layer 3 so the second hand rotates sixty times faster than the minute hand. To do this, select the Rotation transform for Adjustment Layer 3 and choose Animation > Add Expression from the menu.

21. The expression once more needs to be modified so that it reads as follows:

```
this_comp.layer("Adjustment Layer 1").rotation *60
```

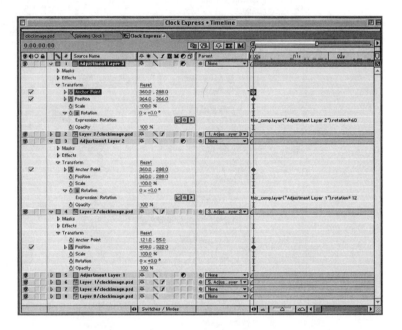

> *Note: In order for this to work the layers have to be positioned correctly. If one of the layers is even only slightly off center the hands may not appear to turn by the amount you expect them to. However, we aren't clock makers, and the hands of the clock won't even be seen through most of this footage, so don't worry about being too precise. As long as it gives the illusion of a working clock you're doing your job.*

Well done!! We now have a clock with a whirring clock face that you have generated using expressions. As you can see, expressions can be very powerful things, and although they may seem a little daunting if you aren't used to scripting or this kind of mathematics, they're really just simple commands to modify the effects After Effects creates. And the jargon of expressions is really no more complicated than the jargon of digital film making: once you get familiar with the phrases, you don't even notice you're using them!

Building the final composition

So far, we've been looking at how we can organize the development of images so that they can be used efficiently and simply in After Effects. By this stage, we should have three elements, which will be used to build the final composition.

- One of these elements was created in a 3D animation package to produce an image sequence of stills.

- Recycling material can be very useful – the live-action video of the fast moving clouds was previously used in **Chapter 6** .

- A pre-composed element was created in Photoshop Elements from a scan of an actual clock. The image of the clock was split into layers consisting of a layer for each hand and one for the clock face. This Photoshop image was then imported into After Effects as a composition file and worked on to animate the hands of the clock face by adding adjustment layers, which became the parents for each hand individually. By the time the clock face composition was completed, there were eight layers in its construction.

Using the clock face composition within the final composition simplifies the construction, and makes navigation of the timeline that bit easier.

Adding clips to the Spinning Clock composition

It's now time to bring everything together into one composition. This will consist of four layers. The base layer, or lowest layer, will contain the star field, which will require rotation. Above this will be the fast moving cloud clip. A TrkMat will be used so that the stars can cut through the blue sky, and then be manipulated so that the image is adjusted to give the impression of changing from day to night. The clock face with moving hands will be placed in the second layer so that as the 3D clock moves, the rim of the clock will obscure parts of the clock face at various times. The clock face layer will need rescaling so that it can fit into the mask shape cut out of the 3D animated clock in the top. The clock face will also need to be adjusted in 3D space so that it matches the movement of the 3D clock as it travels from the background to the foreground in the shot.

Earlier on, we created a composition called Spinning Clock. This is the composition that will be used to build the final sequence.

1. Drag Cloudx2002.mov from the Project window on to the Composition window. Resize it to crop out the two black edges down the side of the image, and the roof top that's intruding from the lower right-hand corner.

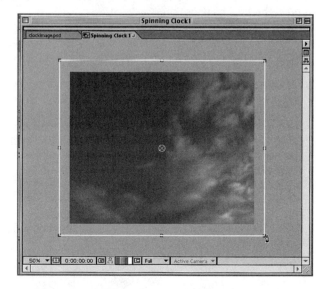

2. The second layer to be added is the 3D animation of the clock contained in the file Clockx.pict.[00000-00125]. The 00000-00125 indicates that there are 125 frames in the animation. Drag this file from the Project window onto the Composition window.

3. The third layer to be added is the clock face animation contained in the composition clockimage.psd. There's a folder with the same name, which contains the five Photoshop layers created in Photoshop Elements earlier. In the Switches panel, click on the 3D Layer switch so that the clock face can be moved using three-dimensional co-ordinates.

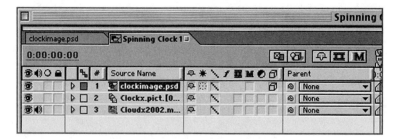

To continue, we need to add a traveling matte to the 3D clock animation in Layer 2 so that the clock face can occasionally be obscured by the rim of the 3D clock as it rotates. But first, the clock face needs to be hidden from view so the mask can be created.

Adding a traveling matte to the 3D animated clock

1. Click the eye icon for Layer 1 to hide the clock face. The clock face will disappear in the Composition window, revealing the 3D clock. We can now begin adding the initial mask by double-clicking on the Composition window. This opens the Layer window for clockx.pict.[00000-00125].

2. Move the timeline marker in the Layer window so that where the clock face would be forms a full circle facing you, this should be at somewhere just under 2.5 seconds. Then set the resolution to 200%.

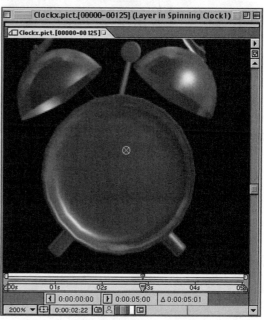

3. Using the Pen tool, create a rough mask around the clock face with six control points. Then fine-tune the shape so that it matches the circumference of the clock face.

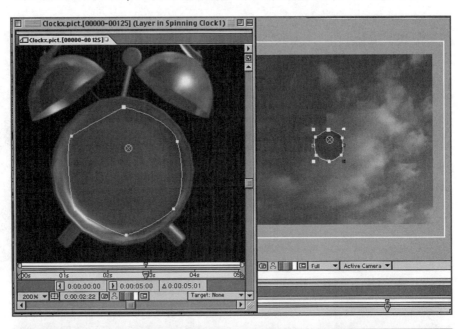

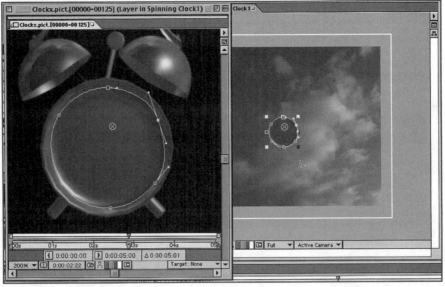

4. In the Composition window, the mask has now cut out the face of the clock, but has hidden the clock bells and body. This needs to be reversed so that the mask cuts out a shape where the face should be, and we can insert the pre-composed clock face from Layer 1 in its place. To reverse the mask, click the triangle in Layer 2 to drop down the Mask, Effects, and Transform list. Then click the triangle beside Mask in Layer 2 to reveal Mask 1. In the switches panel, select Inverted. Now, the face is cut out and the body of the 3D clock appears in the Composition window.

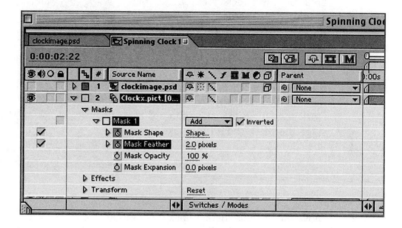

5. Click on the triangle beside Mask 1, to reveal the mask features. Click the stopwatches for Mask Shape and Mask Feather to add keyframes into the timeline. We need to add these keyframes so we can change their values in frames either side of the current keyframe. Set Mask Feather to 2.0 pixels.

6. Next, select the Layer window once more. Click the Previous Frame button to move the timeline marker back a few frames. Watch for any big changes in the position of the clock when it begins to move back and turn. When you need to, change the mask so that it fits the area of the clock face at its new position. Each time you change the mask, move the timeline marker forwards to check that the mask morphs in a manner that tracks the changes exactly. Here you have your traveling matte. Carry on amending the mask as you rotate the clock until the clock face is no longer visible. By this stage the mask should look like a thin line.

7. Move the timeline marker back one more frame. Select the whole mask for that frame, and drag it to the lower edge of the Layer window frame. This will prevent any of the clock face that is replacing the copper, featureless face from accidentally being revealed too soon.

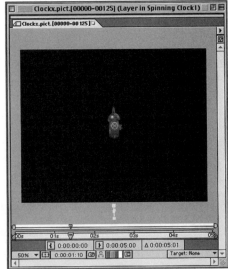

8. Now place the timeline marker at the last keyframe in the timeline, and edit the mask as the clock moves closer to the camera view.

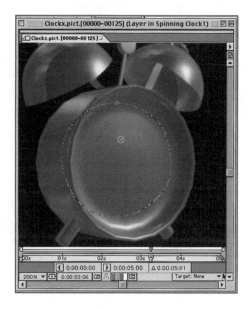

9. Again, once the copper clock face is no longer visible, add a keyframe, move the timeline maker on one more frame, then drag the entire mask to the lower edge of the frame.

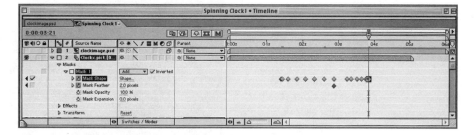

10. The mask is now complete. To ensure there are no accidental changes to it, lock the layer by switching on the padlock in the Audio/Video Features panel of the Timeline window.

We have now come to the part where we need to animate the clock face so that it matches the hole left by the traveling matte.

Adding the clock face

1. Position the timeline marker over the keyframe at the center of the movement of the clock, at the same place the keyframe was added for the Mask Feather in Layer 2.

2. Switch on the eye icon so that the Photoshop clock face in Layer 1 is revealed. Earlier, we made Layer 1 into a 3D layer, so when the layer is selected, the 3D controls become visible. Using the Z control, push the clock face back into the picture, scaling the image so that it is the same size as the 3D clock face.

3. Set the Composition window to 200% so that the animation can be easily manipulated. Then, using the Y and X controls, position the clock face into the 3D clock. The image

is not an exact circle, so you'll need to reduce the height of the layer so that it fits more comfortably.

4. Once the clock face is in position, click the stopwatches for all of the Transforms for Layer 1 to add keyframes into the timeline.

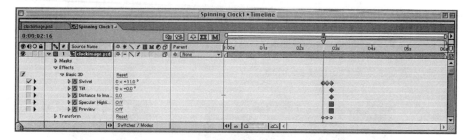

5. On the same frame, apply a Basic 3D effect to allow the clock face to be swiveled as the 3D clock turns. Do this by choosing Effect > Perspective > Basic 3D from the menu.

6. Now move the timeline marker, frame by frame, towards the head of the timeline, mid way between the center of the move and the position where the 3D clock is 90 degrees to the view in the Composition window. As with the creation of the traveling matte, adjust the clock face using a combination of the Swivel control in the Effect Controls palette and the 3D layer controls to fit it into the clock as it moves back to its first position in the timeline.

7. Next, click the triangle beside Position to enable the Speed graph to become visible. Use the control points to pull the clock face into its correct position.

8. Once Layer 1, with clockimage.psd, reaches a Swivel of 0 x +90.00 it is no longer visible. Therefore, no more keyframes need to be added to earlier frames in the sequence, and the timeline marker now needs to be positioned to the point where the clock is face on once more.

9. Move the timeline marker using the Next Frame button. Again, adjust the clock face in using a combination of the Swivel control and the 3D layer controls so that it's set in the correct position.

10. Continue to adjust the clock face by moving the timeline marker forwards until the Swivel control reads 0 x –90.00. Add a final keyframe at this point. Once again, there is no further need to animate the clock face, as it's no longer visible.

11. Click the triangle beside Position to enable the Speed graph to become visible, and use the controls points to pull the clock face into its correct position.

12. To complete the composition, Layer 1, containing pre-composed layer clockimage.psd, needs to be sandwiched between Layer 2 and Layer 3. To do this, select Layer 1 and drag it between the two lower layers, so the thick black line appears between them. Release the mouse, the thick black line disappears, and clockimage.psd becomes Layer 2. The purpose behind moving this layer is to ensure that the clock face is partially hidden behind the rim of the 3D clock as it slowly spins round from left to right.

The star field

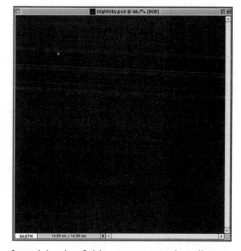

In the initial drawing for the composition, I envisaged a star field in the background. I decided to use a pencil to map out the star field on paper first. Using a child's encyclopedia book, I found a star map. I wanted to use the North Star as the center point, so that I could rotate the stars, as another method of portraying time passing, to complement the clock.

The piece of paper, with dots showing the constellation, was scanned into Photoshop Elements and inverted to create a dark sky with white dots. The information in the book gave an idea of how far away the stars were by providing four different marks to indicate distances. I used this technique to give my stars different strengths.

The image `nightsky.psd` of the star field can be found in the folder you created earlier to transfer the files from the CD-ROM, but if you have access to a scanner, why not create your own star map? Find a star chart and then create a star field using a pencil and some paper. Scan the image into the computer and invert the image so that the pencil dots become white and the white paper becomes black. Save the image as `nightsky2.psd` in the folder on your hard drive with the rest of the files used for this chapter.

Using the star field in After Effects

1. Import `nightsky.psd` into After Effects. Drag the file from the Project window, into the Composition window.

2. At this point, nightsky.psd is in Layer 1, obscuring all the other elements. So move the file to below Cloudx2002.mov.

3. Then, click all the padlocks to deactivate them, and change the Switches/Modes panel from Switches to Modes by clicking on Switches/Modes at the lower edge of the Switches panel.

4. Set Layer 3, which contains Cloudx2002.mov to Exclusion by clicking on the Mode menu in the panel.

5. Leave Layer 4's mode as Normal, but set the TrkMat menu to Luma Inverted Matte "Cloudx2002.mov". This allows the stars to appear in the blue part of the sky, but not in the clouds of Cloudx2002.mov.

   Next, the star field needs to be rotated across the entire length of the timeline.

6. Set the timeline marker to the first frame. Then select Layer 4 (containing nightsky.psd) and scale the image up so that when it is rotated, the image constantly covers the entire frame of the Composition window.

7. Now add a keyframe on the first frame of the composition for Scale and Rotation, and move the timeline marker to the end of the timeline.

8. Then change the Rotation value to 0 x +259.00, which adds a keyframe to this frame in the timeline.

To reveal more of the stars, it's necessary to turn the daytime sky into a night time sky. This is achieved by adding a Hue/Saturation filter to Layer 3.

9. Position the timeline marker near the two-second mark on the timeline and select Effect > Adjust > Hue/Saturation from the menu.

10. Click on the triangles in Layer 3 to reach the Channel Range, and add a keyframe by clicking on the stopwatch icon. At this point, the Hue/Saturation has not been altered, but a keyframe is needed to ensure that there are no visual changes up to this point. Next position the timeline marker near the four-second mark in the timeline.

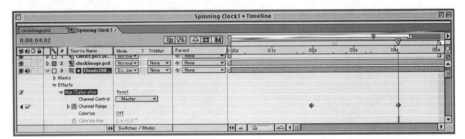

11. At this position, set the Master Lightness slider (in the Effect Controls palette) to -71. This adds a second keyframe in the timeline for the Channel Range. The effect allows some of the clouds to remain visible but reveals more of the stars as they rotate.

Congratulations, our composition is now complete! Play it through and enjoy. If you like, render it out.

Summary

The message throughout this chapter has been the need to design and prepare material before using After Effects. By designing your artwork and visuals before hand, the time you spend using After Effects becomes more efficient and cost-effective. Like most things, if you have a clear picture of what you are trying to achieve, the workflow becomes easier to organize.

Additionally, the tutorials will hopefully have provided you with greater insight into how After Effects can be used. Hopefully, you are beginning to see new ways in which you can realize your ideas with After Effects.

Ultimately, remember that simply sketching out your ideas first with a pencil and paper can help save you many hours of frustration.

Before you go

In previous chapters, we've dealt with every aspect of After Effects, from creating and importing files for use in the package, through to masking, matting, and keying images so that they can be composited together. We've looked at After Effects' filters, and how they can be applied, combined and animated, and we've learnt to use 2D and 3D compositing along with a host of other effects and tools to create effects, new looks for our footage, and stylish graphical animations.

In fact, all the tools of the effects and animation trade should now be at your fingertips. Learning to use them with confidence, subtlety and imagination is the next step, and that comes with experience.

If you're feeling a little overwhelmed with the sheer quantity of information to be taken in, don't worry. After Effects is a huge program, and the tools can seem daunting at first. However, once you get used to what's possible, and how it's achieved, you can start to visualize the way any effect is layered and put together. Soon you'll be able to watch any effect or animation, and see instantly how each layer is created and composited to form the finished shot.

Of course, this is only half the story. In the real world, effects are produced to tight specifications and tight deadlines. You'll need to learn to manage your time on a project, and be able to describe to clients clearly what you can do for them. Being realistic about what can be done with a given budget and a given time is often the difference between a successful piece of work, and one which fails to meet its mark.

The world the After Effects designer inhabits can be one filled with impossible deadlines set by employers who have no idea what's possible, what's easy and what will take weeks. You're the one who will have to make sure everyone knows what they need to provide for you, and what they can expect you to do with it. It's very easy to get carried away with the art of animation, and neglect the organizational side of your work. If you look up from your screen and the time is 2am, then you probably need to re-think your time management.

Do get excited about what you can achieve with After Effects. Be enthused by it, enjoy it, and work hard to stretch its boundaries. After Effects lets you create video effects which would have been beyond the reach of Hollywood only a few years ago, but while you're devising the most innovative effect, animation, or website ever created, do try to get some sleep!

After Effects provides a strong set of tools, and a working environment that lets you use them to their greatest effect. It's now up to you to start devising new ways to combine these tools into projects of your own. Experiment with the package, try out different working methods, and ideas. Push the program to its limits.

After Effects is used in everything from two-second long web animations right up to top Hollywood feature films, so if you can unlock its power, the possibilities are limitless. It's time now to get out there and start using it. Bon voyage!

CS1 Case Study 1: Android Child

During this case study, I will be attempting to demonstrate the procedures I used to create the final composition for a scene in a short drama, in which the main character watches a 3D android walk past her and into a room.

Background story

The scene is part of a seventeen minute drama called *Computer Crazy* starring Mary Moulds and Philip Young, two Northern Irish actors who are currently appearing in several feature films from Ireland.

Computer Crazy was originally written in 1995 as part of an entry into a film competition. Like most projects, it was rejected, but there was sufficient interest by local filmmakers, including myself, for an attempt to be made at producing the project as a digital film.

A lot of the work I had been involved with at that time used graphics and animation. At college, way back in the early eighties, I had been interested in combining animation and live-action, and with computers becoming so powerful by the mid to late nineties, I suddenly found that I had the opportunity to realize some of my ambitions to play with live-action and animation. All I needed was a project.

In 1998, a group of us in Belfast got together to write four shorts. The following summer, we managed to get a cast and crew together to make these films. Philip Young and Mary Moulds were chosen for the key roles in a project called *The Engagement* (this nine minute film can be seen at www.bluesphere.co.uk). Mary's performance won her a 'Best Actress' award in the 'Click-Flick' internet film festival in 2000.

With the enthusiasm generated by *The Engagement*, Philip, Mary and myself teamed up again to produce *Computer Crazy*.

The story line is about a couple's obsessive behavior, which develops when they are enticed to buy a computer. As the computer takes over their lives, it wants to start reproducing. A three second clip of the android; a momentary vision of man and machine combined, was required.

This gave me the opportunity to develop the theme of combining live-action and animation, and also, much later on, a certain case study in an After Effects book!

As so often happens, the design of the android developed by watching the way others had designed androids in the past. And as is so often the case, you kick yourself when you realize that simple ideas are in fact the most effective. In the post-production house I worked for prior to making this film, I had watched a traditional 3D modeler build the characters for his 16mm film using plasticine. From his storyboards, he had determined that one particular model would be shot in mainly close-up and medium shot. This meant he didn't need to build any legs for the character. Having worked out how my own character would appear in *Computer Crazy* through the storyboard, I was able to determine that the same design parameters applied. All that was necessary to build the android was a head, body and arms. This saved me valuable time.

What follows is a case study of the procedure I used to create the shot; compositing the 3D character with the live action.

Preparation

Most of the scenes in the film were designed to be covered by a single shot, which moved with the action. Therefore, each shot had a defined beginning, middle, and end.

For the scene we are going to look at, the script indicates that the character Teresa, played by Mary, was standing by the doorway of a small sitting room:

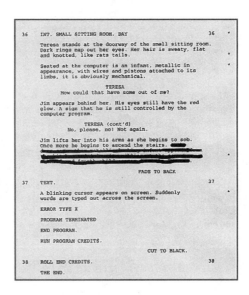

As the two characters need to ascend the stairs at the end of the scene, I decided that a single low-angle shot would suit. By holding the shot for a further thirty or forty seconds after the characters had moved out of vision, the end credits could be played over the same scene. I decided to simplify the scene by just having the infant, an android, walk through the shot very briefly.

Android design

The designs for the android were roughed out on paper. The image of the Frankenstein monster was initially sketched due to the similarities between the two stories.

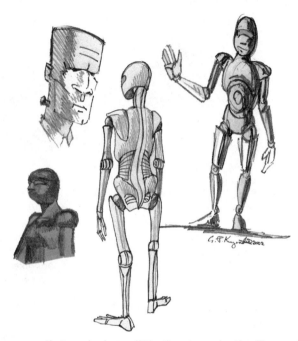

The biggest problems were that we had very little time to make the film, and we had no money (sound familiar?). With these restraints in mind, the more complicated, time consuming designs were rejected. Another consideration in this decision was the fact that the android would only be seen for approximately three seconds in the shot. So it's more of a tease for the audience than something to linger on.

Storyboard

I had visualized most of the scenes in the film in my head, and as I was the cameraman (no-budget usually means you do everything), I found that it was easy enough to work out the shots as I was filming.

However, for the scene with the android, it was useful to have a storyboard image to give an idea of how we were going to treat the shot.

Often, filmmakers are tempted to skip storyboarding elaborate shots, but this is only to their peril. A pre-visualization of even the simplest effects shot can help save valuable time when it comes to producing the effect in After Effects.

For the shot we're discussing here, the storyboard helped me to work out the kind of perspective I was looking for to add drama to the shot. It also helped to get a sense of what the relationship between the live action character and 3D animation would look like. Shading the two characters, to represent where the light source should come from, allowed the live action to be shot more quickly, and the scene to be recreated in the 3D animation package more easily. Storyboards can also help develop a sense of how each sequence develops the storyline of the film, thereby saving valuable time and film stock on location.

The shoot

To give Mary something to react to, we used a six-year-old boy to take the place of the android and walk through the shot. His movements would then become the key action for the 3D android animation to follow.

Once the sequence with Mary and the boy had been shot, a second clip was filmed without Mary and the stand-in. As the action was filmed on a locked off camera, this second clip would be used to replace the boy from the first clip as part of the After Effects composition.

Editing

The film was digitized into Final Cut Pro for editing. Once the end sequence was completed, the edited shot was saved in its cut form so that it could be used in After Effects.

Generating the elements needed to build the final composition

Up to this point, we have looked at how the film came about, and the tasks that were necessary to generate some of the images that will be used to build the final composition. We will now begin to prepare the way to create the remaining elements needed. All of the elements are supplied on the CD-ROM, but if you are interested in generating the elements yourself, then the next few sections will take you through the procedures used to generate the 3D model and animation. First, you should copy all the files relating to 'Case Study One' from the CD-ROM to your hard drive.

Setting up the composition

1. First of all, create a new After Effects project, with the following composition settings:

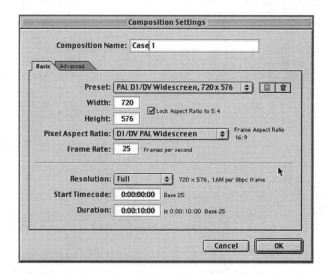

2. Next, we need to import the live action video clip of Mary, which is saved on the CD as `liveaction.mov`. At this point, if the movie file is dragged across to the Composition window, the aspect ratio of the clip will be wrong. This is because the clip was shot in anamorphic 16:9 ratio and the project is currently set as 4:3.

3. To correct, highlight the liveaction.mov file in the Project window and select File > Interpret Footage > Main... from the menu.

4. When the Interpret Footage window opens, change the Pixel Aspect Ratio to D1/DV PAL Widescreen. Then click OK.

5. Drag the liveaction.mov file onto the Composition window. The frame shape should now match that of the composition.

Exporting still images of the boy

The boy in the movie clip is only there as a guide to where the android animation should be positioned. Therefore, by exporting several images of the boy's movement, we can use them as keyframes when we come to generate the action for the 3D android.

> Some 3D animation packages will allow you to use the QuickTime movie as a backdrop but this also takes up a lot of memory. If you are not using a high end system but want to create a motion path based on an image, the following method can provide you with a simple and less memory hungry solution.

1. Move the timeline marker along the timeline, using the Next Frame button in the Time Controls palette, until you can see the first position of the boy entering the frame. Then select Composition > Save Frame As > File... from the menu.

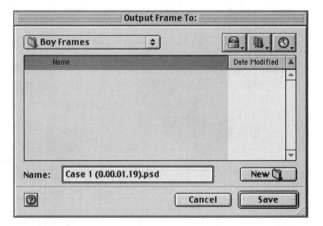

You will notice that the Name of the frame includes the timecode from where its original position is in the timeline. Don't worry if your timecode is different, as it all depends on where you select the frame from.

2.   Click Save, and the Render Queue window will open. The frame you are exporting is
ready to be rendered. The render settings are based on the Current Settings of the
Composition. By clicking on the Based on "Current Settings" text, you can change these.
Set up the Render Settings window as below.

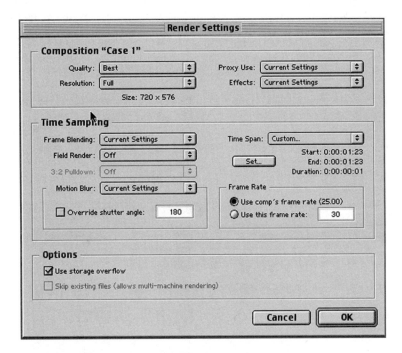

3.   Clicking OK returns you to the Render Queue window. Now click on the Render button.
After a few moments, the file will be rendered.

4.   The first frame has been rendered. Now you will need to repeat the previous 3 steps to
export eleven more frames, plotting the movement of the boy from the current frame,
to when he exits out of view.

> *You don't need to capture every single frame of the boy's movement,
> you only need enough to use as keyframes for the boy's movement.
> So when you position the time marker, make sure you that the frame
> you're capturing is at the end of one movement and the beginning of
> the next, such as when the body moves down as the full weight is put
> onto one foot, or when the body rises as it moves forward.*

Generating a background image

We now need to create a backdrop image for the 3D android to move over, as it passes initially in front of the stairs but behind the door, and then in front of the door, as it enters the room. Remember that for this shot, the camera was locked off so there would be no camera movements. This provides a clean plate allowing easy compositing. If a camera movement had been required, then some sort of computer control rig would have been necessary to record the movement accurately for the live-action camera. This exact movement could then be applied to the camera within the 3D animation package to replicate the same camera move.

1. Move the timeline marker to just a few frames after when the boy exits frame. Then select Composition > Save Frame As > File... from the menu.

2. Once again, this will open the Output Frame To: window. If you are taken straight to the Render window, just click next to the Output To: option to the bottom right of the queue item. Change the name so that it includes the word backdrop, but retains the timecode:

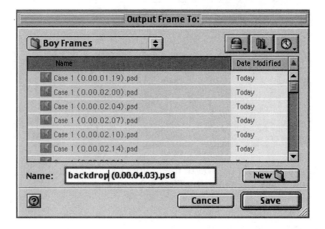

3. Click the Save button, and again, the Render Queue window will open. Change the settings to those we used the first time, and then click the Render button.

4. Save the project and then exit After Effects.

Working in Adobe Photoshop Elements

The next section covers the work that needs to be done to the frames and backdrop we exported from After Effects. These files can be manipulated in any bitmap editing package such as Adobe Photoshop, or Paint Shop Pro. However, for those of you who do not have the full version of Photoshop, its sibling, Photoshop Elements can provide the means for editing these files, and most other material you may want to use for video or composition work.

1. Open Photoshop Elements or your equivalent package. Import all the files you exported from After Effects, except for the backdrop file.

2. For each frame, add a new layer by choosing Layer > New > Layer... from the menu. When the new layer window opens, click OK.

3. In the Layers palette, select the new layer, and choose the Brush tool from the Tool palette.

4. Select a different color for each frame. To do this, click on the color box at the bottom of the tool palette. The Color Picker will appear. Select a new color, then click OK.

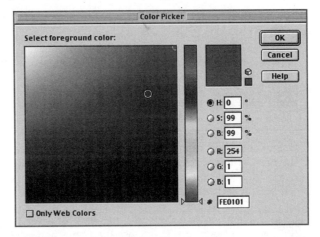

5. Trace a line around the shape of the boy as he appears in each frame.

To make sure that it is the new layer that you are drawing on, and not the background image, click on the eye icon in the Layers palette for the background. The image of the boy and the actress should disappear, leaving just the line you have just drawn.

6. Before moving on to the next frame, place four marks, one in each corner of the frame in the layer with the line drawing. This will help later.

7. Repeat this process for all eleven frames.

Building a single frame with all the line drawing layers

Once your have finished tracing out the figure of the boy, you need to merge each layer into a single layer. This can be done in the backdrop layer.

1. Import the backdrop layer into Photoshop Elements and choose File > Save As….. This opens the Save As… window.

2. In the name field, type Assembly.psd, and check that the format is Photoshop. Then click Save.

3. One by one, select each of the frames, and then select Layer 1. Choose Select > All from the menu. This will select the whole of the frame because of the marks placed at each corner earlier. If you have not put in these corner marks, then the only area selected will be around the shape of the boy that was drawn.

4. Once you're happy that the whole frame size of Layer 1 has been selected, choose Edit > Copy from the menu. Then close the frame, and select Assembly.psd. You can now paste the drawing into the Assembly.psd file by choosing Edit > Paste from the menu.

5. Repeat this process for every one of the eleven frames.

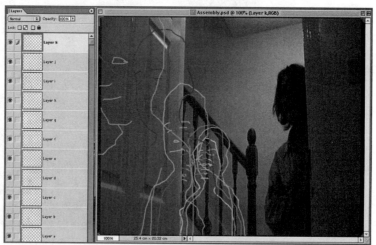

6. Once you have completed the final assembly, you may find that the outline of the boy if too confusing to see. To resolve this, save the file as three separate files – Assembly1.psd, Assembly2.psd and Assembly3.psd. Then open each file independently.

7. In Assembly1.psd, click on the eye icon for the first seven layers to hide them. Then click on the top right hand corner arrow in the Layers palette, and flatten the image. Save the files as a PICT file (ok the specifications in the PICT file options window).

8. Open Assembly2.psd, and hide layers 1 to 4, and layers 8 to 11, then make sure that layers 5 to 7 are showing.

9. Again flatten the image and save it as a PICT file.

10. Open Assembly3.psd, hide layers 1 to 7 and show layers 8 to 11. Flatten the file and save it as a PICT file.

11. At the end of this process, you should have the original Assembly.psd, plus three others, all retaining the eleven layers of the boys outline. On top of this, you should have three PICT files: Assembly1.pct, Assembly2.pct and Assembly3.pct, each showing different sets of layers.

Reducing the resolution of the PICT files

So that the three PICT files do not take up too much memory when used in the 3D model package, we need to decrease their resolution.

1. Close all files currently open, except for Assembly1.pct, Assembly2.pct, and Assembly3.pct and select Assembly1.pct.

2. Choose Image > Resize > Image Size... from the menu. In the image size window, change the width to 384 pixels. The height will change automatically.

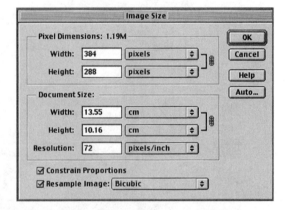

> *The final image needs to be in 16:9 ratio instead of the 4:3 ratio the images are currently in. To convert the image, we need to divide the height by 9 and multiply the result by 16 to give us the new width: 288/9 = 32, 32x16=512.*

3. In the image size window, deselect Constrain Proportions. The two sets of chains should now disappear. One chain connects the Pixel Dimensions width and height, and the other chain connects the Document Size Width and Height.

4. In the Pixel Dimensions width field type in 512.

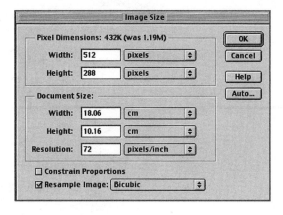

5. Click OK. Assembly1.pct will now be reshaped to its intended 16:9 ratio.

6. Repeat the process for Assembly2.pct, and Assembly3.pct. Remember that the final image size should have a width of 512 pixels and height of 288 pixels.

The 3D character creation

At this stage in the procedure, it is time to look at building the 3D model and animating it.

To build the 3D model, I used Pixels 3D. It's a very useful Mac OS 3D package designed for 3D character animation. However, you should be able to build a similar model in virtually any 3D animation package such as Lightwave, 3D StudioMax, Cinema 4D, Maya, Softimage, and various other packages.

Beginning with pencil drawings

After choosing one of the designs I had sketched out on paper at the beginning of the case study, I produced a side view, and front view drawing of the android.

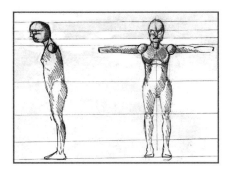

1. First of all, scan the pencil drawing and open it in Photoshop Elements. Then split the image into two square frames 250 x 250 pixels at 72dpi.

2. Save each new file as 2Dside.pct, and 2Dfrnt.pct (these can be found on the CD-ROM).

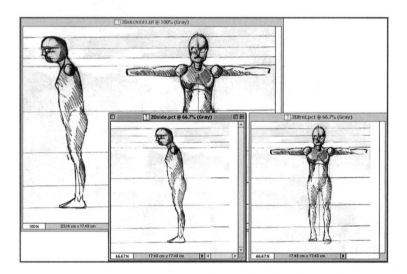

3. Close Photoshop Elements.

3D modeling

We now turn to the 3D animation package. Again use the package you are most familiar with for this section.

1. Open the 3D animation program. In many cases, you will be presented with something similar to the screenshot below.

2. Set the output camera to 16:9 ratio and import the `2Dside.pct` file into the 'right' view and the `2Dfrnt.pct` file into the 'front' view.

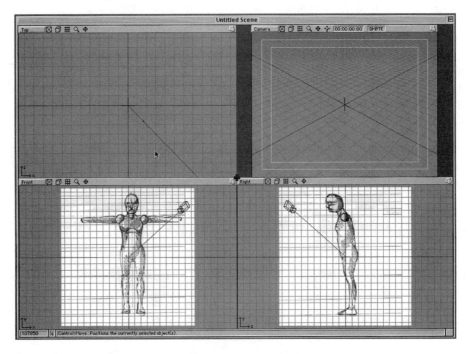

3. Add a cylinder and model it to form the shape of the body. This is accomplished by pulling, pushing, and pinching the various vertices to make the 3D model match the drawings.

> *I used NURBs to do this, as this is the main method of creating shapes in Pixels3D 3.7. In the newest version, polygons can be used.*

4. Add a sphere to form the head. Again, by pushing, pulling, and pinching the vertices, mold the sphere into the shape of the head. To prevent unintentionally altering the body section, it is best to hide the body while working on the head.

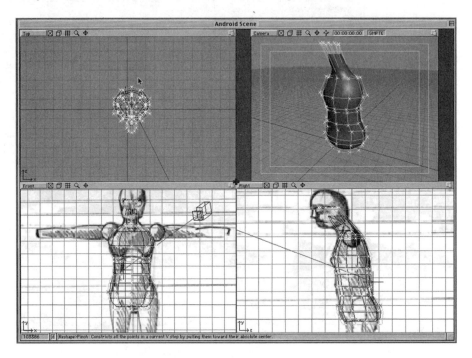

5. Then make the arms out of another cylinder, and mold them to match the pencil drawing. Once you have made one of the arms, you can make the other by duplicating the first. You can do the same with the shoulder, which you can mold from a sphere.

> It's unnecessary to build the hands and legs as they do not appear in the shot. A lot of people, when they begin using 3D, feel compelled to try and recreate every single detail they would find in the real world, when often this is not needed for the shot. Why create an elaborate IK foot setup when the feet wont even be in shot?

6. Gradually, refine the model by continuing to manipulate the vertices until you are happy that the shape of the 3D model matches that of the 2D drawings in the front and right plan.

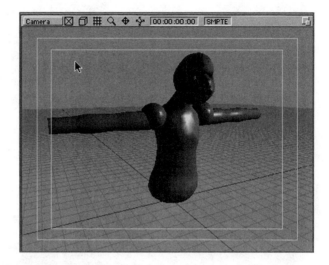

7. Each element can have its name changed. In Pixels 3D, this is done through the object's Info palette. By changing the elements to the names of the object they represent, it makes it easier to locate the various limbs when they need to be animated.

8. Once all the elements are in place, link them together, with the body becoming the anchor point. Some 3D packages show schematics of the model, which can be used to link objects together.

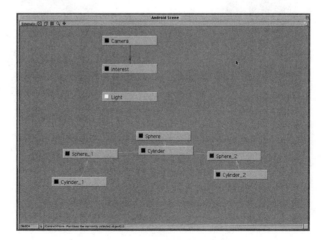

9.   Attach Inverse-Kinetic chains to the arms to enable the model to be animated.

> *In the hierarchy of the model, the body is the main parent. The shoulder, followed by the upper arm, and then the lower arm become the child objects to the previous. By using Inverse Kinetics, I was able to move the whole of the arm and shoulder by simply moving the lower arm. If I had used Forward Kinetics I would have needed to rotate the shoulder to move the upper and lower arm. The next step would have been to rotate the upper arm, then the lower arm. This process would have take three actions instead of the one using Inverse Kinetics.*

10.   Next, color each shape of the model by applying a Color Shade.

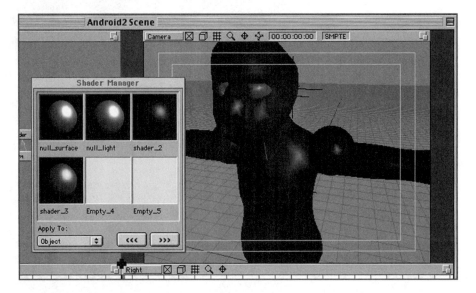

11.   Using the same method to add the 2D drawings to the 'front' and 'right' views, we now add Assembly1.psd, Assembly2.psd, and Assembly3.psd to the image store, and place them into the background of the Camera view, one at a time as we need them.

12. Position the model at its starting point, and then open the 3D animation program's timeline, and begin to position the model at each keyframe marked on the background image. Use the timecode reference on each of the frames that was exported from After Effects. It's very useful to write out a list of them, or add them into a spreadsheet and print the list out as a reference.

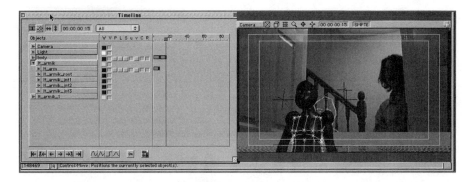

13. Once you have the keyframes added to the timeline, you can render out a test movie to see if the model is moving correctly. Adjustments may need to be made with the arms to make them swing correctly.

14. Another thing to consider is the lighting of the model, now that it is animated. You can set the timeline marker in the animation program to the first frame, then add, and position a light using the 'top', 'front', and 'right' views. When the program was initially opened, a light may have already been set up. You should adjust this, and any extras you place into the scene so that they match the light of the background still image.

As a reference, I tried to imitate the lighting set up used on set, which included a light to represent the light bulb in the hall, and some less intensive, more bluish light from the room the android was moving into. The light bulb in the hall is tungsten, which has a color temperature of about 3200 degrees Kelvin, making the light look orange. Therefore, the light cast across the android needs to have an orange tint to it to replicate the light bulb from the hall. Remember, the better you can get your 3D lighting to match your original footage, the easier the compositing.

> *Color temperature is based on the color a 'black body' or perfect radiator would appear if heated up to a given temperature. Therefore a light bulb glowing at 3200 degrees Kelvin looks the same as the color of a perfect radiator heated up to 3200 degrees Kelvin. Sun light during the day has a color temperature of about 5500 degrees Kelvin.*

15. Once you have completed your lighting modifications, render out another low-resolution test movie.

> *In Pixels3D Studio the background image is not included in the rendered image. Instead, an alpha channel is created so that the background image can be included when using After Effects.*

16. If you're happy with the result, output the animation as a series of PICT files. Set the various Render options, and click OK.

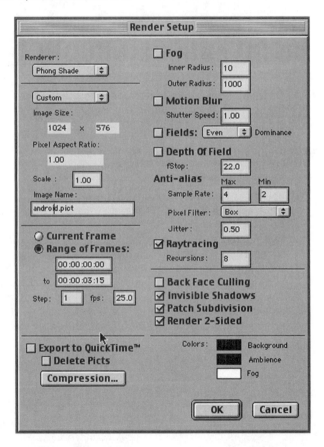

17. Then select the method your 3D program uses to render the files, choose a new folder to store all the images in, name the PICT files, and click OK.

Once the PICT files have been rendered out, we should have all of the media files we need to build the After Effects composition! You can find a folder named Final Render on the CD-ROM. This contains the rendered files for the Android animation, which we use as a PICT file sequence in After Effects.

> In 3D, trying to replicate all of the subtle layers of real world movement can be an enormous task. Often keyframes and interpolations need to be adjusted between frames, because the computer tends to want to choose the shortest route, and this can make movement look stiff and robotic. However, in this case, a bit of a robotic feel is actually what we are after. This makes the animation task, for this project, significantly faster than if we were trying to animate a lead character like those in the recent Final Fantasy feature film.

Working in After Effects

We can now re-open the After Effects project we created earlier. In the Project window, you should already see the liveaction.mov clip. Now we need to add the background image, and the android PICT file sequence.

Importing the media into After Effects

1. From the menu, choose File > Import > Multiple Files... and locate the backdrop (0.00.04.03).psd from the Boy Frames folder. Import the file.

2. Now locate cchild.pict.00000 from the Final Render folder. This is the first frame of the PICT file sequence. Check the box beside PICT sequence towards the lower-left hand side of the window, and click Import.

3. Select the Premultiplied – Matted with Color radio button from the Interpret Footage window, followed by OK.

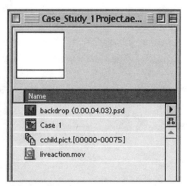

Now we have our files!

Creating mattes

Next, we need to open the backdrop file to add a mask so that we can see Mary, but hide the boy. Then we need to create a mask that will allow us the see the android move from behind the door, and then pass in front of the door.

1. Drag backdrop (0.00.04.03).psd onto the Composition window. If you find that the frame does not fit correctly, then leave it in the Project window, but make sure that it is highlighted.

2. Choose File > Interpret Footage > Main... from the menu. When the Interpret Footage window opens, you need to change the Pixel Aspect Ratio to D1/DV PAL Widescreen, then click OK.

3. The image should now completely fill the frame in the Composition window, so drag it in. You will also see backdrop (0.00.04.03).psd appear as a new layer in the timeline.

4. Double click on the image in the Composition window to open the Layer window. Then use the Pen tool to create a shape, which covers the door but does not cover Mary, and close the Layer window.

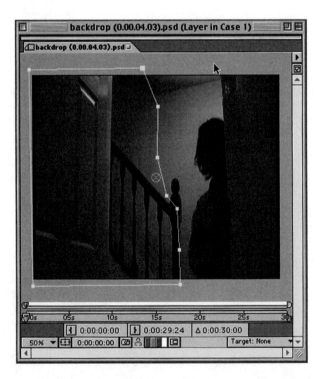

5. Now drag backdrop(0.00.04.03).psd from the Project window onto the Composition window again to add another layer. Double click on the Composition window to open the Layer window.

6. This time use the Pen tool to create a mask that is the same shape as the door, and close the Layer window.

Building layers

By this stage, you will have noticed that we currently have three layers showing in the Timeline window.

We now have to add the android animation to the composition.

1. Drag the cchild.pict.[00000-00075] file onto the composition window. You will notice that the android sits on top of the door. Also, at this point we are seeing the still images we are going to use to mask the boy from the live-action movie.

2. Click on the eye icons for layers 2 & 3 so that only the live-action and the android are visible.

3. We now need to match the movement of the boy with the android. To do this, move the timeline marker to the position where the boy is about to leave the frame after walking through the scene. Then use the mouse to slide the clip in the first layer so that the android matches the position of the boy.

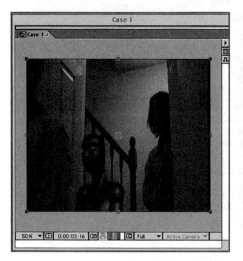 

4. Click on the gray box to reveal the eye icon for layers 2 & 3. Now the boy from the live-action clip should disappear.

5. Next, select Layer 1 with the cchild.pict.[00000-00075] in it and choose Edit > Duplicate from the menu to duplicate the layer with the android animation.

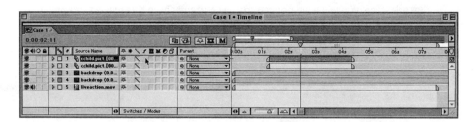

6. Move the timeline marker to the position where the android has just cleared the edge of the door and slide the end marker of layer 2 towards the timeline marker.

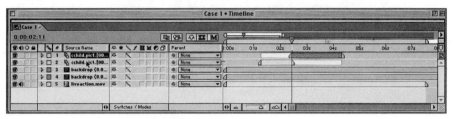

7. Then, slide the start marker of layer 1 up to the timeline marker, select layer 2, and drag it between layer 3 and layer 4.

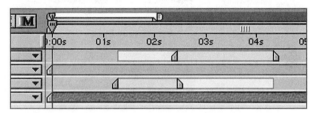

8. Now hit the Previous Frame button on the Time Control palette, and you should see the android move behind the door.

Adding Feather Edges to the Masks

At the moment, the mask is too harsh and needs to be softened.

1. Select the new layer 2 and drop down the list by clicking on the arrow to the left of the layer number. Do the same with the next two arrows relating to the Masks and Mask 1, and set the timeline marker to the beginning of the composition.

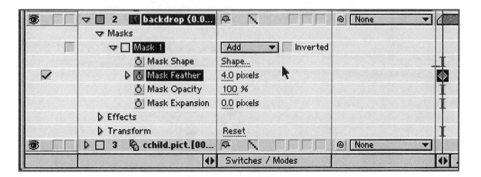

2. Click on the stopwatch associated with Mask Feather, and set the pixels to 4.0.

3. Select layer 4 and repeat the process, but this time set the mask feather to 118.0.

Adding a shadow of the android onto the door

The only thing missing from the door is the android's shadow.

1. Select layer 1, and go to Effects > Perspective > Drop Shadow.

2. Click on the arrow beside the layer 1 number. This will reveal Masks, Effects, and Transforms.

3. Now move the timeline marker to the start marker for layer 1, and drop down the effects list by clicking on the arrow beside it.

4. Set the Opacity to 0%, Direction to 0 x +263.0, Distance to 167.0, and softness to 39.0. Then click on all of the stopwatches for these four options. This will add four keyframes to the timeline.

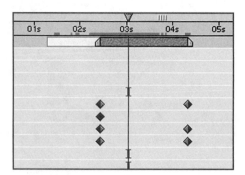

5. Now move the timeline marker to the end marker for layer 1, and change the Opacity to 25%; Distance to 400.0, and Softness to 41.0. Click on the gray box in the keyframe navigator for each of these options to add keyframes for these settings into the timeline.

6. Now set the composition window resolution to Third, and play the movie. This will give you the chance to see how the whole composition is working. If there are any elements that you are not happy with, tweak the various masks and effects until you have the desired look.

Rendering the composition

Once you're happy with the way the composition is working, you need to render the composition into a QuickTime movie.

1. Select Composition > Make Movie... from the menu.

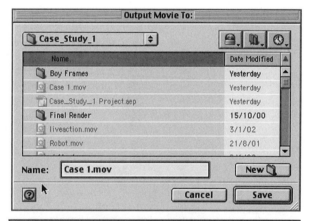

2. Choose the folder to which you want to save the QuickTime movie, name the file Case 1.mov, and click Save. The Render Queue window will appear. Click on Current Settings.

3. Next, the Render Settings window will appear. Set Quality to Best and Resolution to Full. Then click OK. Field rendering is not necessary for this composition as the video was shot in frame mode on a Canon XL-1.

> *If you have changed any settings during the building of the composition, it's always a good idea to check these, and set them to the highest quality possible. You should make this part of your 'final-rendering-procedure'. If you neglect to do this, you may find that the settings are lower than you expected, and the final render needs to be re-done to correct the error. Unfortunately, it is often after the longest renders that you discover the problem, so be warned!*

4. You'll now be returned to the Render Queue window.

> *If you click on the arrow beside* Output Module, *you'll be shown where the file is going to be rendered to, and more importantly, the type of CODEC that will be used for the final render. At the moment,* Animation Compressor *is being used. However, as most of the files are in DV PAL, it is best to output using this compressor so that the final movie can be inserted into an existing edit, or output directly to miniDV.*

5. Click on Lossless beside Output Module in the Render Queue window. The Output Module Settings window will open. Select Import into project when done. This will open the rendered file in the current project once it is rendered.

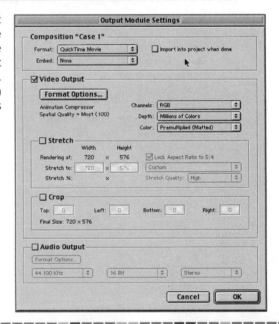

6.   Now click on Format Options in the Video Output panel, and the Compression Settings window will open. Click on Animation and select DV PAL from the drop down menu that appears. Then click OK.

7.   This returns you to the Output Module Settings window. Click OK and you are once again presented with the Render Queue window. All that is necessary to do now is click on the Render button and the rendering will begin.

8.   The estimated time for rendering will appear after a moment or two. On my iMac 400mHz machine with 256Mb RAM the estimated time is eight minutes.

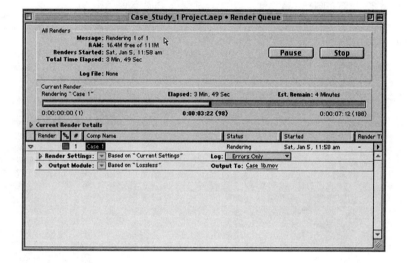

This brings us to the end of Case Study 1.

For those of you who may be interested in using Pixels3D studio, version 4 is now available and can be purchased at http://www.pixels.net. *Computer Crazy* can be seen at www.bluesphere.co.uk. If you're interested in finding out more details about Mary Moulds, her agent Patrick Duncan can be contacted via his web site at www.dealersagencyireland.com.

CS2 Case Study 2

The following case study will look at how to use After Effects to produce a web page banner for Blue Sphere Productions Ltd.

Blue Sphere Productions Ltd. is a company I set up to produce both short and feature length films. The idea behind the web site is to inform like-minded people of the progress we are making with a number of different projects, and to present some of the completed films such as *The Engagement*, *Computer Crazy*, and *One Night*. Each of these shorts were produced on digital video. Another aspect of the site is to promote the idea of continuing to make celluloid projects.

With this in mind, I wanted the banner to represent both the digital, and celluloid interests of the company. To view the actual banner used, visit www.bluesphere.co.uk.

Designing the sequence

The design brief for the banner was simply to produce something visually interesting using the text Blue Sphere Productions Ltd.

Standing by the 'K.I.S.S.' (keep it simple stupid) principle, it was decided to keep the banner as simple as possible by not using the 3D logo animation used in our video promotional material. Early versions of the banner had contained the logo, and the file size became too large to download in a reasonable amount of time. Using similar flat graphics, with a minimum number of colors, allowed the banner to flow more smoothly, and still remain a small file.

I wanted the banner to have the company name, and decided to look at what kind of motion could be applied to the three words that made up the name and ways to, at some point, have the whole name appear. This way, I could tease out the name in segments, and finish with the full name assembled together so it could be read as a whole. The start and finish had to be the same so that the banner would loop without there appearing to be a jump cut. The length of the sequence I felt should be restricted to two to three seconds. This length is small enough to keep the file size small, but long enough for the banner to appear and easily be read.

I decided to use a different font for each element of the banner, to represent the diverse activities undertaken by the company in the work it does. Another aspect of the design was to include scratches, and to add hairs, to give the impression of celluloid film.

The fonts chosen for the banner included Bodoni MT Ultra Bold, Chicago, Comic Sans MS, and Helvetica. Bodoni MT Ultra Bold was used to give a sense of the boldness injected into the work we do. Chicago is a typical font used often within the Mac OS system, so it was decided this should be used for the main title to represent the fact that Power Mac are the computers used in post production. Comic Sans MS has a sense of fun about its shape and form, so this was chosen to represent the kind of atmosphere we like to create on each shoot. We used Helvetica in italics to give a sense of the importance of meeting deadlines.

I then worked out the dimensions of the banner to be 468 pixels wide, by 60 pixels high. I found this size provided enough room to portray the information I wanted to have in the banner, but also left enough room for a side menu bar and a frame to contain the various web pages used in the site.

A five frame storyboard was drawn up in pencil, scanned in, and the last two frames were inverted in Photoshop so that we could see the black background with white text.

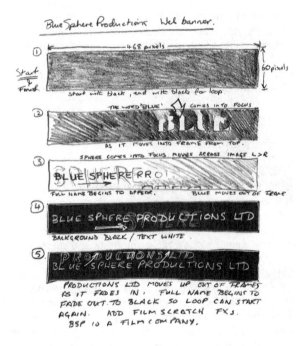

As it's natural for us to read text from left to right, I decided that the movement across the banner should follow the same convention. The storyboard therefore indicates the direction in which the text should travel.

Producing the layers

The next stage was to create the picture files. These included the background, and four text files, which were all created in Photoshop Elements. Essentially you could use any program you like, but to recreate this case study from scratch, you need to create files like so exactly as below.

Background

The background specifications consist of an image size with a width of 468 pixels by a height of 60 pixels. The resolution for internet graphics doesn't need to be set any higher than 72dpi. You should use Only Web Colors when choosing colors from the Color Picker. I used #003366, which is a shade of blue.

Full title

The full title of the production company was produced using the image size of 468 pixels wide by 60 pixels high. The background was left transparent so that it would be used as an alpha channel in After Effects. I wanted the main title to stand out against the other images of separate pieces of text, animating across a motion path. For the main title, I chose the font Chicago with a point size of 28. The text was given a center justification, and was white in color.

'Productions ltd'

This was again transparent, and had the same width, but a height of 100 pixels, and the text was written in Comic Sans MS Bold, with a size of 48pt.

'Blue'

'Blue' had a taller setting, at 150 pixels, and was in Bodini MT Extra Bold at 72pt.

'Sphere'

Finally, 'Sphere', was similar to 'Blue', but the text was in Helevetica Bold Oblique.

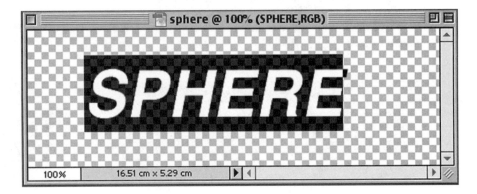

The journey continues in After Effects

We now move to After Effects to continue to build the banner. The following is a description of what I did to create my own banner, but I've written them as steps so that you can follow them to experiment with your own projects and ideas.

Getting started

1. To get started, open a new project, and import all of the picture files you created. Then open a new composition, with the settings as in the following screenshot:

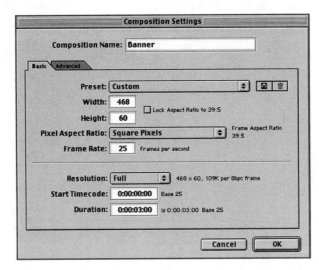

2. Select C2bgnd.psd from the Project window, and drag it onto the Composition window. At the beginning of the timeline, add a keyframe with an Opacity of 50%.

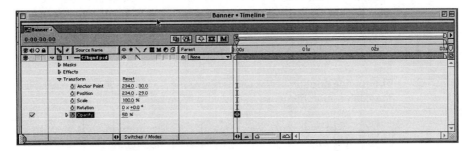

'Blue'

Now that we have a background and composition ready, it's time to start animating the test we made.

1. Select blue.psd from the project window, and drag it onto the composition window. You'll notice that the text just about fits the height of the composition frame.

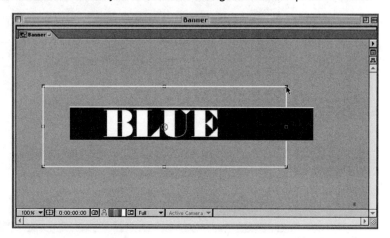

2. To make it fit better, reduce the size of the layer. You may be asking why the layer wasn't created the same size as the background. This is because the intention was to use it larger, but once I brought the material into After Effects I felt it didn't work so well. If I had made the image the same size, and had then decided to increase the size of the 'Blue' text, the image would have become more pixelated. As it is easy enough to reduce the size and retain quality, I always create larger images to give me more choice once I am working in After Effects.

3. The starting position of the text is above the frame, so we need to drag the word above the composition frame, so that it's out of view.

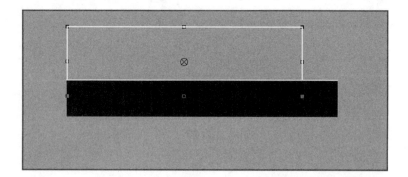

4. We then need to set a position keyframe for this, at 0 seconds on the timeline.

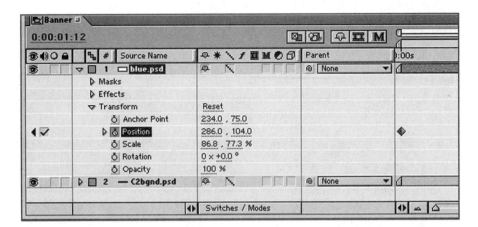

5. Move the timeline marker to about one and a half seconds into the timeline. Then returning to the Composition window, drag the white outline rectangle to below the composition frame. The motion path will now be visible, and a keyframe will have been added to the timeline.

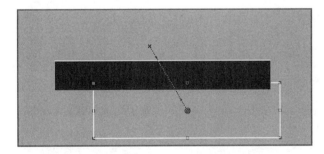

6. Select the control levers on the motion path, and form a curved line so the 'Blue' text moves in an arc. This will create a more interesting move than just a straight motion.

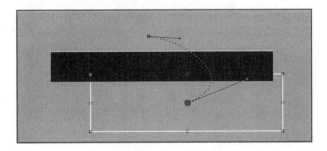

Adding fades to blue.psd

Now we're going to add a fade in and a fade out.

1. Position the timeline marker at a point where the word 'Blue' is clearly visible, and is fully in frame, and add an Opacity keyframe with a value of 100%.

2. Use the first frame button on the Time Controls palette to position the timeline marker on the first frame, and change the Opacity to 0%.

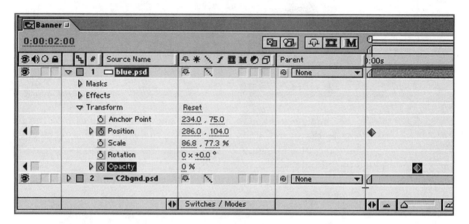

3. Position the timeline marker on the second keyframe for the position transform, and again change the Opacity value to 0%. This will add a third keyframe in the timeline for the Opacity transform.

   You'll notice that the text is virtually opaque all the way through the motion path where it is visible in the Composition window.

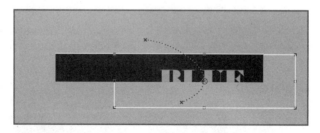

4. Now adjust the first and third Opacity keyframes so that the text only becomes visible for a short while once it's half way into the frame. To do this you need to drag both keyframes towards the second.

Adding a Gaussian Blur effect to blue.psd

We will now add the Gaussian Blur effect to the 'Blue' text.

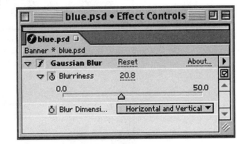

1. Position the timeline marker at the keyframe where the Opacity is set at 100%, click Effect > Blur & Sharpen > Gaussian Blur, and add a keyframe with no blurriness.

2. Move the timeline marker to the first frame, and then use the slider in the Effect Controls palette to set the Blurriness to 20.8.

3. Now move to the last keyframe for the position of the 'Blue' text, and set the value to 20.8 so that a third keyframe is added to the Blurriness of the Gaussian Blur effect.

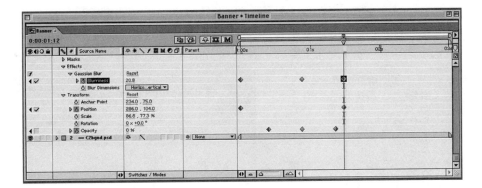

Time to move on to the next bit of text. To save the first two frames from being accidentally moved, it's a good idea to lock them in place at this point.

'Sphere'

The next step is to add the sphere.psd file to the composition. So drag it into the composition, starting at the first frame.

1. Again it's a bit big, so we need to reduce the image size by clicking the corner of the white outline rectangle.

2. With the timeline marker pointing at the first frame, click on the text itself and drag the layer to the left hand edge of the composition window. Now add a position keyframe. Then place the timeline marker onto the two-second point in the timeline.

3. Next, drag the layer in the composition window so that it is moved out of the right of frame.

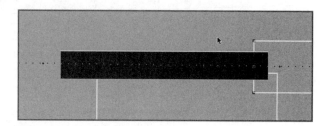

Making adjustments to the 'Sphere' text

You'll notice that 'Sphere' appears too soon and crosses 'Blue'. We want the individual words to be completely separate, so the position of the 'Sphere' text needs to be altered so that it doesn't cross over the 'Blue' text.

1. Position the timeline marker around the one second point in the timeline. Here the two pieces of text have crossed over.

2. Click on the first keyframe for the Position of sphere.psd, and then drag it towards the timeline marker. Position the keyframe so that the word 'Sphere' is no longer crossing over the word 'Blue'.

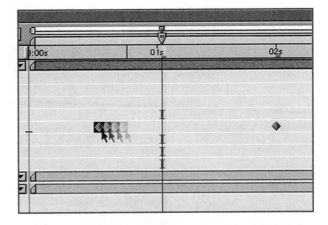

3. Now when you play the piece, you should be able to see that the two pieces of text no longer cross each other.

Adding the first Opacity keyframe for the sphere.psd layer

Next, we will set the point where the text 'Sphere' needs to be sharp, and then add a fade in, and a fade out.

1. Set the timeline marker to a point on the timeline where you can see the right edge of the white outline for the sphere.psd layer touch the left edge of the Composition window.

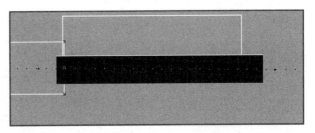

2. Add a keyframe for Opacity here, and set it to 0%. Then move the timeline marker fowards until you can see the whole of the text 'Sphere'; and add a keyframe, but this time with 100% Opacity.

3. Now move the timeline marker towards the end of the timeline so that only the 'S' is visible. Again we need here a keyframe with the Opacity set to 0%.

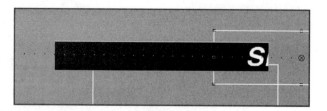

Adding a motion blur to the sphere.psd layer

For the sphere.psd layer, we will add a directional blur filter to add a bit of interesting variation to the visuals. Remember this is a creative process, sometimes there are no other reasons for doing things than they are pleasing to the eye.

1. Position the timeline marker on the center keyframe of the three in the timeline for Opacity. Then choose Effect > Blur & Sharpen > Directional Blur from the menu.

2. Under Directional Blur in the timeline, add keyframes for both Direction and Blur Length.

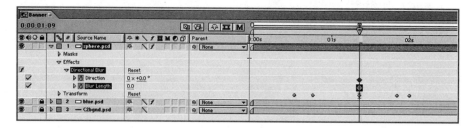

3. Now position the timeline marker at the first keyframe where the 'Sphere' text is at 0% Opacity. Here, set the Direction to 0 x –70.0o and Blur Length to 20.0.

4. Next, place the timeline marker at the keyframe towards the end of the timeline, where the 'Sphere' text is set to 0% Opacity, and repeat step 16.

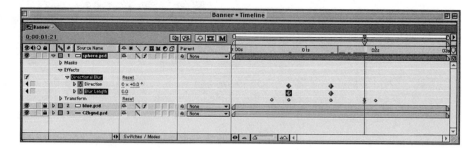

'productions ltd'

We now need to add the 'productions ltd' text layer to the composition.

1. Drag the production.psd file into the composition at frame one, and position it roughly as in the following screenshot.

2. Set the timeline marker so that the composition window looks something like the next screenshot. Here you should set keyframes for both Position and Opacity, leaving Opacity at 100%.

3. Drag the timeline marker toward the end of the timeline, to a point where the 'Sphere' text is at 0% Opacity. Add keyframes here as before.

4. Move the timeline marker to midway between the two second point, and the end of the timeline. Here, change Opacity to 0%.

5. Then add another keyframe with 0% Opacity at the point where the 'Sphere' text overlaps the 'productions ltd' text, from the letter 'U', as below.

Adding a Caustics effect to production.psd

So far, we've used two blur effects, one on each of the previous texts. This time, we'll use Caustics, to create the illusion of water. The reason for adding a water type effects came about because the aesthetic of the piece was beginning to remind me of liquid, or the film 'Sphere'. You can find this under Simulation in the Effect drop down menu.

1. Set the timeline marker to the third keyframe of production.psd, and select Caustics from the Effects menu.

2. Open up Caustics on the timeline via the arrows. You will be presented with Bottom, Water, Sky, Lighting and Material.

3. Click on the Water triangle. Set Water Surface to 1, production.psd Wave Height to 0.000, Smoothing to 24.000, Water Depth to 0.170, Refractive Index to 1.150, Surface Opacity to 0.000, and Caustics Strength to 0.120.

4. For the Surface Color, use the Syringe tool to select the color of the background in the Composition window. Then click on all of the stopwatches in the Water drop down list.

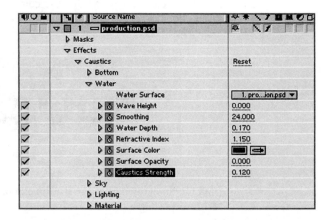

5. Click on the Sky triangle. Set Sky to None, Scaling to 1.000, Repeat Mode to Reflected, If Layer Size Differs to Center, Intensity to 0.010, and Convergence to 0.120. Then click on all of the stopwatches in this list.

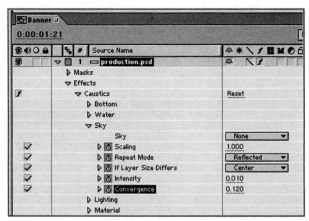

6. Click on the triangle beside Sky to close the list.

7. Next, click on the Lighting triangle. Set Light Type to Point Source, Light Intensity to 1.00, Light Position to 234.0,50.0, Light Height to 1.000, and Ambient Light to 0.25.

8. Again, use the syringe to set the Light Color the same as the background color in the Composition window.

9. Click on all the stopwatches for the Lighting settings.

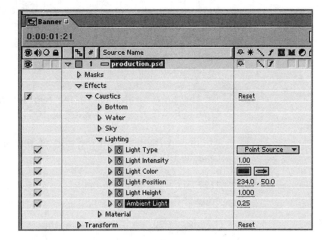

10. Next, move the timeline marker to the previous keyframe, where the production.psd is still at 100% Opacity. This will enable you to apply the effect and see the result as you change each setting.

11. Change the Water settings as follows: Wave Height to 0.120, Smoothing to 38.000, Water Depth to 0.990, Refractive Index to 2.000, Surface Opacity to 0.000, and Caustics Strength to 0.040.

12. Select the keyframes that have just been added, and drag them to the first transform keyframe.

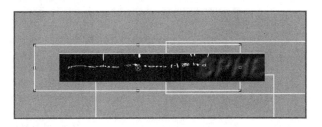

The full title

We've now come to the point where we add the final piece of text.

1. Place the timeline marker at the first frame. Drag the file Fulltitle.psd from the Project window, onto the composition. You'll find that it is the same size as the composition frame.

2. Set the timeline marker to the two second position on the timeline, and place an Opacity keyframe with a value of 100%.

3. About ten frames from the end of the timeline, set a keyframe where the value of Opacity is 0%.

4. Then place the timeline marker to about ten frames from the beginning of the timeline and set the value of Opacity to 0%.

Modifying the composition

At this point, a lot of the text elements are competing with one another for attention. To counteract this a little, we want to change some of the values for the Opacity of three layers, and add a motion path to the production.psd layer. As you make the following modifications to each layer, it helps to keep all the other layers locked.

1. On the blue.psd layer, change the keyframe with the Opacity set at 100% to 50%.

2. On sphere.psd, reset the Opacity keyframe, currently set at 100%, to 50%.

3. When you reach the Opacity transform in the production.psd layer, you should discover that there are two keyframes with the value of 100%. Change both of these to 50%. Then place the timeline marker at the first set of keyframes associated with this layer.

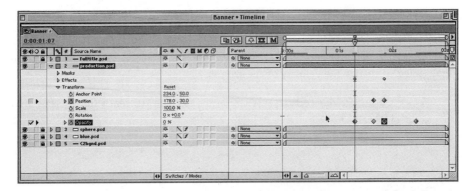

In the Composition window, you should see the production.psd layer with dark squares in each corner and in the middle of the white outline rectangle.

4. Drag the layer in the Composition window so that the outline rectangle is just below the full title. You will see a motion path has been formed, because of the two previous keyframes we set for Position earlier.

5. Set the timeline marker to the last Opacity keyframe.

6. Once again, drag the layer in the Composition window, this time so that the lower line of the white outline is just above the 'Blue Sphere Productions Ltd' text.

7. If you play the composition, you will find that 'production ltd' moves, then stops, then moves on again. What we want is a continuous move. Therefore, we need to delete the two middle keyframes associated with Position.

Changing the velocity of the fade in of the main title

As you preview the composition, you'll notice that the main title text fades in too quickly. We're now going to change the velocity of the fade in.

1. On the Fulltitle.psd layer, click on the triangles to reach the Opacity transform, and open out the Value and Velocity graphs.

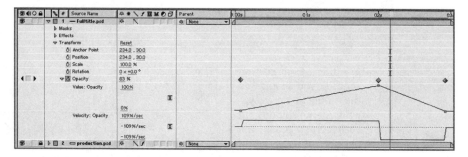

2. Select Value: Opacity, and then lengthen the control levers by dragging them towards the second keyframe.

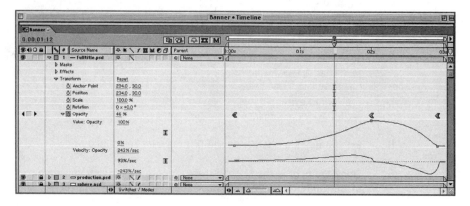

The 'Blue Sphere Productions Ltd' text should now fade in more gently, while still allowing the piece of text time to be viewed before it fades.

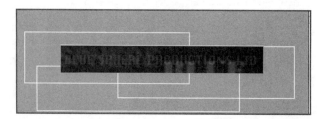

Let's get ready to render

You should now be ready to render the file out as an animated GIF. Set the quality to best, and the resolution to full within the current settings of the Render Queue window. Then, within the Lossless settings, set the format to Animated GIF, and check the looping box in the Animated GIF Options window.

The rendering on my iMac took about 30 seconds to complete.

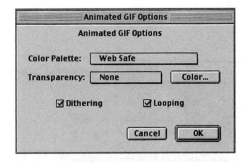

Using HTML to add the animated GIF file to a web page

We now need to view the animated GIF file in a web browser. To do this, you can simply import a graphic file into something like Dreamweaver. Alternatively, you can write the following HTML code in a word processor, and save as a text only file, named `whateveryoulike.html`.

```html
<html>
  <head>
    <title>RevAE5 Case Study 2</title>
  </head>
  <body>
    <img src="Banner.gif" width="468" height="60">
  </body>
</html>
```

Making sure that this file is in the same folder as `Banner.gif`, double click on the HTML file, and your default browser should open up and start looping your animation.

Well, that's the job complete!

The design of the actual banner basically evolved as the piece was being created. As is often the case with much of the work I have done for the past eighteen years, the client is often not sure what they want, as the graphical elements of their production are usually the last thing they think about. The client is usually relying on the designer to come up with ideas, and to be creative. Sometime this creative process is just a case of throwing out a few ideas, and trying things to see if they work or not. With the banner for this website, something simple, eye-catching, and that enabled the company name to be read was all that was required. The end solution met these criteria, and the people who have visited the site have been impressed by what they've seen. Again, it was important to keep things simple so the work could be done quickly and efficiently.

CS3 Case Study 3

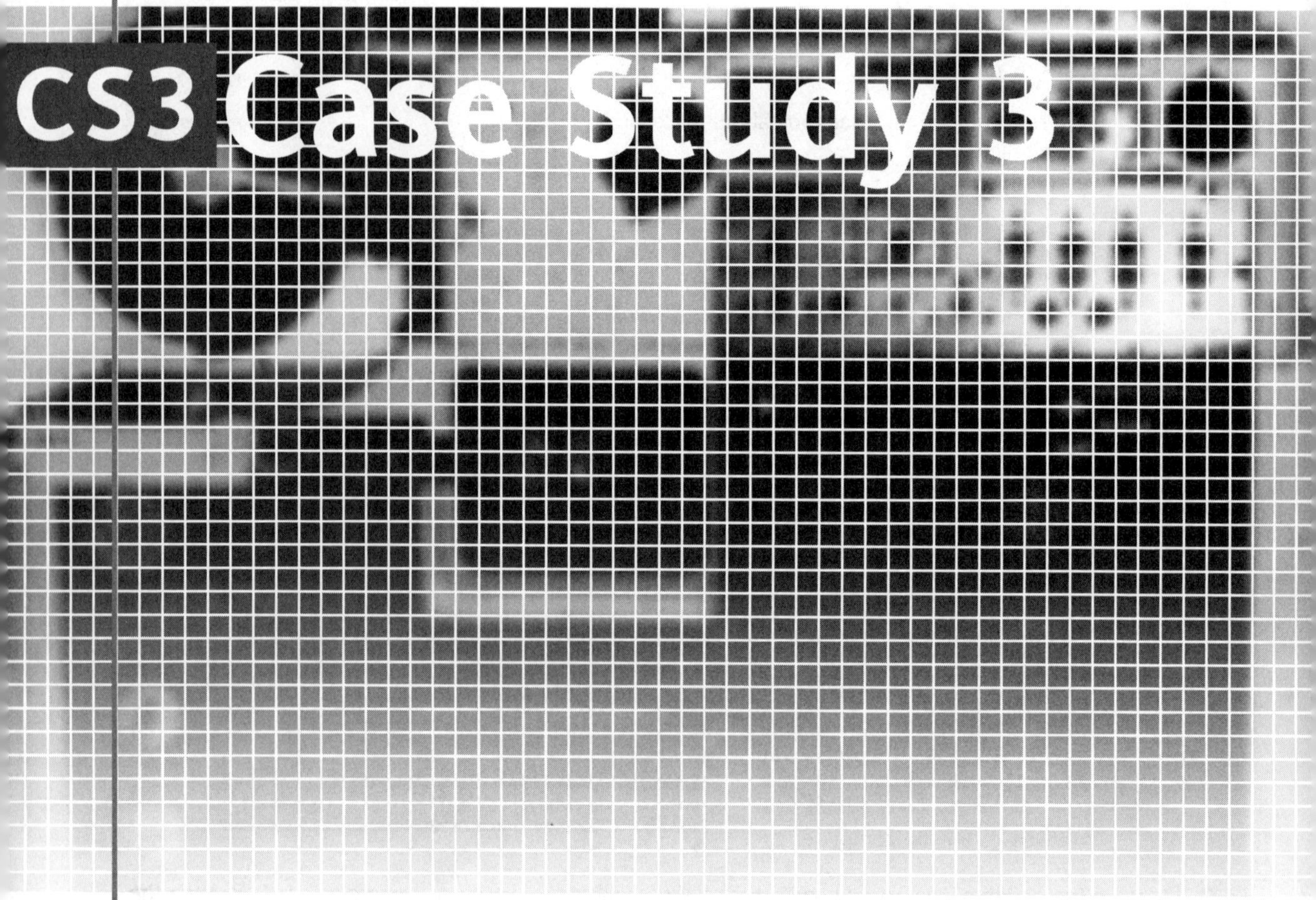

The brief

O-music, o-generator video presentation for viral e-mail / web broadcast.

O-generator is an intuitive piece of music software, to be released by o-music. It will be available in various musical styles, and appeal to a range of users, from young teenagers to experienced amateur musicians.

As part of the initial awareness campaign, The New Media Works wanted to produce an appealing video that could be web broadcast from the o-music site, www.o-music.tv. The video had to capture the excitement and flavor of what can be produced with o-generator.

The finished video is on the CD-ROM if you want to take a sneaky peak at how it ended up.

The idea

After having great fun playing with various o-generator samples, we felt the best way to tease the senses of prospective o-generator users would be to create an MTV styled promotional video. By producing an advertising biased video, the focus will fall heavily with the brand.

The feel

The music software is capable of producing a huge range of styles, from Samba to Soul. Rather than literally showing the styles in the video, we felt an eclectic audio mix with hints of the styles could be used in the music track. On the image side, we wanted a mix of high-energy visuals that are punchy and contrasting, switching quickly to create a fast paced edit. To enhance this feeling, the fast flashing imagery is juxtaposed with ambient slower visuals, underneath some simple messages about the software.

The messages

Although the feel is an important part of what needs to be said, we still needed to literally explain what the software is about, and what it can be used for. To help make this easier, we scribbled out a storyboard.

Storyboard part 1

The storyboard at this stage isn't too concerned about time, or the total length of the video. We just use it to get the messages down in the right order.

The text we'll use goes something like this:

1. Count in on beats '1' to '4'.

2. 'See it', 'hear it', 'feel it'.

3. 'Generate a note', 'a beat', 'a rhythm', 'and a tune'.

4. 'Generate funk...', 'Rock...', 'Jazz...', 'Samba...', 'Latin...', 'Bhangra...', 'Pop...', 'Blues...'

5. 'O-GENERATOR', 'See it', 'hear it', 'feel it', 'www.o-music.tv.

The soundtrack

We're starting to build an idea, so at this stage we source the music track we want to use. Matt (resident music maker) is continuously playing around with different music and styles. He has a rough idea of something already put together, so we can use this, and tighten up the timing of our story to the track.

In AE, we need to import the track and analyze it to see where the main beats and breaks are.

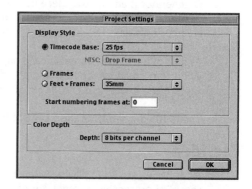

We launched AE, and set up the project. In the Project Settings window, we set up the time base to the PAL standard of 25fps.

Then we created a new composition at 320*240 pixels, 25fps, and 0:02:00:00 minutes long:

We chose to create a composition at 320*240 (4:3 ratio) as it's a user friendly size for web download, and also, considering future possibilities, we could scale up the entire composition to full screen pal 768x576 and keep everything to the same proportion.

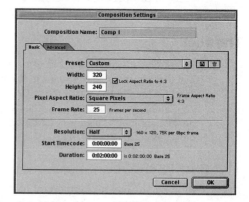

We then imported the audio: Track 01.aif. We dragged this file into the Comp 1 window. In the timeline for the composition, we opened the layer to show the audio and effects layers, then opened the waveform layer inside of the audio layer to show the waveform in the timeline.

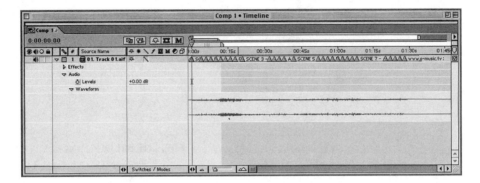

Before we listened to the track, we needed to adjust the preview preferences in the menu, Edit > Preferences > Previews.... Here, we changed the audio preview to 0:02:00:00. We then chose Composition > Preview > Audio Preview. Now we could see the playback head passing over the beats, and monitor the style changes in the timeline waveform. We needed to put in annotated markers where the beats and changes happen in the audio track. We do this to help define both the amount of time a visual element is on screen for, and when it appears.

We dragged the time marker in the Timeline window, to our first main beat, at 0:00:04:00, and then with the audio layer selected, chose Layer > Add Marker. We double clicked on the marker and added the comment Beat 1. This will be the beginning of our textual count-in.

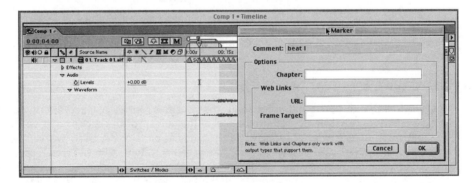

We then needed to repeat this process to add the rest of the markers, and note down the time at which they are inserted. We ended up with a list like this:

TIME	MARKER COMMENT
0:00:06:00	BEAT 2
0:00:08:00	BEAT 3
0:00:10:00	BEAT 4
0:00:14:00	SEE IT
0:00:16:00	HEAR IT
0:00:18:00	FEEL IT
0:00:21:00	AMBIENT BREAK
0:00:32:00	A NOTE
0:00:34:00	A BEAT
0:00:36:00	A RHYTHM
0:00:38:00	A TUNE
0:00:42:00	AMBIENT BREAK
0:00:54:00	FUNK
0:00:56:00	ROCK
0:00:58:00	DANCE
0:01:00:00	POP
0:01:02:00	BLUES
0:01:04:00	SAMBA
0:01:06:00	LATIN
0:01:08:00	AMBIENT BREAK
0:01:20:00	O-GENERATOR
0:01:22:00	SEE IT
0:01:24:00	HEAR IT
0:01:26:00	FEEL IT
0:01:28:00	WWW.O-MUSIC.TV

We now had a better understanding of the track, and could start to scribble down ideas for supporting visuals to shoot on DV, and consider at what point in time the various messages could come in.

Storyboard part 2

The storyboard, with timing and notes about the visuals, is roughly mapped out on paper. We try to tie the ideas as closely as possible to the feel of the music. For the background, we have an idea to shoot two different types of footage. On the ambient parts of the track, we want slow passive shots, and to contrast with this, we'll shoot fast paced activity for the heavy percussion sections. We decided that by randomly moving the camera, and constantly walking around with it, the shot would appear erratic and jumpy enough for the fast paced section, and to counteract this, the more ambient sections would consist of slow, well controlled panning. The messages and associated graphics are then going to sit over the top of, and work with the backgrounds.

To help segment work later on in the project, we mark the storyboard up into a number of scenes. These scenes will then become individual projects.

With the storyboard mapped out, we can now add it to the audio track to create a rough animatic. An animatic is a preliminary version of a video/animation/television commercial in which substituted content is used instead of live footage and real objects. This enables you to get a much more realistic idea of timing and content placement before wasting too much time/money creating content that may never be used. If we need to make any changes in direction, this stage really helps us see that.

Animatic

We used Photoshop to scan in the storyboard, crop out each frame, and number them as individual files to act as a temporary place holder for the graphics.

We then opened up the project with the audio track and its markers and imported the folder of storyboard pictures.

At this point, we renamed some of the markers with scene numbers as in the following table. This helps to easily identify the scenes in the timeline.

TIME	MARKER COMMENT
0:00:00:00	SCENE 1
0:00:04:00	BEAT 1
0:00:06:00	BEAT 2
0:00:08:00	BEAT 3
0:00:10:00	BEAT 4
0:00:12:00	SCENE 2
0:00:14:00	SEE IT
0:00:16:00	HEAR IT
0:00:18:00	FEEL IT
0:00:21:00	SCENE 3 - AMBIENT BREAK
0:00:32:00	SCENE 4 - A NOTE
0:00:34:00	A BEAT
0:00:36:00	A RHYTHM
0:00:38:00	A TUNE
0:00:42:00	SCENE 5 - AMBIENT BREAK
0:00:52:00	SCENE 6 - STREET SCENE
0:00:54:00	FUNK
0:00:56:00	ROCK
0:00:58:00	DANCE
0:01:00:00	POP
0:01:02:00	BLUES
0:01:04:00	SAMBA
0:01:06:00	LATIN
0:01:08:00	SCENE 7 - AMBIENT BREAK
0:01:20:00	SCENE 8 - O-GENERATOR
0:01:22:00	SEE IT
0:01:24:00	HEAR IT
0:01:26:00	FEEL IT
0:01:28:00	WWW.O-MUSIC.TV

Each storyboard file was then placed at the appropriate point in the Timeline window. To do this, the first scanned storyboard image was dragged to the Timeline window and placed at marker Beat 1. We then moved the time marker to before the next marker, and double clicked on the layer with the scanned storyboard image. This window shows us the in and out points for this clip/layer. Clicking on the out point icon sets the out point for this clip. We then repeated this process for the following times/markers and clip numbers.

PIC NO.	TIME	MARKER COMMENT
001.JPG	0:00:00:00	SCENE 1
002.JPG	0:00:04:00	BEAT 1
003.JPG	0:00:06:00	BEAT 2
004.JPG	0:00:08:00	BEAT 3
005.JPG	0:00:10:00	BEAT 4
006.JPG	0:00:12:00	SCENE 2
007.JPG	0:00:14:00	SEE IT
008.JPG	0:00:16:00	HEAR IT
009.JPG	0:00:18:00	FEEL IT
010.JPG	0:00:21:00	SCENE 3 - AMBIENT BREAK
011.JPG	0:00:32:00	SCENE 4 - A NOTE
012.JPG	0:00:34:00	A BEAT
013.JPG	0:00:36:00	A RHYTHM
014.JPG	0:00:38:00	A TUNE
015.JPG	0:00:42:00	SCENE 5 - AMBIENT BREAK
016.JPG	0:00:52:00	SCENE 6 - STREET SCENE
017.JPG	0:00:54:00	FUNK
018.JPG	0:00:56:00	ROCK
019.JPG	0:00:58:00	DANCE
020.JPG	0:01:00:00	POP
021.JPG	0:01:02:00	BLUES
022.JPG	0:01:04:00	SAMBA
023.JPG	0:01:06:00	LATIN
024.JPG	0:01:08:00	SCENE 7 - AMBIENT BREAK
025.JPG	0:01:20:00	SCENE 8 - O-GENERATOR
026.JPG	0:01:22:00	SEE IT
027.JPG	0:01:24:00	HEAR IT
028.JPG	0:01:26:00	FEEL IT
029.JPG	0:01:28:00	WWW.O-MUSIC.TV

Render movie/RAM preview

This is where we start to enjoy the fruits of our labor, and see the animatic for the first time. The Composition window was set to Half resolution, and we then chose Composition > Preview > RAM Preview.

You can now see why we took our time to find the right parts of the audio track to apply the visuals to. The whole thing starts to gel together, and it gives us a great indication of how to produce the different types of media to go into the video.

Creating media sources

As with any project of this nature, we like to experiment and gather more film footage and digital stills than we actually need. It's only when the final edit comes together, that we decide on the pieces of footage we want to use.

Filming techniques

We went out into the local streets to capture video and photographic footage. Remember, we had two different styles of background video footage to capture. Rather than doing unnecessary work in AE, we try to capture the footage, as closely as possible to how it should finally appear. We have a Sony miniDV TRV900E that, used in the right way, can create some great effects on its own. The effects we wanted can be achieved using any reasonable video camera.

The first footage to get was the ambient sections. We found a busy street, switched the focus on the camera, so that everything was out of focus and recorded head shots of people walking along the street. We used the same out of focus technique to shoot slow panning shots of the interior and exterior of buildings.

Next, we wanted the high energy backgrounds. We captured this by setting the camera shutter speed to 3 frames per second with auto focus. We then walked up the street, moving the camera around randomly. What you end up with is each frame motion blurred, which when seen in sequence gives all the feeling of activity we were after.

While we are out and about with the camera, we used the opportunity to gather any extra footage, experimenting with exposures and situations to see if anything interesting comes out. In case they are needed (you never know!), we also took a digital stills camera, to shoot interesting signage or buildings.

Video capture

Back at the studio, we hooked the video camera up to iMovie 2 via firewire on the Mac. iMovie 2 (http://www.apple.com/imovie/) is ideal for grabbing this type of footage, as it is very easy to work with clips of video. With on-screen buttons providing remote camera control for capturing, recording, playing, rewinding, fast-forwarding, and pausing, you can preview video from the camcorder on the computer screen, so we use this function to capture the bits of footage we feel are most appropriate, and try to keep them to the length they are used in each scene of our AE project. iMovie 2 saves each clip in its project batch folder in DV format. These are then ready to put in the current AE project folder for use in this project.

Illustrator graphics

We prepared all the line and text graphics in Illustrator and Freehand. The first thing to note here is how AE handles these graphics when they are imported. If you had an Illustrator file that had just the word BEAT in it, and you put a blur effect on it, the effect would only happen inside the bounds of the text. To get around this, we prepare each Illustrator graphic with a box that's bigger than the graphic it's holding. The box has a thin stroke width on it, but no fill.

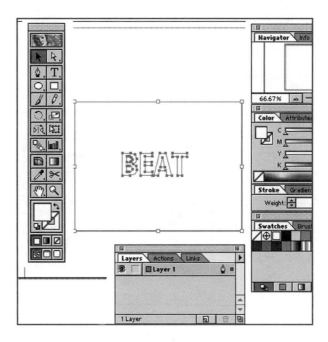

Then, when this is imported into AE, we can use the layers mask to crop out the bounding box, leaving the graphic/text still showing. If the blur effect is then applied, it behaves more as we expect it to.

Creating the scenes 1-8

When all the graphics had been prepared, we were ready to start creating the scenes. Each scene is built as its own AE project. Eventually, all the separate scenes/projects are imported into a master for the final edit. Splitting the scenes into individual projects helps us distribute the workload.

To make sure we're all doing the same thing, the easiest thing to do is to duplicate our animatic project, and rename it scene_01. We don't need the storyboard images in Scene 1 project any more, so we can delete them from the Comp 1 Timeline and Project window.

We can then quit out of AE and duplicate the scene_01 project eight more times, renaming each one scene_02 - 09 (9 is the master composition). We are now ready to build each scene.

Constructing scene 1

As we start scene_01, it's worth considering how the graphics used will fit with the track. We decided the pace of the tune we are using should control the graphics.

If you listen to the music on the finished movie (available on the CD), you will notice that it's broken up into beats of 4. It seemed natural then, to emphasize this in the graphics. Fundamentally, it's visually counting in the music track.

Layout of the composition

As you can see in the screenshot below, the timeline (comp_01) for scene_01.aep contains the following compositions:

- number_01

- number_02

- number_03

- number_04

and in addition there is:

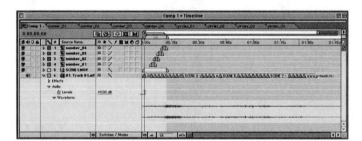

- SCENE1.MOV and

- 01.Track 01.aif

You'll notice that the scene is broken up in time by the segments we allocated in the storyboard (and animatic). This scene is 12 seconds in length, which is governed by the length of the video (SCENE1.MOV – the yellow layer in the timeline).

Following the storyboard in reference to the events that happen, you will notice that there's a gap of 4 seconds, which is pure video and no effects. On 4 seconds, the number 1 is introduced in keeping with the beat. This pattern is repeated on 6 seconds, 8 seconds and 10 seconds.

Text layers

Within the main timeline, the composition number_01 begins at 4 seconds and is set to 2 seconds in length.

The composition consists of two Illustrator files and another composition (which is used as a matte effect, but don't worry about the matte effect for a minute, since we will first discuss the effects used on the layer c_bold_01).

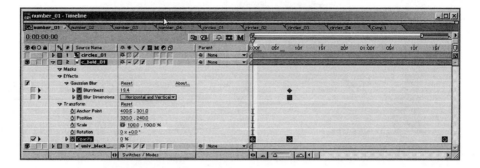

If you look at the keyframes in the timeline, you will notice we have only used two effects for the c_bols_01 layer, Gaussian Blur and Opacity. The c_bols_01 layer contains an image of the number '1'.

The layer that holds the blur has a single effect that sets the amount of blur, and the blur dimensions. These are set to 19.4 and Horizontal and Vertical respectively.

> To repeat this on a clean composition of your own, go to Effects > Blur and Sharpen > Gaussian Blur. *Just how the blur is used is up to you, but it can be applied over as many keyframes as you want. Remember, though, that using effects like blurring is very processor heavy when it comes to rendering.*

Now if we look at the Opacity of this layer (c_bold_01), you'll notice that a keyframe at 0:00:00:00 sets the Opacity to 0%, by adding another at 0:00:00:08 (at 100%), the layer will gently fade in over a short amount of time. Further along the timeline (at 0:00:01:17) we insert another keyframe with a value of 0% so the image fades out slowly and disappears as the beat does.

Used as a simple text effect, this works very nicely. The layer beneath this one, however, is a little more complicated. univ_black_01 uses a composition as a matte channel (or mask).

Set matte

The layer called univ_black_01 contains an outlined font from Illustrator. If you check the parameters of this layer, we have not used anything like those used in the previous text layer.

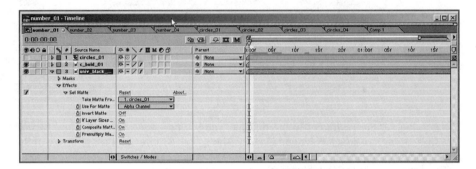

Instead, we have set the text layer to use the composition circles_01 as a matte. Going to Effect > Effect Controls opens a pop-up window that displays effects used on that particular layer/channel, and gives us a bit more information about the matte used.

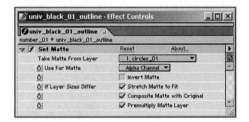

Under the name of the effect used (Set Matte), you'll notice the Take Matte From Layer option. Next to this, there's a menu that allows you to pick whatever layer you want as the matte.

To get univ_black_01 to work as a matte, we needed to make sure the eye icon on the layer circles_01 had been turned off.

Circles_01

Two Illustrator files exist in this composition: circle_fill, and circle_outline.

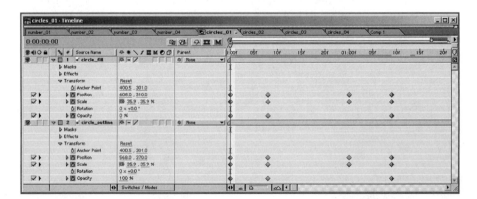

The circle_fill layer consists of a filled circle shape, whilst circle_outline is an outlined version of the same shape. Both follow roughly the same route, but are offset to add more depth.

In this case, we have changed the Position, Scale, and Opacity of the layers over time. You will notice that keyframes exist in the same place in time for both layers, so that they will move in sync.

The actual movement of the layers was constructed as follows:

1. We shifted the position of the circle_fill off-screen in the first frame, and added keyframes for the new Position. We also set the Scale to 35.9%, and the Opacity to 0%.

2. On the 8th frame, we added another set of keyframes for Position, Scale, and Opacity, changing the values slightly to get the circles moving and scaling on the screen. We then did the same at the 1 second mark, and then again at the 1 second and 9 frame mark, where we also set the Opacity value to 0%.

3. We set the Transform properties of the circle_outline layer to follow the same path as circle_fill, but slightly altered the value of each keyframe to create more depth. The only other difference was that at 0:00:01:09, we want the outlined circle to stay on the screen at 50% Opacity.

Once we had completed what will be our matte composition, we went back to the number_01 composition, and scrolled along the timeline (making sure circles_01 was switched off) to preview how the matte effect was masking the text. The use of the circles matte produced a really interesting effect on the text. We went with it.

All we needed to do now was repeat this process for the other number compositions, 02 - 04. Once this was done, we went back to the main composition comp_1 and dragged the new compositions, numbers_01, numbers_02, numbers_03, and numbers_04, into the timeline from the Library window.

Since we had markers in place on the audio layer, we could easily see how to place the compositions exactly in place at their starting point.

Constructing scene 2

In the previous section, we referred to building the timeline and using and embedding other compositions. Hopefully, you will now be able to see how these compositions work with one another.

Scene 2 is created in much the same way. However in this case, only one composition has a matte, rather than all of them, as before.

You can use this effect as much or as little as you like, just remember it all adds to the rendering time at the end of the project. This is another good reason to think through the project, as we have done, by creating the animatic. Doing this allowed us to get an idea of the content and effects we might want to use (or not use!).

Layout of the composition

If you refer to the storyboard, there's a gap of 2 seconds at the end of scene 1, where the video plays through without any effects over the top. This helps when it comes to piecing all the scenes together, since we will not have any difficult edits to line up.

Following the 2 second gap in scene 1, scene 2 begins with a further 2 seconds, in which outlined circles introduce the 'see it, hear it, feel it' section.

The main timeline

Let's look at the main timeline (Comp_02) and decipher what's going on each of the layers/channels.

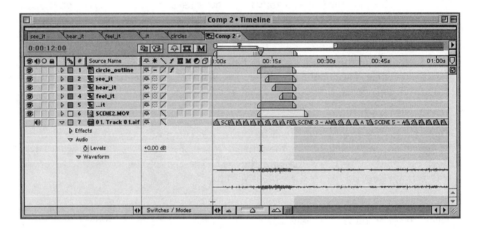

Refer to the music layer, 01. Track 01.aif and you'll notice that at 0:00:12:00, we have the circle outline layer animating throughout this scene until 0:00:20:20. This layer uses a blur effect, Position, Scale, and Opacity animation.

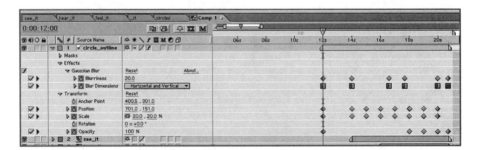

As the circle animates in, we thought it might be nice to blur it against the already hectic background, to help add more depth. To achieve this, at 0:00:12:00 we added a Gaussian Blur with a Blurriness of 20, and Horizontal and Vertical dimensions. We also added keyframes to the

Position, Scale, and Opacity channels, so it animates from the right, into the center, while growing from 20% to 150% when it reaches the next set of keyframes at 0:00:14:00. At this point, we set the Gaussian Blur to 0 Blurriness to give an illusion of focus.

Over the next couple of seconds, we needed to shift the focus from the circle to the text clips that will appear. At 0:00:15:00, we added more keyframes in the position and scale channels to reduce its size and position. At 0:00:16:00 we reduced it still further. We repeated this process up until 0:00:19:28, at which point, we fade and blur the circle out until 0:00:20:20.

See_it, hear_it, and feel_it

Underneath the circle_outline layer in the main timeline are 3 more compositions: see_it, hear_it, and feel_it. It's important that these compositions are synched to come in on each beat, at 2-second intervals.

Let's ignore (just for now!) how these were constructed, and first turn our attention to the composition it, which includes the composition circles inside of it.

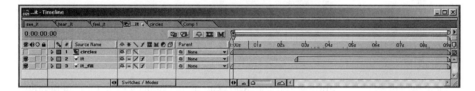

Setting the matte

Inside the composition ...it, there is another composition named circles. In addition to this, there are two Illustrator files, one solid representation of the word 'it', it_fill, and one outlined version, it.

Persisting with the ideas we used in scene 1, we decided to also use a matte in scene 2. The matte used in this composition was circles, a circle composition similar to that used earlier. However, this time, we applied the matte in a different way to create a slightly different effect; we used Set Matte on both of the layers.

Referring to the storyboard, you will see that scene 2 is just around 9 seconds in length. Therefore, we first check the length of the composition we'll be setting up.

We then selected the layer it_fill and went to Effect > Channel > Set Matte to apply the effect to the layer. This opened up the Effect Controls window, where we specified that the circles layer was to be used as the matte. We then did the same with the layer called it.

Independently to the matte effects, it_fill is set in place using the Position, Scale, and Opacity keyframes. Also, to create some difference between the two text files, we gave it_fill a Gaussian Blur (Blurriness: 30, and Direction: Horizontal and Vertical effect) set at 0:00:00:00, which remains constant throughout.

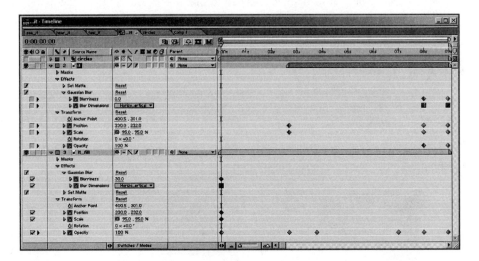

Opacity values change throughout the layer. The actual opacity of it_fill is dependent on how the circle matte is working against the two Illustrator files. At 0:00:02:20, the Opacity is set at 100%, this changes to 0% at 0:00:03:22, and back to 100% at 0:00:07:00. Changing the Opacity value like this creates different effects contrasting with what is happening in the foreground / background. Finally, the layer fades back to 0% at 0:00:08:00.

To add to the difference between the filled text (it_fill) and outlined text (it), we bought in the outlined text later in the timeline, at 0:00:02:20.

it remains static, and is only affected by the matte up until 0:00:08:00, when a blur effect is applied, and the layer is faded out over the final second.

Inside our matte layer, the composition, circles, a filled circle shape animates around the screen affecting the text layers as it animates. This is a simple animation that uses Position, Scale, and Opacity. Starting off screen, and sized at 20%, at 0:00:02:00 it is scaled to 150%, as it is brought to the center of the frame. At this size, the entire text file is revealed. The size and position of the circle fluctuate up until 0:00:08:00, where the circle holds at a Scale value of 150% for the final second.

Text compositions – see it, hear it and feel it

Inside the composition see_it, there are a series of keyframes that animate the text file around in keeping with the feel of the music.

We set the Position keyframe to where we want the text to begin, and Opacity to 0% at 0:00:00:00. We then changed the Opacity setting to 100% at 0:00:00:01 to give the impression that the music has prompted the text. Over the next second, (0:00:01:20) the text jigs around to add pace to the presentation. At this point, we want this to fade back as the next piece of text springs on, so we change its Position and Opacity at 0:00:03:00, to get it to animate out of the way and disappear.

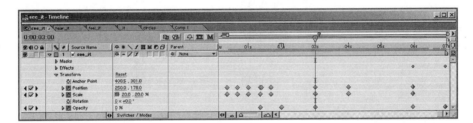

The composition then continues to move and fade up to 50% Opacity until it fades and blurs out at 0:00:06:00.

Each of the remaining compositions follows the same route. However, when these are introduced into the main timeline for scene 2, we want to alter the compositions' properties a little more.

The main timeline

Now that we'd created these compositions, dragging them onto the main timeline, guided by the markers on the audio layer allowed us to plan effects to the actual sound events. Notice that all of the compositions sit directly under the labels on the audio track.

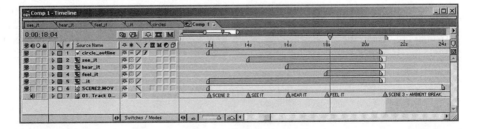

At the moment, the compositions see_it, hear_it, and feel_it already change in opacity. However, in keeping with the timing of the tune at this point (0:00:18:04), we want the graphics to be erratic, and flash on and off.

At 0:00:18:04, the Opacity of the graphics is set at 100%, at 0:00:18:07, in the main timeline, we change this to 0%. This repeats over time to the beat of the music up until 0:00:19:16, as follows:

Time	Opacity
0:00:18:04	100%
0:00:18:07	0%
0:00:18:10	100%
0:00:18:14	100%
0:00:18:16	0%
0:00:18:20	100%
0:00:18:22	100%
0:00:18:25	0%
0:00:18:28	100%
0:00:19:02	100%
0:00:19:04	0%
0:00:19:08	100%
0:00:19:10	100%
0:00:19:13	0%
0:00:19:16	100%

Once these effects have played though on the timeline, the remainder of the scene plays through the effects we set up in our individual compositions earlier on.

Constructing scene 3

This scene is the first of the two more ambient scenes, and to visualize this, we need to take the pace of the animation right down as the music becomes more chilled. The use of blurred buildings as the basis of this shot allows soft geometric forms to softly come through, and the camera panning accentuates the feeling of a more ambient state.

Animation

First of all, we imported a five-second shot of a building. The shot was taken shooting from top to bottom. We felt that an opposite motion (bottom to top) better suited this particular section of the tune. So the first thing we did was to place the video in its correct position on the timeline, starting at 21 seconds, and time stretched this from 5 seconds to minus 11 seconds. This will stretch the clip so that it lasts as long as we want it to, and also, being a negative value, it will play the clip backwards.

We wanted to use circles on top of this video in an interesting and fairly abstract way. This was to subtly introduce the viewer to the appearance of the product, and allow the motion of the grouped circles to reflect the ambient state of the tune.

To make up the ring group animation layer, we used Illustrator to create a ring of circles as white outlines. We then brought the layer into After Effects.

To add a bit of depth and spatial quality, we decided to use the Basic 3D tool, which allowed us to alter the layer's Swivel, Tilt, and Distance to Image. By changing these values, you can apply simple motion with perspective over time.

In this instance, we used the Basic 3D tool to introduce the ring from the distance, and change its perspective as it became closer to the viewer. We decided to confine this part of the animation to two seconds (the entire length of the layer was 30 seconds)

What we did was to give our 3D values to our ring graphic, and then duplicate it as required. First off, we started at 00:00 in the animate rings composition, which had the rings off in the distance and gave it the Basic 3D values of:

Swivel :	0 (revolutions) x -90°
Tilt :	0 (revolutions) x -90°
Distance from image :	100

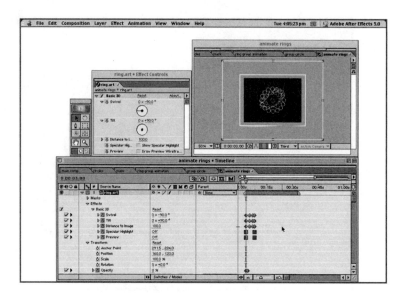

The other Basic 3D values were left as a constant. To introduce this smoothly, we faded in the ring from 0% Opacity to 100% over 1 second.

The final values for the ring (at the 2 second mark) were as follows :

Swivel :	0 (revolutions) x -0°
	(this value is given to it at 1
	second to help visibility)
Tilt :	0 (revolutions) x -0°
Distance from image :	0.0

This basically meant that the image was now flat on. To enhance the effect, we duplicated the layer 3 times, and offset, and overlapped our current ring at one-second intervals with the new ones within the same composition. We wanted to create a formation of four concentric rings, so we changed the scale of each ring to the values of:

Layer 1 :	100%
Layer 2:	65%
Layer 3 :	40%
Layer 4:	25%

As these files were all in one composition, we imported that composition into a new one, ring group animation, so we were able manipulate the whole thing as one.

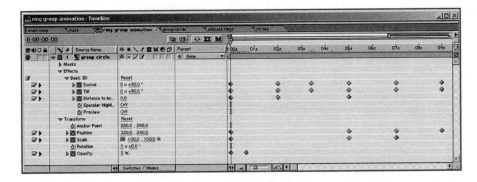

We gave the composition some more Basic 3D values, which started at 00:00. At five seconds, all the Basic 3D effects were reset, ready for the final part of the animation to occur over the next four seconds.

In this final part of the scene, the composition was scaled upwards, and then the whole sequence was reversed, and disappeared just before the breakdown of the tune occurred. Again, It was important to get the flow of animation correct to the style of the music, and to experiment with different values to see which result's work best.

Finally, to lie this across the background video, we used two very simple techniques that added depth and texture to this scene. First off, we chose the Set Matte effect on the scene3.mov layer, and got this layer to Take Matte From Layer: 1. ring group animation. We then hid this layer so that we could see the Layer Matte coming through. What we did next, was to duplicate scene3.mov, and take off the layer matte on this layer. The effect was invisible at this stage, but it was there. All we needed to do was to create some contrast by a constant enhancement to the layers Brightness & Contrast. We used the values of:

Brightness :	100.0
Contrast :	44.2

We could now see the concentric rings beginning to stand out. This scene was now complete.

Constructing scene 4

To allow for more accurate and easier compositing of the scene, we made the main composition in last for the full length of the video (1:35 minutes), and started the scene at its real starting point, (32 seconds).

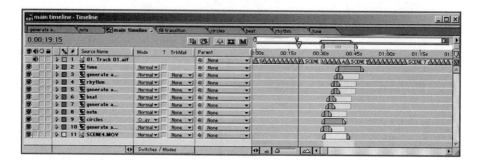

By looking at our storyboard, we could see that scene 4 lasted from 31 seconds to 42 seconds., and that it would consist of text on top of fast paced abstractly shot video. We found it easier to prepare all of our source files before we opened up After Effects.

For this scene we required individual files of text that read:

- GENERATE A

- NOTE

- BEAT

- RHYTHM

- TUNE

We also wanted to use two simple graphics for

- beat_ring (a circle outline)

- beat_ring_fill (a filled circle shape)

As mentioned before, we created these Illustrator files with a large bounding box so that we had more control of the files once we imported them into After Effects.

Animation

We previewed the audio first, and got a feel of the pace of the background movie and music. We saw that we needed the text to appear with a punchy rhythmical feel. Also, the key words of 'NOTE', 'BEAT', 'RHYTHM', and 'TUNE' were to be introduced by 'GENERATE A'.

First off, we set the composition generate a... to be just 10 seconds, as we knew it would not be on screen for any longer that that. To create a repetitive beat feel for this section, we simply changed the position of the text over time. We created the punchy feel by duplicating the layer, and moving it along in the timeline to create a 1 frame gap between the layers. This is a great technique for producing a quick on and off flash.

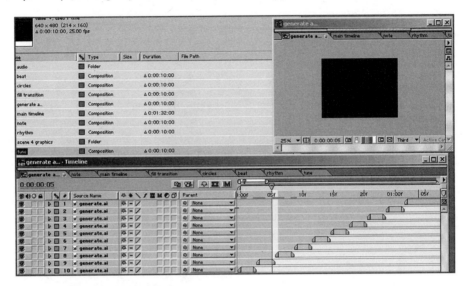

To enhance this technique, small positional changes were made between the sequential layers. The layer was actually repeated 9 times before the final layer's (layer 1) Opacity faded from 100% to 0%. In total, generate a... ran for 2:02 seconds. This gave us enough time for the phrase to be read on its own, in conjunction with 'NOTE', 'BEAT', and so on. This composition was ultimately repeated to introduce each new word.

We then looked at creating the composition 'NOTE', and decided that we wanted to bring in the circles again, in a subtle, but purposeful way. So we used a circle to reveal the key words quickly, which we felt acted as a visual description of the musical beat itself.

To introduce the word, 'NOTE', we had the word Scaling from 80% to 100%, and we changed its Opacity from 0% to 100%. Both of these values changed in quick succession over 5 frames. We used a separate circle composition to mask our 'NOTE' composition, fill transition.

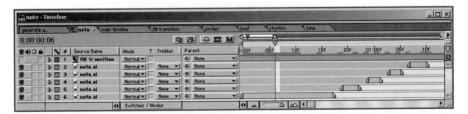

We created the composition fill transition by simply having the Illustrator file beat_ring_fill on the timeline Scaling from 10% to 300%, where it covers the whole screen.

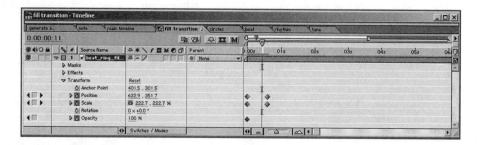

We then brought this composition into the note composition, and placed an effect on it so that it would act as a mask. We chose the Set Matte on the bottom layer, and got this layer to Take Matte From Layer: 1. fill transition.

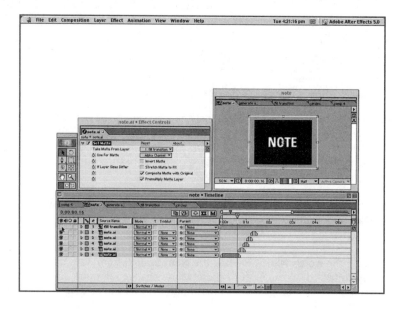

We then hid this layer by turning it off, and checked the animation by using a RAM preview. We saw that the circle now quickly revealed the word 'NOTE'. This was exactly the effect we were after. We repeated this technique and applied it in new compositions for each of the three remaining words. The easiest way we found to do this was to simply copy and paste keyframes from one composition into the next

We enhanced the rhythmical feel to this section by introducing an outlined circle, beat_ring.ai, which again played on the beat of the percussion based tune. To help build up this section, and relate to the words, we introduced one circle with 'NOTE', two with a 'BEAT', three with 'RHYTHM', and four with 'TUNE'.

In the circles composition, we simply scaled and positioned files, and flashed them on and off, using the same layered and gap effect as we used to introduce the key words. Again this worked well with the tune and the background video.

All the compositions were then placed on the main timeline composition, in relation to the storyboard. We always used RAM previews to check the timing of our compositions.

> *RAM previews are a great way to check an area of work, as opposed to rendering a test movie each time. Within a RAM preview area, After Effects caches the work span, and only small changes that are made within that area are re-rendered as part of another preview, again saving valuable time.*

Finally, we added a layer effect to the circles composition on the main timeline, by changing the circles layer mode. We did this by clicking on the Switches/Modes button on the bottom of the timeline, which enabled us to change the mode from Normal to Overlay. These work in a very similar way to those in Photoshop. The only other values that we changed are Position and Scale.

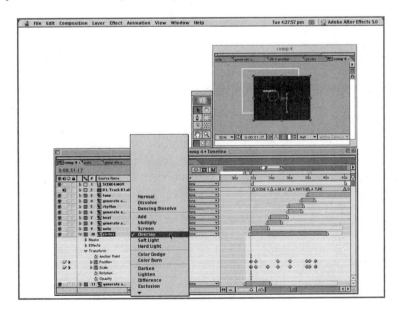

Constructing scene 5

Scene 5 needed to be the visual and audio opposite to scene 6. We wanted to take the playback head device from the o-generator software (a series of three circles), and fit it with the ambient sound. The playback head does a circular motion around the beats in o-generator, so this fits in perfectly with the relaxed feeling for this scene. Because the rest of the video uses very abstracted backgrounds, we felt it would be nice to get a reality check here (but not too much), so we cut and edited a simple shot of people arriving at the top of an escalator, and saved the shot as SCENE5.MOV.

The graphics were prepared in illustrator, as with previous scenes, the only difference being that to keep the line circles and fill circles sharp, and positioned in the correct place, they need to be scaled in Illustrator by 200%. You'll notice that the sweep of the circles rotates around a pivot point. This pivot point is actually the center of the bounding box that is created in the Illustrator files, which means the rotation automatically rotates around this point.

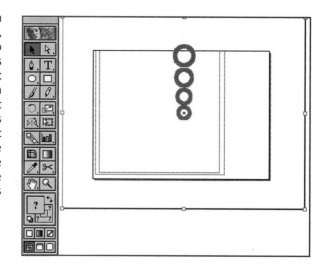

The name of the composition already in this project, needed changing to comp 5. The first thing we did with the background footage, SCENE5.MOV, was to put it into a new composition, video edit. We took a copy of the audio track with the annotated markers on it, and pasted it into the video edit comp. Like all the other scenes, this gave us an accurate position in time for the start of scene 5 in the overall video.

The SCENE5.MOV layer was positioned to start at the marker SCENE 5, and scaled in the layer's Transform settings to 70%. Then it was Time Stretched to speed it up by 30%. We switched the audio icon on the layer off, and duplicated the layer. The new layer was then positioned to start at 0:00:46:12. To give the background a little more energy, we decided to chop up, repeat, reverse, speed up, and slow down bits of SCENE5.MOV.

We duplicated the layer again, and positioned it at 0:00:46:19. We then Time Stretched it to -30%, in effect reversing the sequence. The time marker was then positioned at 0:00:47:24. Double clicking on the layer, we then clicked on the in-point icon. The time marker was then set to 0:00:48:14 to create the out point. The layer was duplicated again, positioned at 0:00:48:14 and its Time Stretch was set to 15%, to speed it up even further. This process was then repeated with different in and out points, and stretch factors on the rest of the layers.

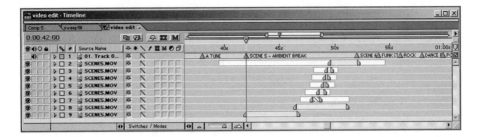

The main timeline (comp 5) for this scene uses the video edit composition, affected in two different ways.

■ one of them is simply blurred

■ the other is masked using another composition

This composition used as a mask is sweepfill, and it contains one of the two Illustrator files used in the scene.

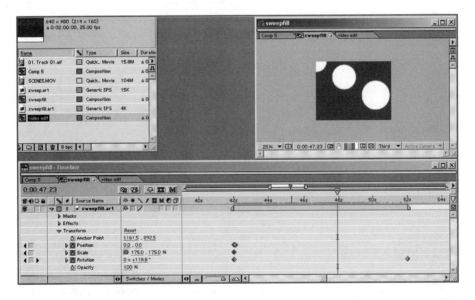

Sweepfill.art was dragged into the sweepfill composition to start at 0:00:42:00. We then opened up the layer, and set a keyframe for the Rotation property to 30°. Its Position was set to 0, 0 and the Scale was set to 175%. We then moved the time marker to 0:00:52:00, double clicked on the layer, and set the out point here. Returning to the timeline, we set a new keyframe for the Rotation property at 180°. We then wanted to copy the layer's attributes to another Illustrator layer in comp 5. To do this, we selected the four keyframe icons, and copied them.

In comp 5, we dragged sweep.art from the Project window to the timeline at 0:00:42:00. Then pasted the previously copied properties from the clipboard. Again, we then moved the time marker to 0:00:52:00, double clicked on the layer, and set the out point here. The only other thing we changed on the sweep.art layer was its Opacity; that was set to 65%.

We then dragged the video edit comp, and sweepfill from the Project window, and placed them in comp 5 at 0:00:00:00.

We duplicated video edit, so that we had two copies of it. The lower layer of video edit had a Gaussian Blur effect put on it, and the upper video edit layer is left to become the sharp, in focus, rotating circles you can see in the final film. This was achieved by switching the sweepfill layer off, and using it as a matte on the video edit layer. With the video edit layer selected, we chose Effect > Channel > Set Matte. In the Take Matte From option, we chose 1.sweepfill, and then for Use For Matte, we chose Alpha Channel.

Constructing scene 6

This scene played a very important part, in that it visually described the tune at its most built up section, and it also described the type of music that can be created through the o-generator. Once again, we animated this very closely to the beat that occurred throughout that period of the tune.

We wanted to introduce the viewer to the information bit by bit, and we did this by splitting the phrase in a similar fashion to how we approached things in scene 3. By this, we mean that it will say 'GENERATE' first (not 'GENERATE A'), followed closely by a music type. We worked out that we had roughly two seconds to introduce the word 'GENERATE', and then the music type, before the next one needed to appear. We worked this out by the structure of the tune in, knowing that the text would appear on every forth beat.

Animation

We used a technique here that brought on each item in the same way, and thought it worthwhile to take our time and get the first one exactly right. From there we could just copy and paste the properties onto future frames.

A piece of advice here, in this technique, we thought it better not to use keyframes in each layers' properties. We chose to use the cut (in and out points) between layers to act as a break in transition. It's easier not to use keyframes here, as you will constantly need to check that you are not putting additional ones in where they are not wanted.

To start with, we looked at animating generate_music.ai, and decided to introduce it by having it positioned constantly to the center of the screen, at 100% Opacity for 10 frames (2/5 second). After this, we wanted it to appear flashy and rhythmic in relation to the music, so we introduced the use of shorter frames and breaks between them. Also, we changed the Position and Scale transforms to enhance the effect.

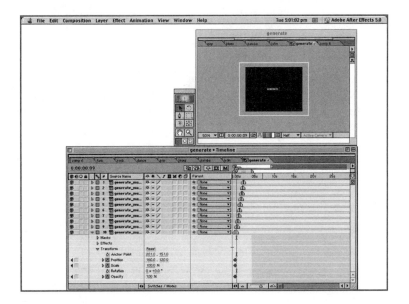

For example, we positioned generate_music.ai on layer two after a two-frame break, and changed the property values slightly, so that it created a bit of motion and contrast between the following frames. This process was repeated a further 8 times with the Scale, Opacity, and Position changed slightly each time. We kept each clip to just three frames, with a two frame break.

This composition will be used to introduce 'GENERATE' before each music type on the first four bars of this composition, and the third four bars to enhanced the feeling of rhythm and repetition.

We approached the introduction of each music type in a similar way to 'GENERATE', but used a slower animation process that picked out the more 'flow-y' parts of the tune. For this, we used the same relationship between Scale, Opacity, and Position, but without any frame gaps.

We started with the 'FUNK' composition.

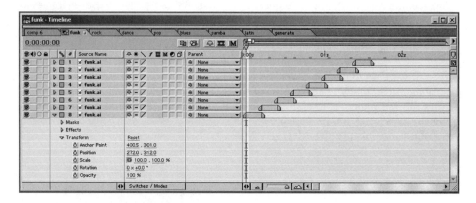

The composition began with funk.ai being placed roughly in the center of the screen, and at full Opacity. This remained constantly on the timeline, at a set position, for just 5 frames. Layer 8's out point is set on frame 5, and layer 7 starts at the same frame, but at a different Scale, Opacity, and Position. This process was then repeated six more times, leaving the composition one second and fifteen frames long.

Once again, we were able to copy and paste these key frame values directly onto our other 'music style' compositions where needed.

On the main timeline, comp 6, the position of compositions generate, funk, generate, and rock were lined up with the audio file to get the correct timing on the edit.

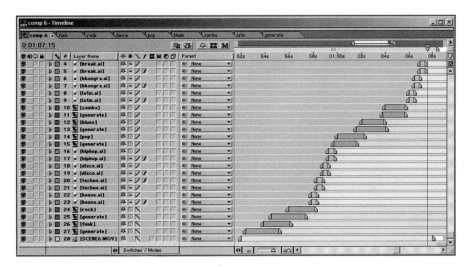

We then introduced something a bit different, in that we used a series of four different music types ('HOUSE', 'TECHNO', 'DISCO', and 'HIP HOP') that were introduced on screen quickly, and attached to each large beat that occurred to the four beats within this bar of music. Each of the four different music types was given a different position in the frame, rather than any individual animation. To visually support this, a juxtaposed duplicate layer was used, that was positioned away from the original layer. We placed a blur effect on this second layer, and on all of the blurred layers, we used a consistent Gaussian Blur value of 8.0, and dropped the Opacity to 50%.

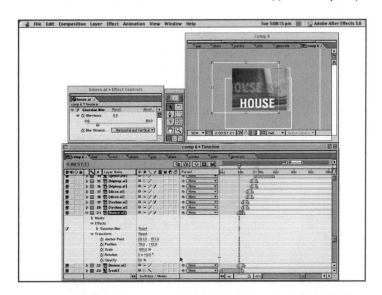

After this, we drop in a further six compositions, in a very similar way to our first 4 compositions, and to finish comp 6, we have four final music types, latin.ai, bhangra.ai, break.ai, and soul.ai displayed in a similar way to house.ai, techno.ai, disco.ai, and hiphop.ai.

Constructing scene 7

This scene was very similar to scene three; and we found the quickest way to create the scene's composition was to duplicate the project, comp3.aep, and rename it comp7.aep. We opened up the file, and replaced the footage file of the scene3.mov with that of scene7.mov.

> To replace the movie footage, we clicked on the layer in the timeline that we wanted to replace and go to File > Replace Footage > File....

We then saw that the appropriate effect was now occurring over our background movie. We felt, however, that we needed to slow scene7.mov down just a little to work better with the background, so we used a simple Time Stretch, and turned a 10 second clip into a 12 second clip.

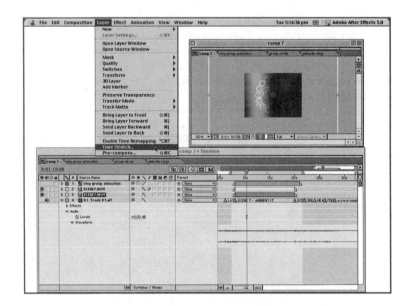

Constructing scene 8

If you check with the storyboard, you'll notice the similarities between what appears in scene 2 and scene 8. At this point, we duplicated scene 2, and renamed it 'scene 8'. We then replaced the background movie footage with footage for scene 8.

Once the video file was replaced, we selected all of the layers and dragged them along the timeline, so that the beginning lined up with the scene 8 marker located in the audio track.

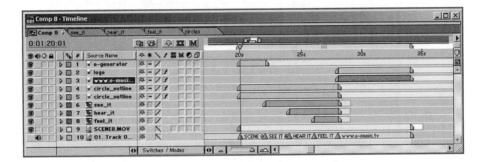

You will notice in the screenshot above, that there are 4 new layers in this composition, that weren't there in scene 2. Three of these are new, and the layer circle_outline has been duplicated and altered slightly.

Layout of the composition

Check how the timeline is constructed in the screenshot below. You will see that elements are aligned to markers in the audio layer, and as before, we have shifted the compositions see_it, hear_it, and feel_it to line up with the beat. Later we will explain how we added extra effects to these compositions.

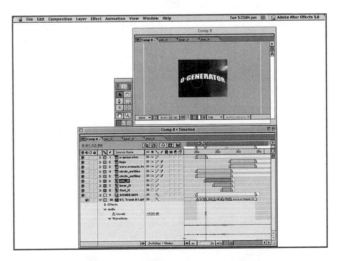

This scene begins at 0:01:20:00, and introduces the logo 'O-GENERATOR'. This layer punches in right at the start of the scene, scaled at 80%, and remains relatively untouched.

Also starting at 0:01:20:00 are the circle_outline layers. One of these is untouched from scene 2, but the other is a duplicate, and slightly altered to set up some foreground texture.

If you can cast your mind back to scene_02, you will remember that the circle_outline layer's Positioned, Scale, Opacity, and Blurriness were altered over time. So at this point, we had two circle_outline layers, in exactly the same place on the timeline, and using the exact same effects.

The idea was to get these layers working off each other, and interacting in quite a random way, to make the final shot look more dynamic. To do this, we positioned the playback head to whichever keyframe we would like to manipulate, and started re-positioning, re-scaling, and changing the blur values.

What follows shows how the duplicated layer differs from the original.

0:01:20:00	gaussian blur amount is reduced to 11.5% and repositioned to the left of the screen
0:01:21:01	scaled to 115%, remaining on the left of screen.
0:01:22:01	scaled 20% of original and repositioned.
0:01:23:01	scaled 80% and repositioned
0:01:23:19	blur value altered.
0:01:24:01	repositioned and scaled.
0:01:25:01	repositioned and scaled.
0:01:26:01	repositioned, opacity changed and scaled.
0:01:27:00	repositioned and scaled.
0:01:27:21	repositioned and scaled.

See_it, hear_it, and feel_it compositions

You will notice in the see_it composition below, that we have removed the circles composition, as we no longer needed the matte effect. However, we have replaced it with an Illustrator file of an outlined font.

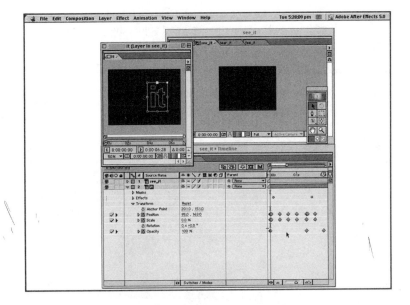

This will follow the movements of the layer see_it (containing the word 'see') exactly, as the keyframes have just been copied and pasted from one layer to the other. The new layer was then just placed on the right of the first layer in the Composition window, to read:

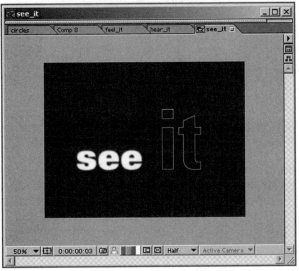

The remaining compositions, hear_it, and feel_it, were modified in exactly the same way. All we have to do now is go back to the main timeline and adjust the time that these compositions remain on screen.

Introducing the logo and web link

Ok, we're almost there now. In line with the marker www.o-music.tv we have two layers containing the logo and web address.

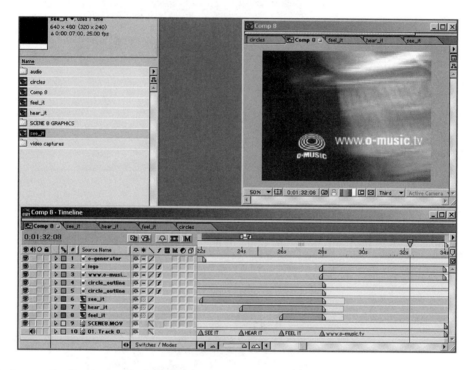

Having set the Position and Scale for the items on the first frame to what we find aesthetically pleasing, we then created an effect to bring them into the frame.

First of all, we set the Opacity in the first frame of the two layers to 0%, we then moved one second further along the timeline, and re-set the Opacity to 100%. Then, over the first two seconds of the layers (from 0:01:28:00 to 0:01:30:00), we added a Gaussian Blur, and altered the keyframe values at 0:01:28:00 to 40% Blurriness, and at 0:01:30:00 to 0% Blurriness.

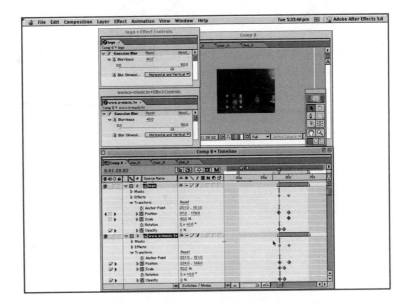

This effect gently brings in the layers. Then from 0:01:30:00 - 0:01:33:28, the logo and website address stay on screen.

Master composition

All the hard work had been done, and we just had to import all of our completed scene projects into our MASTER.aep before we could see the first glimpse of our finished movie. We created MASTER.aep by simply duplicating SCENE_01.aep, removing the unnecessary files, and just leaving the audio track.

We re-named our composition master comp, and imported each individual scene's project file, in much the same way as importing any other file. Once we had all our projects within the project file we were ready to place scene 1 onto the composition timeline, making sure that the playback head was at 0:00:00. We repeated this step for the other seven remaining scenes, again making sure the playback head was at 0:00:00. We turned off each composition's audio, as this was sourced from the main audio file. If we kept the sound channel turned on, each layer's audio would be mixed together as part of our final render. We didn't want this, as we were happy with the audio as it was.

We were now ready to render.

Render from After Effects

We found it better to render out the final movie at its full size, and with no compression on the video and audio. The reason for this is that we used further software (Terrain Cleaner 5.0) to compress the video. In After Effects, we used Best quality and Full resolution in our render settings:

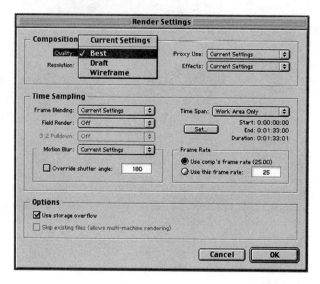

We used the following video format options:

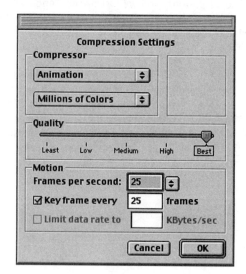

And we set up our Output Module Settings as follows:

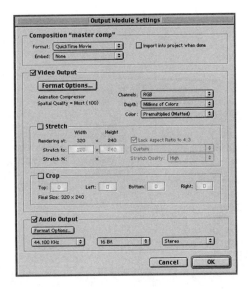

Then we sent o_music.mov to render.

Video compression

Before we began the process of compression, once we had rendered our video, we needed to consider exactly where the final video was going to be shown. In this instance, it was via the web / viral email campaign, so we needed to get maximum compression with the least amount of loss in quality as possible.

We look at various sizes of videos, with a variety of compression rates, and eventually we used the Sorrenson 3 compression at 12.5fps, with MP3 audio. By using Cleaner 5.0 in this way, we brought the 320*240 file of 470MB down to 4.1MB, at the same movie size – just slightly more manageable! We also rendered out a secondary file at a smaller size of 240*180, which was 3.0MB.

Now we have been through the whole process of creating this movie, take another look at the finished version and see how we've answered the brief. We've (hopefully!) produced a funky high energy video that both promotes the product's abilities, and also drives the o-music brand. We've let the music lead us, and worked the visual direction to the note, the beat, the tune, and the rhythm.

And that's it! Hope you enjoyed this NMW case study. Remember that one of the most important aspects of a successful AE project is the amount of planning and thought you put into the idea. It will almost definitely save you time during the creation of a video, and ensure you get what you want from After Effects.

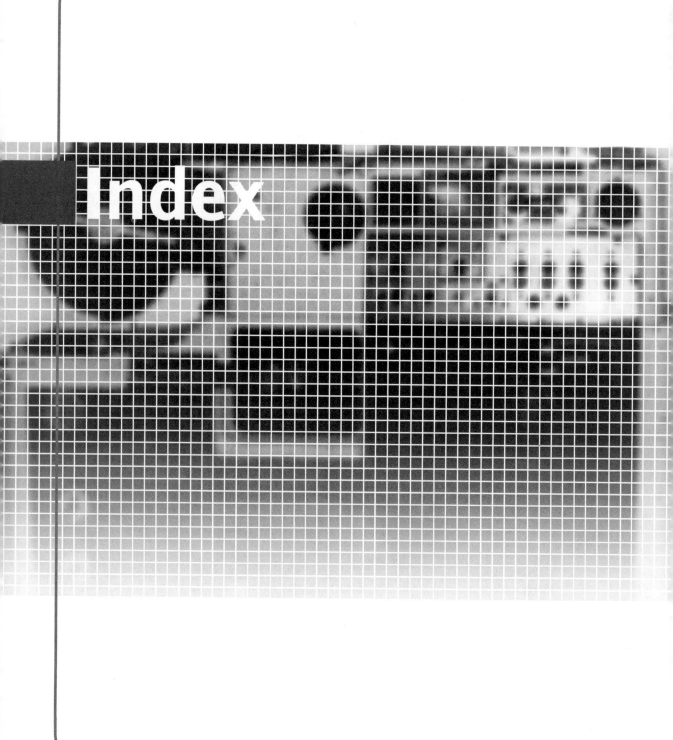

Index

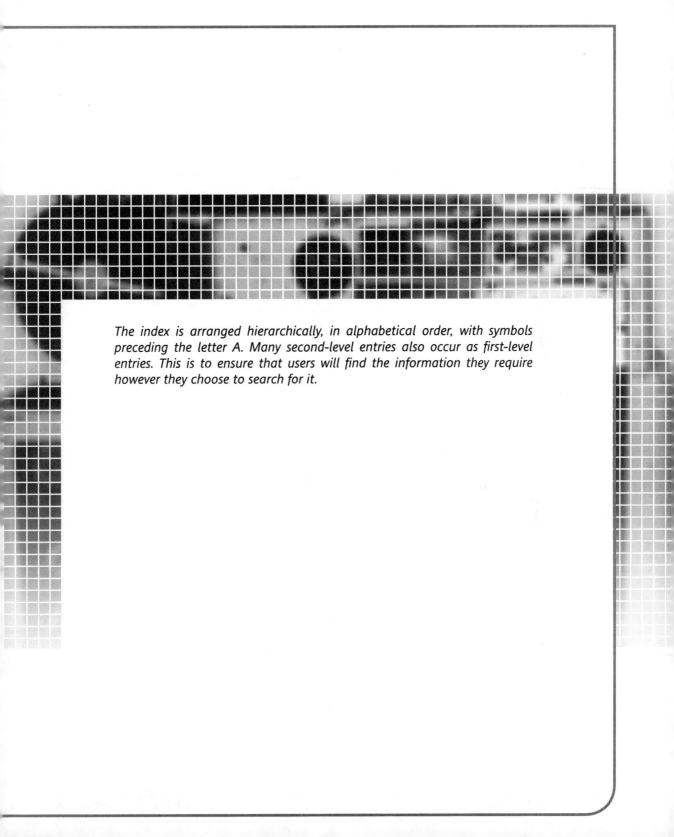

The index is arranged hierarchically, in alphabetical order, with symbols preceding the letter A. Many second-level entries also occur as first-level entries. This is to ensure that users will find the information they require however they choose to search for it.

Notes

Notes

Notes

Notes

DESIGNER TO DESIGNER™

friends of ED writes books for you. Any suggestions, or ideas about how you want information given in your ideal book will be studied by our team.

Your comments are valued by friends of ED.

For technical support please contact support@friendsofed.com.

Freephone in USA	800.873.9769
Fax	312.893.8001
UK contact: Tel:	0121.258.8858
Fax:	0121.258.8868

Registration Code : _____

Revolutionary After Effects 5.5 - Registration Card

Name ....

Address ....

City ....State/Region ....

Country ....Postcode/Zip ....

E-mail ....

Profession: film student ☐ freelance filmmaker ☐

part of an agency ☐ inhouse editor ☐

other (please specify) ....

Age: Under 20 ☐ 20-25 ☐ 25-30 ☐ 30-40 ☐ over 40 ☐

Do you use: mac ☐ pc ☐ both ☐

How did you hear about this book?...

Book review (name)..

Advertisement (name) ....

Recommendation ....

Catalog ....

Other ....

Where did you buy this book? ....

Bookstore (name) ....City........................

Computer Store (name)...

Mail Order...

Other...

How did you rate the overall content of this book?

Excellent ☐   Good ☐

Average ☐   Poor ☐

What applications/technologies do you intend to learn in the near future?..

....

What did you find most useful about this book? ....

....

What did you find the least useful about this book? ....

....

Please add any additional comments ....

....

What other subjects will you buy a computer book on soon?

....

....

What is the best computer book you have used this year?

....

....

Note: This information will only be used to keep you updated about new friends of ED titles and will not be used for any other purpose or passed to any other third party.

friendsof

DESIGNER TO DESIGNER™

NB. If you post the bounce back card below in the UK, please send it to:

friends of ED Ltd.,
30 Lincoln Road,
Olton,
Birmingham.
B27 6PA

BUSINESS REPLY MAIL

FIRST CLASS   *PERMIT #64*   *CHICAGO, IL*

POSTAGE WILL BE PAID BY ADDRESSEE

friends of ED,
29 S. La Salle St.
Suite 520
Chicago Il 60603-USA